MARTYR'S MANUAL

MARTYR'S MANUAL

The Brilliant, Tragic, and Inspiring Message of Hebrews

Wayne Brouwer

WIPF & STOCK · Eugene, Oregon

Wipf & Stock
An Imprint of Wipf and Stock Publishers
199 W. 8th Ave., Suite 3
Eugene, OR 97401

www.wipfandstock.com

PAPERBACK ISBN: 978-1-5326-8198-1
HARDCOVER ISBN: 978-1-5326-8199-8
EBOOK ISBN: 978-1-5326-8200-1

Manufactured in the U.S.A.   APRIL 23, 2019

To Ross Hoekstra, Brandon Huston, Steve Mann, Mark Rich,
Marcy Rudins, Karen Vande Bunte, Adam Van Der Stoep,
and Steve Zeoli, who shared this journey of investigation
and camaraderie with me.

Martyr

(from μαρτυρ)

A Greek word that for centuries simply meant witness.

A Greek word that changed meaning because of Jesus' people.

A Greek word that came to mean "one who is persecuted, probably to the death," because of her or his steadfast witness about Jesus.

Martyr.

Contents

Preface

"WRITE THIS IN YOUR Bibles . . ."

I couldn't believe it. Sacrilege. Desecration. Write in our Holy Bibles?

And I respected the man. I didn't like him, but I respected him. He was my sixth-grade teacher, the first man I had endured at the head of the classroom. A stern man, a disciplinarian. We were used to nice teachers, women teachers who looked and sounded like our moms. Sure, they put us in our places at times, but they were kind. Mr. Lobbes was imposing: chiseled features, black suits every day, thin black ties. He was one of the first "Men in Black" I knew, long before I ever went to my first movie.

"Find Hebrews 11 in your Bibles."

We shuffled and paged, looking to the ones who actually knew where to find things in their Bibles. We pretended familiarity with the sacred tomes, their fake-leather, dimpled covers and red-edged tissue leaves. Eventually we all were there, open Bibles on our school desks.

Heroes of Faith

"Now, take your pens and write 'Heroes of Faith' at the top of the page."

I hesitated. Would God really want me to do this? Would my minister approve? More important, what would my parents say?

But he was our teacher. Our stern, Christian school teacher. Our first male, authoritarian teacher.

So I wrote the words. "Heroes of Faith." My 12-year-old scrawl is still there.

In the old King James language, with the voice of a prophet, he began to read:

> Now faith is the substance of things hoped for, the evidence of things not seen.
>> For by it the elders obtained a good report.

Through faith we understand that the worlds were framed by the word of God, so that things which are seen were not made of things which do appear.

By faith Abel offered unto God a more excellent sacrifice than Cain, by which he obtained witness that he was righteous, God testifying of his gifts: and by it he being dead yet speaketh.

By faith Enoch was translated that he should not see death; and was not found, because God had translated him: for before his translation he had this testimony, that he pleased God.

But without faith it is impossible to please him: for he that cometh to God must believe that he is, and that he is a rewarder of them that diligently seek him.

By faith Noah, being warned of God of things not seen as yet, moved with fear, prepared an ark to the saving of his house; by the which he condemned the world, and became heir of the righteousness which is by faith.

By faith Abraham, when he was called to go out into a place which he should after receive for an inheritance, obeyed; and he went out, not knowing whither he went.

By faith he sojourned in the land of promise, as in a strange country, dwelling in tabernacles with Isaac and Jacob, the heirs with him of the same promise:

For he looked for a city which hath foundations, whose builder and maker is God.

Through faith also Sara herself received strength to conceive seed, and was delivered of a child when she was past age, because she judged him faithful who had promised.

Therefore sprang there even of one, and him as good as dead, so many as the stars of the sky in multitude, and as the sand which is by the sea shore innumerable.

These all died in faith, not having received the promises, but having seen them afar off, and were persuaded of them, and embraced them, and confessed that they were strangers and pilgrims on the earth.

For they that say such things declare plainly that they seek a country.

And truly, if they had been mindful of that country from whence they came out, they might have had opportunity to have returned.

But now they desire a better country, that is, an heavenly: wherefore God is not ashamed to be called their God: for he hath prepared for them a city.

By faith Abraham, when he was tried, offered up Isaac: and he that had received the promises offered up his only begotten son,

Of whom it was said, That in Isaac shall thy seed be called:

Accounting that God was able to raise him up, even from the dead; from whence also he received him in a figure.

By faith Isaac blessed Jacob and Esau concerning things to come.

By faith Jacob, when he was a dying, blessed both the sons of Joseph; and worshipped, leaning upon the top of his staff.

By faith Joseph, when he died, made mention of the departing of the children of Israel; and gave commandment concerning his bones.

By faith Moses, when he was born, was hid three months of his parents, because they saw he was a proper child; and they were not afraid of the king's commandment.

By faith Moses, when he was come to years, refused to be called the son of Pharaoh's daughter;

Choosing rather to suffer affliction with the people of God, than to enjoy the pleasures of sin for a season;

Esteeming the reproach of Christ greater riches than the treasures in Egypt: for he had respect unto the recompence of the reward.

By faith he forsook Egypt, not fearing the wrath of the king: for he endured, as seeing him who is invisible.

Through faith he kept the passover, and the sprinkling of blood, lest he that destroyed the firstborn should touch them.

By faith they passed through the Red sea as by dry land: which the Egyptians assaying to do were drowned.

By faith the walls of Jericho fell down, after they were compassed about seven days.

By faith the harlot Rahab perished not with them that believed not, when she had received the spies with peace.

And what shall I more say? for the time would fail me to tell of Gedeon, and of Barak, and of Samson, and of Jephthae; of David also, and Samuel, and of the prophets:

Who through faith subdued kingdoms, wrought righteousness, obtained promises, stopped the mouths of lions.

Quenched the violence of fire, escaped the edge of the sword, out of weakness were made strong, waxed valiant in fight, turned to flight the armies of the aliens.

Women received their dead raised to life again: and others were tortured, not accepting deliverance; that they might obtain a better resurrection:

And others had trial of cruel mockings and scourgings, yea, moreover of bonds and imprisonment:

> They were stoned, they were sawn asunder, were tempted, were slain with the sword: they wandered about in sheepskins and goatskins; being destitute, afflicted, tormented;
>
> (Of whom the world was not worthy:) they wandered in deserts, and in mountains, and in dens and caves of the earth.
>
> And these all, having obtained a good report through faith, received not the promise:
>
> God having provided some better thing for us, that they without us should not be made perfect.

We were mesmerized. In an age before fantasy superheroes had taken to the big screen, here were snippets of stories that boiled our blood and intrigued our imaginations. Here were reminders of men and women of courage who lived for much and died for more. I was into this. I *had* to read Hebrews.

From Disappointment to Intrigue to Terrifying Exhilaration

So I did. But it was tough sledding. There were some nice turns of phrase at the beginning and a few intriguing asides, yet they were dominated mostly by incomprehensible quotes and syllogistic theology. The end didn't seem to justify the means. The book of Hebrews became mostly a foreigner to me, an alien living within my Bible but not part of my "canon within the canon." Luke I loved, Paul I pilfered, John I juiced, Peter I plied, but Hebrews I hesitated.

The slumbering lasted for decades. A few lines from Hebrews 11 could stir my faith, yet the book as a whole remained off-putting. Until the summer of 2004, that is, when an editor of a scholarly journal sent Kenneth Schenck's *Understanding the Book of Hebrews: The Story Behind the Sermon*[1] for me to review. Duty transitioned to desire as I read Schenck's words, and then re-opened Hebrews. The old passions were ignited, this time for the whole book, the complete story, the entire journey. Schenck helped me understand the context, the drama, the crisis behind this seemingly tame tome, and I was hooked. When I wrote my own introduction to the Bible,[2] the chapter on Hebrews burned both the keyboard and the pages. Recently, a student told me she altered her career trajectory during the single hour I spoke about Hebrews in class. "I'll never forget it," she said. "It changed my life."

I hope this book gets to you too. Hebrews, I mean.

WAYNE BROUWER

1. Schenck, *Understanding the Book.*
2. Brouwer, *Covenant Documents.*

Introduction

HEBREWS IS A DIFFERENT kind of writing. They are all unique, of course, every one of the sixty-six books of the Bible, like children in a family. But among the limited genres of New Testament literature, Hebrews stands out. It is not a letter, like that of Paul or John or Peter, since it has no salutations, no personal references until the very end, and the author does not introduce her/himself. It is not a Gospel, for though the person of Jesus pops up on every page, his life and teachings are nowhere to be found. It is not a history book, even though it specializes in history lessons, reviewing events both recent and remote. At times, it almost feels like an apocalypse, but only until Revelation puts that theory to rest.

Many call it a sermon. Some declare it to be a treatise. Others simply announce it as a teaching.

While it slides between the cracks of our literary categories, there is still very much that we can say about Hebrews and the world into which it draws us:

- It assumes that:

    - its hearers are deeply and profoundly and practicing Jews.

    - the Hebrew Scriptures (Old Testament) matter deeply and have foundational authority.

    - God is moving history along from creation to Abraham, to Moses and the Sinai covenant, to Israel, to the prophets, to Jesus, to now. And the story is not finished. A climactic, culminating, cataclysmic conclusion is just two pages ahead on the calendar.

    - pain and persecution are ramping up rapidly, and targeted on these readers.

- It quotes:

    - Scripture (the Old Testament) forty times, nearly always from the Septuagint (the Greek translation of the Hebrew Bible), and often with unique variations. Not only that, but it alludes to other Scripture passages another fifty times or so.

- ◆ Psalms, most of all among the Old Testament writings.
- It constantly interweaves:
  - ◆ exposition (*explaining the meaning of Scripture passages*): 1:1–14; 2:5–8; 3:2–6; 3:14–19; 4:2–10; 5:1–10; 6:13–15; 7:1–22; 8:3–9:10; 9:16–22; 10:1–18; 11.
  - ◆ exhortation (*applying meanings and values to life situations*): 2:1–4; 3:1; 3:7–13; 4:1; 4:11–16; 5:11–6:12; 6:16–20; 7:23–8:2; 9:11–15; 9:23–28; 10:19–39; 12–13.
- It remembers:
  - ◆ events from a few years back in the experiences of this particular community.
  - ◆ the history of Israel.
  - ◆ the big names among the leaders of God's people.
  - ◆ the nuances of context that shape specific Scripture references.
- It motivates through:
  - ◆ teaching.
  - ◆ argument.
  - ◆ embarrassment.
  - ◆ intimidation.
  - ◆ inspiration.
  - ◆ encouragement.
  - ◆ analogy.

Most of all, Hebrews is a finely-tuned rhetorical piece that never gets boring. It shifts gears constantly to slow down considerations, focus temporarily on key figures, ratchet up engagement challenges, accelerate illustrations, stop in wonder at big image visions, and beat out in tempo lists of ethical behaviors. In a word, it is brilliant.

But the brilliance of Hebrews sidetracks those who become enamored by it, for Hebrews was written in a crisis that does not allow for meandering strolls by literary critics. It is not Mussorgsky's *Pictures at an Exhibition*, with the pacing of a musical moment paused by each scene artistically presented in expansive isolation down the corridors of a museum gallery. Hebrews is urgent. Hebrews is demanding. Hebrews requires response, without dalliance. And there is no margin: do or die. Listen or lose. Get with it or get lost. As we make our way through Hebrews, each chapter of this book has four sections:

- The Text—The New Revised Standard Version of each successive unit from the book of Hebrews, provided without internal chapter or verse references so that the text will read somewhat in the manner it was first intended. Old Testament quotations will be identified in footnotes.

- The Backstory—A more theological investigation of the terms and ideas within that section of the text.

- Where Have We Come So Far?—A running summary of the message of Hebrews through this point in our study.

- The Message—A broader reflection on the key themes as they continue to impact us today.

The reason for this structure is rooted within Hebrews itself. The entire text of the treatise is an interweaving of exposition ("The Backstory") and exhortation ("The Message"). So we will follow the author's lead, and engage his message in the manner he himself intended.[1]

The purpose of studying Hebrews in this way is to keep the text central, while always remembering the flow of the writer's intentions and message, and then to reflect on the text both deeply (to ensure that we are not reading our own wishes into it) and broadly (to assist us in making contemporary connections). Sometimes in our Bible studies we only discuss the last of these and forget that if we do not keep the others in mind, we will only find what we are looking for and not necessarily what God, through this author, wished for us to know or be challenged by.

---

1. I refer to the author of Hebrews in masculine pronouns, based on the masculine self-reference of the writer in Hebrews 11:32—"What more shall I say?"

Chapter 1

A New Voice

The Text: Hebrews 1:1–4

God Has Spoken by His Son

LONG AGO GOD SPOKE to our ancestors in many and various ways by the prophets, but in these last days he has spoken to us by a Son whom he appointed heir of all things, through whom he also created the worlds. He is the reflection of God's glory and the exact imprint of God's very being, and he sustains all things by his powerful word. When he had made purification for sins, he sat down at the right hand of the majesty on high, having become much superior to angels as the name he has inherited is more excellent than theirs.[1]

The Backstory: God Speaks

A young girl was furiously jamming crayons to her paper, energetically making line and swirls. She grabbed for new colors with only brief seconds of reflection, and filled the sheet with hues and shades.

"What are you drawing?" asked her mom.

"I'm making a picture of God," she said proudly.

---

1. All biblical quotations are from the New Revised Standard Version (NRSV Bible Translation Committee, 1989). While other translations have attractive vocabularies, dynamic equivalencies, and stylistics, the NRSV achieves a uniquely close correspondence between Hebrew (Old Testament) or Greek (New Testament) words and the consistent English cognates it uses to represent them.

"But nobody knows what God looks like," her mom replied gently.

"They will when I'm done," came the emphatic reply.

Mysterious God

We don't know what God looks like. We don't know how the spiritual essence of God exists, moves, or flows around us. We are less than microbes over against what we understand to be God's immense greatness.

The difference between God and us is so profound that it sometimes makes us question whether there actually is a God: maybe a divine figure of some kind is only a wish or a hope or a projection of our own insecurities. Someone has imagined us like a colony of mice living in the bottom of a huge, old upright piano. The place is dry and strong and safe, and we huddle together for warmth after our forays for food and nest linings.

Now and again we are startled and soothed by music that flows through our world. Sometimes it hammers us with staccato rhythms. Sometimes it causes our hearts to race with majestic passion. Sometimes it lulls us into romance and rest. But whatever the music is, we do not cause it, even though it is part of our world.

Sometimes a brave young mouse among us sneaks and crawls and climbs the dusty passageways that extend over our world. Now and again reports come back to us of complex mechanical systems that shape our home—wires and hammers and gears and levers. When the music comes, these things whirl to life and jump around with a frenzy that makes the melodies to which we have grown accustomed. While we would like to know how these things happen, we cannot find answers. We believe these are part of the mystery that shelters us. We think, in fact, that the music is somehow the voice of the Creator calling out to us. More than that, we cannot say.

One time a fearless explorer among us traced a path further than any previous mouse had gone. We were sure we would never see him again. So when he did return, we gathered around him while he caught his breath and told us of his journey of discovery.

He had actually seen the Creator, he said with wild excitement. The Creator was really nothing more than a big mouse, banging on a part of our world where smooth white rocks formed a pavement. Somehow the music and the strokes of the Creator went together.

Many thought that the mystery had been solved by this brave young scientist. Perhaps there really was no creator. Perhaps we were just smaller versions of another branch of our species too big to fit into our snug corner.

Perhaps the music was not a conundrum any longer, but merely the mechanical rattling of familiar things.

Mysterious Selves

And so, we continue on here, in our little world, listening to the music that comes and goes. Some of us still think it is the voice of our Creator, singing to us of love, of warning, or of passion. Others among us hear only the pounding of hammers and the vibration of strings, and tell us with dispassionate scientific certainty that there is no Creator. We and other beings not that different from us, they say, are masters of our own fate, propagating ourselves in a world we need to make and remake.

How will we know? Is there a truth larger than our experiences? If there is a Creator, will such a being actually be able to connect with us?

The story has its limits, of course. But it does remind us of the problem of our finiteness in a world that seeks and worships the infinity of a great Creator God. While our quests for God have rarely fully satisfied us, and certainly have not produced complete agreement about a common religious knowledge among our human race, the Bible keeps pulling us with a great spiritual attraction.

If the connection between us and God cannot be fully linked from our side of the equation, what might God do to enter our arena? How might God speak or make music so that we can hear the divine voice?

Different Ears

A husband and wife went to a marriage counselor because they were always tied up in arguments. The first session went badly because the two of them were constantly throwing accusations against one another, so the therapist said that at the beginning of their next appointment he would first see the wife for fifteen minutes, and then the husband, and then they would spend the rest of the time together reflecting on the dynamics of their relationship.

After the wife expressed her disappointment in her husband, she said to the counselor, "It's all his fault." Moved by her passionate descriptions of their marriage, the therapist nodded in agreement. "You're probably right," he said.

Of course, the husband had a different version of life in their home. By the time his fifteen minutes ended he had reached fever pitch as well. "It's all her fault," he cried. And again, the love doctor was swayed: "You're probably right."

Gathering both into his office for their final reflections, the counselor began by saying, "I've come to the conclusion that each of you is right about the other."

Startled and amazed, the husband sputtered back, "But that can't be. We can't both be right."

To which the therapist thoughtfully nodded and said, "You know, you're right."

We Hear with Our Hearts

We live in a pluralized world where all opinions seem valid, and the only perspective about which we are intolerant is intolerance itself. So, when we compare our views of reality, few of us dare to back all the way into the ultimate questions of origins and worldviews.

Yet it is impossible to read the Bible without admitting that it has a definite opinion about these things. Atheism is not an option from the biblical point of view, nor are several other ideas about values and gods in our world.

There are really only several major worldviews behind all of the smaller philosophies we hold to within the human race. It is important to reflect on these up front, as we think about the Bible and its message.

Scientific Naturalism

First, there are Naturalistic Closed System perspectives. For these, our world is self-contained, with no external source of information available to us, no "God" or gods, and no revelation other than that which we discover from the nuanced clues imbedded in the matter and energy that swirl around us.

Human life, from this viewpoint, is at best accidental. We have no more meaning than any other object or substance on our planet. Were chemicals to have been combined in other ways and acted upon by differing forces or energies there might not be any human race whatsoever, or there may well have developed a species or several which differed wildly from what we have become familiar with as we look in the mirror.

Living Universe

A second major grouping of worldviews, which we might call Intelligent Closed System perspectives, starts at the same reference point—a closed system environment where what we see is what we get. There is no god-like spirit hovering outside and above and beyond the universe accessible to us. But unlike the undirected randomness found in the previous worldview collection, this perspective believes that life itself, probably combined with time, forms the intelligence that drives the system.

So it is, from this collective worldview family, that life and time are understood together to be the intelligence which shapes the universal system. These are the creative edge that shape existence in a closed system. From this perspective, human life is meaningful insofar as it plays out its role and obeys its "designed" purposes—aligning with activities that sustain life and refraining from any nonsense that would pretend to circumvent time. We have no eternally transcendent purpose or existence, but while we are here we need to fit with our environment and promote life in all forms rather than destroy it.

Creator and Creatures in Conversation

We recognize these worldview perspectives around us. They are in competition with one other worldview collection, the one often simply known as "religious," and might be labeled as Creator/creature open system. This third worldview group believes that there is a Creator God who exists outside and before the system of reality in which we are housed, and that this God shaped the system so that it has inherent meaning and purpose. Existence is planned and intended by God. Human life is honored as a unique facet of created reality, formed to occupy a place of primary influence in the world as we know it, and reflecting attributes of the character of the Creator. Moreover, human life has been compromised in some way, and this accounts for the tragic and senseless elements of our daily walk. Furthermore, the Creator did not and does not abandon this world system to chance or fate, but invests in the renewal and redemption of all things: human life and also the other dimensions of reality. Within this worldview the Bible is one dimension of the divine-human redemptive link, ensuring that whoever God is will not be forgotten among us, and that whatever God is doing will not be lost in the hectic shuffle of human social shifts.

We must acknowledge these worldviews as we enter a study of the Bible. We cannot prove one worldview over against another. Nor can we force someone to shift from the paradigm of one perspective to that of another. But we cannot talk with meaning about the Bible without at some points admitting our philosophic stance. One may not say that Jesus is Savior or Redeemer and at the same time announce that the Bible is merely the product of human reflections about the problem of evil. In this case, not everybody can be right.

If There Is a God, What Is God Saying?

When I was a radio announcer during my college days our station began a late-night contemporary Christian music program, one of the first in the nation. We talked about the format for a while and discussed the content. And, of course, we debated what to call the show.

An early suggestion was "The Solid Rock Hour." Though the double entendre in that title was marvelous ("rock" for the style of some of the music, and "solid rock" as a picture of Jesus Christ), the name itself didn't ring with any contemporary feel. Our final choice was ILLUMINATION, and both the name and the program became a major hit.

"Illumination" speaks of darkness and shadows while at the same time pointing to the growing clarity produced by light and insight. There is a lot of spirituality contained in thoughts of illumination.

It certainly expresses well the God-talk of the Bible: darkness and chaos lurk until God speaks light and life; the psalmist wanders through the valley of the shadow of death with the testimony "The Lord is my Light and my salvation" on his lips; Jesus appears as the Light of God entering a dark world; and when he hangs on the cross, darkness steals the light away and the shades of Hades appear to take over for a time—yet, on Easter morning, resurrection comes with the dawn. For these reasons and more, John says that "God is Light," and Paul tells us to live as "Children of the Light."

The Dawn of Understanding

C. S. Lewis captured the tension of light and darkness in spiritual combat in his space trilogy about Venus. The planet Mars, in his tale, is populated by an ancient race of God's creatures who never gave in to the lure of evil, and remain holy and just. Earth, as we know, has fallen under the domain of the dark shadows, and the great Creator has posted warning signs around it in space. It is off limits to other races, quarantined until the end of time.

Venus, though, is a freshly birthed planet with a more recent "Paradise" story of creaturely development. A newly formed pair similar to Earth's Adam and Eve dance about in innocent delight.

The evil power in the universe will not allow a divine masterpiece to go long unmarred, however, and he sends a vicious Earth scientist named Weston to introduce sin on Venus by corrupting its Lord and Lady. In a countermove, the great Creator sends an ambassador of his own to Venus. The universe holds its breath as the future of this bright world hangs in the balance.

In these novels Lewis pictured the tension in every human heart. Like Adam and Eve at Earth's creation, and like the Lord and Lady of Venus, we are surrounded by dark powers, yet long for the light of redemption and love. Most of our lives we struggle to see more clearly.

Still, life gets lost for us, often, in the shadows. But grace breaks through, now and again, in moments of insight and illumination, and those are the moments we have to hang on to. That is why John 3:16 has become one of the most widely known verses of the Bible. It summarizes the scriptural message as that of God looking for us in love.

Like a mother who brings a child into this world, God is protective of the lives birthed on planet Earth. When sin stains and decadence destroys, God's first thought is to rescue and redeem and recover the children God so dearly loves.

Prophetic Anticipations

This is a theme repeated throughout the Bible. If God is saying anything through its pages, at least this much is clear: it is the whisper of divine love. The writer of Hebrews knows this, and points to the words of the prophets as a reminder.

Israel's prophets often appear, at first glance, to be strange creatures. A number of them harangue with incessant tirades (e.g., Amos), making us uncomfortable to spend too much time with such grumpy old men. Some are constant political gadflies (e.g., Jeremiah), always taking positions opposite of those in power. Others veer off into strange visions that are worlds removed from our everyday life (e.g., Zechariah), chafing readers with their oddness. There are even a few who have very compromised personal lives (e.g., Hosea), leading us to suspect more than a little psychologizing in their soap opera-ish theology.

Still, there is an inherent consistency of message and focus among all of these diverse religious ruminations and rantings. First of all, the prophetic sermons are invariably rooted in the web of relationships created by the Sinai covenant. Israel belongs to Yahweh, and her lifestyle must be shaped by the stipulations of that suzerain-vassal treaty. Obedience to Yahweh triggers the blessings of the Sinai covenant, while disobedience is the first reason for Israel's experiences of its curses: drought, war, famine, enemy occupation, destruction of cities and fields, deportation, etc. For this reason, the prophetic writings are laced with moral diatribes that carry a strong emphasis on social ethics.

This is not to say that Israel was held to a different behavioral standard than would otherwise be expected among the nations of the earth. Rather, through Israel's lifestyle there was supposed to flow a witness toward its neighbors, revealing the unique splendor of her God. By looking at the people of Yahweh, living in Canaan, other tribes and nations were to gain a sense of the true character of life when it was experienced in harmony with the forgotten Creator of all. As such, the public actions of Israel were crucial to its covenant existence. Both Isaiah and Micah succinctly summarized it in this way:

> In the last days the mountain of the Lord's temple will be established as chief among the mountains; it will be raised above the hills, and all nations will stream to it. Many peoples will come and say, "Come, let us go up to the mountain of the Lord, to the house of the God of Jacob. He will teach us his ways, so that we may walk in his paths." The law will go out from Zion, the word of the Lord from Jerusalem. He will judge between the nations and will settle disputes for many peoples. They will beat their swords into plowshares and their spears into pruning hooks. Nation will not take up sword against nation, nor will they train for war anymore. Come, O house of Jacob, let us walk in the light of the Lord (Isaiah 2:2–5; nearly identical is Micah 4:1–5).

Political Policy

Second, the function and message of prophecy were very political. Since Yahweh alone was Israel's sovereign, for the nation to come under the domination of other political powers was always seen as a divine scourge which resulted from the application of the covenant curses due to Israel's disobedience. How Israel handled its international relations showed plainly whether she trusted Yahweh, or if she had otherwise become enamored with power and politics rooted in lesser gods. Constantly, the prophets asked whether Israel was Yahweh's witnessing people, or if she was merely another nation with no particular mission or divine purpose. Israel's self-understanding was thus always very religious and, at the same time, invariably political.

It is in this light that the typical prophetic litany against the nations surrounding Israel must be read. These other social and political entities were assessed for public moral behavior by Yahweh alongside Israel because Yahweh was the Creator of all, and continued to be Lord of the nations.

All countries are chided for their own internal social sins, as well as for their inappropriate aggressions toward one another, including—and especially for—their treatment of Israel. While they may be used by Yahweh as a temporary tool of chastisement, punishing Israel according to the covenant curses, they might never presume to hold dominance over either Israel or her God. This typical hubris of nations was regularly condemned as idolatrous by the prophets, and any society afflicted by it would receive divine retribution in its own turn.

Apocalyptic Anticipations

Third, as the epochs of Israel's political fortunes unfolded, the message of the prophets became increasingly apocalyptic. There was a growing sense that because things had not gone the way they should have, producing heartfelt and on-going national repentance and covenant restoration, Yahweh will have to intervene directly again, in a manner similar to that during the time of Moses. When Yahweh interrupts human history the next time, however, along with judgments on the wickedness of the nations of the world, Israel will also fall heavily under divine punishment. But because Yahweh is on a mission to restore the fallen world, this next major divine intervention will be paired with a focus on establishing a new world order as well, even while the old is falling away under the conflagration. In this coming messianic age, everything in both society and the natural realm will finally function in the manner the Creator had intended in the beginning. Furthermore, because Yahweh is faithful to promises made, Israel will not be forgotten, and a remnant of God's servant-nation will be at the center of all this renewal, restoration, and great joy.

This increasingly forward-looking thrust of prophecy leads some to think of it as primarily foretelling, a kind of crystal ball gaze into the future. In reality, however, the nature of prophecy in ancient Israel is more forthtelling: declaring again the meaning of the ancient Sinai Covenant, explaining the mission of Yahweh (and thus Israel also) as witness to the world, and describing the implications of the morality envisioned by the suzerainvassal treaty stipulations. Included in this forth-telling is the anticipation of how things will look when everything is renewed. This becomes the basis for the "new covenant" of Jeremiah and Ezekiel. This forms the background to the prophecies about the "new heavens and new earth" in Isaiah. This shapes the contours of the messianic age described by Isaiah, Ezekiel, Joel, Micah, and Zechariah.

The growing clarity of the prophetic message is best seen when these divinely called and authorized covenant spokespersons are reviewed in historical sequence. While not all aspects of each prophetic experience is fully known, a great amount can be learned from the information provided within most of the prophecies. In large outline, the biblical prophets can be grouped in eras spanning about a century each.

Eleventh-to-Ninth-Century Prophetic Beginnings: Royal Advisers

The earliest prophets have several things in common. First, they are closely attached to the royal dynasties and function significantly as political, moral, and religious advisers. Second, few of their words are written down for posterity. Third, they seem to have close connections vocationally with either the extended royal household or the priestly families who cared for the tabernacle and later the temple. Samuel is the archetype of these prophets, according to 1 Samuel 3, and appears to have given name and status to the role of prophecy in the nation as a whole.[2]

Others in this group include Nathan, who has direct and easy access to King David;[3] Ahijah, who seems to have been significantly responsible for the partition of the nation of Israel after the death of King Solomon,[4] and later spoke a strong word of judgment against the king he had ensconced;[5] and the nameless prophets of 1 Kings 13, who talk with the kings and advise them. Each plays a direct role in the political life of the nation, but does so as an acknowledged representative for Israel's true King, Yahweh. For them, there is no distinction between the religious and political dimensions of society.

Eighth-Century Prophets: Loyal Opposition

Things appear to have changed significantly for prophets in the eighth century. While Isaiah was expressing the passion and purposes of Yahweh with lyric eloquence in the south, prophecy took on a decidedly angry character in the north. The powerful team of Elijah and Elisha railed against the royal pair of Ahab and Jezebel[6] for their anti-Yahweh religious stance and their

2. See 1 Sam 9.

3. 2 Sam 7, 12.

4. 1 Kgs 11:29–39.

5. 1 Kgs 14.

6. 1 Kgs 17—2 Kgs 9.

anti-Sinai covenant betrayal of people like Naboth.[7] Micaiah joined their entourage for one brief incident,[8] lending credence to their pronouncements of judgment, even while having direct access to the royal council room.

The most enduring voices from this era belong, however, to those members of "the Twelve" minor prophets, whose words were recorded in blunt detail. Amos left his large estate near Tekoa in Judah to travel northward into the territory of its sibling rival, Israel, around the year 760 BC. He explored the expansive prevalence of social sins in that realm which, he made clear, would soon result in divine judgment upon these people. According to Amos:

- There was a growing economic gap between very rich and very poor, accentuated by the callousness of the wealthy (6:4–6).

- Public worship had become repetitions of superficial liturgical acts (4:4–5; 5:21–23).

- The rich were stealing the lands of the poor through criminal lending practices, coupled with repossessions when impossible borrowing terms caused inevitable loan repayment defaults (2:6; 8:4, 6).

- Law courts were routinely denying justice to the helpless, simply because they could not pay bribes and had no social standing (2:7; 5:10, 12).

- In the marketplace, the poor were constantly cheated (8:5).

- Throughout the nation, there was overt conspicuous consumption (4:1).

- Added to these were blatant debauchery and other forms of an immoral lifestyle (6:5–6).

All in all, the word from Yahweh through Amos was dark, gloomy, and pointedly judgmental. Because of his pithy precision, coupled with verbal economy, Amos has become the model of street-corner prophets who rail against their societies in epigrammatic diatribes.

The same message is communicated in a very different tone and manner by Hosea, a contemporary of Amos. Hosea also spoke in the Northern Kingdom, but probably as a resident of that community. His oral and written communications are dated to the years 750–723 BC because of the rulers identified within the prophecy's pages.

---

7. 1 Kgs 21.

8. 1 Kgs 22.

Hosea has a very bad marriage. His wife, Gomer, was a prostitute before they wed, and bore at least two sons during their time together. It is uncertain, though, whether these children were biologically related to Hosea, since Gomer was not one to stay in her marriage bed at night. Her escapades and his faithful pleadings, which sound more like a soap opera than a biblical drama, become the analogy for Yahweh's relationship with Israel. Through the voice of Hosea, Yahweh poignantly reviews the past, detailing the amazing story of love that had brought young Israel into a very privileged and powerful position among the nations of the world. But this reminiscence grows bitter as both Hosea and Yahweh mourn their scorned loves, and weep for their respective wives, who are each destroying themselves and their families.

Although more polished and less dramatic, the message of another contemporary is much the same. Micah orated his prophecies over a period of about five decades, from 740–690 BC. He begins this ministry in the North, but after Israel was destroyed by the Assyrians in 722 BC, he heads south and uses the terrifying international political threat as a warning to Judah. God is faithful, Micah intones, but Israel (and also Judah) has been unfaithful to the Sinai covenant. Therefore, judgment is surely coming. Indeed, precisely during Micah's prophecies, it arrives in vengeful force against the Northern Kingdom, wiping it out of existence.

A truly strange incident was also unfolding on another front, during the years of these prophets. Jonah was commissioned by Yahweh to travel all the way to Nineveh, capital of the dreaded Assyrians, and speak a message of divine judgment against this aggressive civilization. One might think that any loyal Israelite would gladly rise to such a task. After all, Assyria was the great political enemy of the day, constantly threatening life in Canaan. Jonah, however, is wise enough to understand the heart of Yahweh. It is not God's desire to destroy the Assyrians, he knew, but rather to bring them, along with all the other nations of the world, into a larger family of peoples who were returning to their Creator in worship and submission and the recovery of full human joy.

So Jonah tries to evade his task by getting as far away from Nineveh as possible. In the famous story told in Jonah 1–2, Yahweh pursues Jonah on the high seas, causes a storm that nearly swamps his ship, and preserves the prophet from suicide-by-drowning in the belly of a large fish. Yet, when Jonah finally resumes his unwelcome mission to Nineveh, his suspicions come true, as the people of that great city actually repent for a time. God's promised judgment is put on hold, and Jonah cries like a spoiled brat.

The meaning of the tale is clear, however, and genuinely prophetic: Although the Creator's world has turned against its maker, Yahweh has prepared Israel as a special missionary people; through it, as promised to Abram in Genesis 12, all the nations of the earth will be blessed. The tiny book of Jonah is one of the greatest affirmations of the missional nature of the redemptive covenant established by Yahweh with Israel at Mount Sinai.

Seventh-Century Prophets: Doomsayers

By the time the seventh century BC rolls around, the prophets are rarely welcome in the royal palaces, even though all that is left of once-proud and expansive Israel is the tiny, mountainous territory of Judah. During the 600s, although Assyria keeps threatening Jerusalem, it is increasingly occupied in defending itself against its rebellious eastern province of Babylon. During these years, while Jeremiah develops his gloomy diatribes in the heart of the capital city, several among "the Twelve" also make brief statements about coming judgment. Zephaniah (630–610 BC) provides a few paragraphs against Judah and the nations that surround it (chapters 1–2), couching the imminent intervention of Yahweh in the increasingly common term, "the Day of the Lord." In a final, somewhat lengthier chapter, Zephaniah turns his attention toward restoration and renewal, pointing to a future time when the fortunes of Yahweh's people would be made full once again.

Also, for just a brief moment (probably around 615 BC), Nahum renews the mission of Jonah against Nineveh and the Assyrians. This time, however, there is no outcome of repentance and restoration. Instead, the short-lived turnabout that had followed Jonah's challenge evaporated entirely, and Nahum declares irreversible divine judgment against this fierce kingdom, which had wreaked so much havoc on its neighbors in the Fertile Crescent. Yahweh's word through Nahum would come true a few years later when the Assyrians are trounced by the Babylonians, first in the destruction of the capital city of Nineveh (612 BC), then at their secondary administrative center, Harran (610 BC), and decisively in the battle of Carchemish (605 BC), where even the allied armies of Egypt prove insufficient to turn the Chaldean tide.

> Finally, during this era as well, comes the disconcerting dialogue between Habakkuk and Yahweh. Formulated around the year 600 B.C., just as Babylon is rapidly overwhelming the whimpering remnants of the old Assyrian regime, Habakkuk asks Yahweh a series of questions that are answered in ways that almost bring more pain than the situations they are supposed to resolve. If summarized, the conversation would sound something like this:

Habakkuk: "Why do you ignore the social evils that plague our land (Judah)?" (1:1–4)

Yahweh: "I'm working on it. Very soon now, I will bring punishment through my dreaded scourge, the growing Babylonian conquest machine that is rolling through the area." (1:5–11)

Habakkuk: "O God, no! You can't do that! They are even worse than the most evil among us! How can you talk about balancing the scales of justice with such an unfair sentence?!" (1:12–2:1)

Yahweh: "I understand your frustration. That's why I'm giving you a message for all to hear. The sins of my people are terrible, and require drastic measures. For this reason, I am bringing the Babylonians against them. But the Babylonians, too, are my people, and will come under my judgment for the wickedness they perform. In the end, all will bow to me, as is appropriate when nations come to know that I am the only true God." (2:2–20)

At this point, Habakkuk breaks into a song of confidence and trust (chapter 3) that rivals anything found in the Psalms. Habakkuk charts the terrifying movements of Yahweh on Earth, bringing death and destruction as the divine judgments swirl. But in the end, Habakkuk raises a marvelous testimony of faith:

"Though the fig tree does not bud and there are no grapes on the vines, though the olive crop fails and the fields produce no food, though there are no sheep in the pen and no cattle in the stalls, yet I will rejoice in the Lord, I will be joyful in God my Savior. The Sovereign Lord is my strength; he makes my feet like the feet of a deer, he enables me to go on the heights" (Habakkuk 3:17–19).

Sixth-Century (Exilic) Prophets: Messianic Optimists

The prophets of the sixth century BC were mostly engulfed by the occupation of Judah and its quick demise (Jerusalem was destroyed in 586 BC), along with the subsequent Babylonian exile, in which the bulk of the remaining population was deported. During these years, as we saw in the prophecies of Ezekiel and Daniel, the center of action shifts from Jerusalem to Babylon. There is only one tiny prophetic reflection from back in the homeland. Obadiah, whose name means "Servant of Yahweh," tosses off a brief—but strident—condemnation of Edom. This nation, which emerged from the same family as Israel by way of Jacob's fraternal twin Esau, had played gadfly to Yahweh's covenant nation for many centuries. Now, through the prophet's voice, Yahweh berates it for the pride and willful cunning that leveraged Judah's demise for its own gain. When the Babylonians marshaled the deportees out of Jerusalem in 586 BC, the looters of Edom raided and scavenged that troubled city. Moreover, as the stragglers were being shepherded down the road to exile, sharpshooters among Edom's bowmen sat on the hillsides and picked them off in an unholy target practice. For these reasons, according to Obadiah, divine judgment will soon destroy Edom's red-rock strongholds.

While Obadiah's vision is too short to encompass the many dimensions of messianic optimism found in other prophets of his age, there is contained within it a firm confidence that Yahweh is still active among the nations. Once again, the "Day of the Lord" (verses 15–21) emerges as the catchall phrase for Yahweh's looming intervention that will redress injustice with divine punishment, and will usher in the renewed covenant order, spreading out from its epicenter in Jerusalem to the ends of the earth.

Fifth-Century (Post-Exilic) Prophets: Cheerleaders and Apocalyptic Moralists

Four among "the Twelve" remained after the first five centuries of Israelite prophecy were swallowed up into the Babylonian exile. Haggai and Zechariah appear on the scene at exactly the same time (summer and fall of 520 BC); the former issues four brief messages from Yahweh on three separate days that year, while the latter continues to have visions for another two calendar cycles. Malachi shows up a generation or two later, and Joel's prophecy marks the conclusion of Old Testament revelations sometime after.

Haggai is a cheerleader. He returns from Babylon to Palestine with the first wave of freed exiles under the leadership of Zerubbabel in 536 BC. Although it took a while for the community to get its bearings, eventually there was a push to sift among the stones still left at the site of Solomon's Temple, and rebuild a house for Yahweh there. In 520 BC, Haggai urges the workers on with divine encouragement. No obstacle can stand in the way of this central task, neither disobedient lifestyles,[9] fainthearted leadership,[10] poverty,[11] ritual defilement,[12] or the rattling sabers of bellicose nations.[13] Under Haggai's promptings and Zerubbabel's governing, the temple is rebuilt

---

9. Hag 1:2–11.

10. Hag 1:12–14.

11. Hag 2:1–9.

12. Hag 2:10–19.

13. Hag 2:20–23.

in the next four years. By 516 BC, it stands again, only a mean miniature compared to the glorious structure created generations before by Solomon in his seven-year building project. Nevertheless, with Haggai's oratorical help, Yahweh's house is reborn.

The visions of Zechariah begin in exactly the same year as Haggai's brief prophecies (520 BC). But Zechariah's temperament is more like a combination of Jeremiah and Ezekiel; his graphic descriptions of Yahweh's revelations involve strange creatures, heavenly scenes, and amazingly cartoonish episodes, in which Yahweh's kingdom is confirmed as chief among the nations. Because of a change in literary style after chapter 8, Zechariah 9–14 is sometimes viewed as emerging from a second voice.

While Haggai's messages were quick, pointed, and easily understood in their references to the work of the day, Zechariah's allegorical pronouncements seem only obliquely connected to his contemporary setting. They pick up on the problems experienced by the post-exilic community, but then shimmer off into grand apocalyptic visions, with no fixed chronology or tidy resolutions. Still, Zechariah's lofty homilies serve well to remind the tiny and lackluster community that these people remain essential to Yahweh's original missionary purpose for Israel. Thus, the Sinai covenant and its stipulations continue to be Israel's greatest treasure, and the source of its public identity.[14]

About sixty years after Haggai's and Zechariah's brief prophetic careers, Malachi comes on the scene. His name means "My Messenger," and may well have been a nickname either given to him by Yahweh or assumed by the man himself in the course of his activities as spokesperson for God. As was true in Habakkuk's situation, Malachi's prophetic utterances take on the form of a dialogue. Here, however, the parties in conversation are not the prophet and Yahweh, but rather Yahweh and the people. Yahweh instigates the interlocutions, interrupting daily life around Jerusalem with a series of searing questions:

> "Why have you people turned away from me?" (1:2–14)

> "Why have you priests failed to honor me?" (2:1–9)

> "Why do you divorce your wives?" (2:10–16)

> "Why do you think I'm not coming back to my Temple?" (2:17–3:5)

> "Why have you withheld tithes and offerings?" (3:6–15)

---

14. See Zech 8:18–23.

These issues match the problems Ezra and Nehemiah struggled with and affirm Malachi's dates as contemporary with those leaders. Even the covenant renewal ceremony of Nehemiah 8–10 may have been the occasion for the brief note in Malachi 3:16, which tells of a scroll of testimony being penned by repentant Jews, who wished to repossess their identity as the community of Yahweh.

It is likely that the short prophecy of Joel was written after Malachi's days, but the position of Malachi at the end of "the Twelve" is perfectly understandable. For Jews, it closed off the post-exilic rebuilding of the temple. Now, the community waited with eager anticipation for Yahweh to return again in the Shekinah glory cloud that first descended on Mount Sinai into the tabernacle, and later came to dwell in Solomon's Temple. Malachi's final vocalization of Yahweh's speech promised a speedy arrival of the divine presence.

For Christians of the New Testament age, Malachi's prophecy was viewed directly in connection with the Gospels. The messianic church community quickly interpreted Jesus as the embodiment of Yahweh's returning glory. In fact, the Gospel according to Matthew, which stands at the head of the New Testament, makes a very deliberate effort to choreograph the travels of Jesus in such a way that his arrival at the temple on the week of the final Passover is understood as the return of divine glory to the house of Yahweh, which has been left in the hands of clueless caretakers.[15]

The prophecy of Joel, although given a position early in the collection of "the Twelve," was probably penned sometime in the last half of the fifth century BC. Biblical scholars have moved it all over the map of prophetic chronology, precisely because it contains no temporal referents other than the terrible plague of locusts that shaped its contents. The sweeping devastation of successive waves of locusts devouring the entire crop in Palestine that year caused Joel to hear a higher word of judgment against the nation of Yahweh. Partly because it contains no mention of kings, and also because of some words and language forms that seem more in tune with nuances of later Hebrew and post-exilic times,[16] many now believe it was written sometime after Malachi.

It is really not very important to place Joel in a historical setting. In fact, Joel's prophecy is a marvelous summary and distillation of all points of theology scattered throughout the rest of the prophets. After the strident tattoo of approaching judgment, still in rhythm with the grinding march of the locust plague, Joel sees a critical and decisive turn of history taking

15. See Matt 21.

16. See, for instance, the note in Joel 3:4–6.

place when Yahweh breathes new life across the face of the Earth. Every-thing turns on the imminent "Day of the Lord."[17]

On this note, the Old Testament closes. The Creator remains on a mis-sion to recover the lost citizens of the kingdom of heaven, as well as renew the painfully twisted elements of nature. In order to make this restoration happen, the family of Abraham was enlisted as a witnessing partner. Unfor-tunately, the nation of Israel proved to be unequal to the task, and the divine redemptive enterprise limped toward an inglorious demise, even while the prophets were seeing and stating grander visions of the coming age. In the end, a muted—but stirring—prophetic voice charmed the hearts of all who waited in longing for the imminent "Day of the Lord."

A New Thing: The Trinity

So Jesus is the latest, greatest messenger of God. But he is also more, and that is what the entire book of Hebrews will be about.

This is where the complexity of prophetic voices, trumped by Jesus, takes a further new turn. The writer of Hebrews says clearly—to Jewish ears, somewhat gratingly—about Jesus: "He is the reflection of God's glory and the exact imprint of God's very being, and he sustains all things by his powerful word. When he had made purification for sins, he sat down at the right hand of the Majesty on high."[18] This could be viewed as blasphemy, since it equates the identity of the man Jesus with the full and indescribable *shekinah* glory of the one Creator God of Israel's history and heritage.[19] Jesus does not flow out of the radiance of God's glory, but he is that radiance itself. Jesus is not an imitation of the character of God, but rather he is "the exact imprint of God's very being." Jesus does not merely assist God (as do the angels) in sustaining the created order, but he is instead the one who actu-ally sustains them himself by the divine word which he speaks.

There can be no clearer language than this. At the very opening of this treatise, the writer of Hebrews unmistakably identifies Jesus with the God of glory worship monotheistically by the Jew and their Israelite forebears. This is either blasphemy (as Paul thought before he met Jesus on the road to Damascus),[20] or it is a startling new insight which only became apparent in this world at the coming of Jesus.

17. Joel 2:11.
18. Heb 1:3.
19. See Deut 6:4.
20. See Acts 9, 22, and 26.

Competing Voices

The early Christian church wrestled with this growing awareness under the conversations revolving around two questions. First, since Jesus was obviously human, how should we understand the divinity to which Jesus connected himself? Was the man Jesus fully divine?

There were a number of honest, deeply Christian answers provided by early church leaders. Paul of Samosata (200–275) kept true to the typical Jewish line of divinely raised up human deliverers, and declared that Jesus was a really good man who had been uniquely adopted (and so characterized since Paul's expressions as "adoptionism") by God for the work of salvation, and was equipped to that work by a special infusion of the divine Spirit. Jesus was fully human, and remained so. But he was unusually called and prepared for the great deliverance God brought about.[21]

Sabellius (lived around 200) entered the conversations from across the room. For him, Jesus was only one of God's multiple manners of appearance. In other words, there is no "Trinity" in the deity, but only several different masks which the one God wears while connecting with humanity. We call his views "modalism" today.

A third strong voice in the debates came from Arius, lingering in ecclesiastical consciousness as most forceful and famous among these. Arius (250–336) wanted to preserve the deep foundation of biblical monotheism, while desiring, at the same time, to highlight the uniqueness of Jesus. His solution was to talk of Jesus as the first creation of God, identical in almost every aspect with the Father, yet originating from the Father.[22] Identified theologically as "subordinationism," Arius' views were fiercely opposed by Athanasius, and resoundingly condemned by the Councils of Nicea (325) and Constantinople (381).

With Jesus' divinity safeguarded, the questions about his personhood shifted in the third to the fifth centuries. Now the issue became, "Is the divine Christ fully human?" Again, there were a number of answers posed. In his enthusiasm to defend the divinity of Jesus, Apollonaris of Laodicea (late fourth century) asserted that the logos of God dominated the person who appeared on earth, making the presumed man from Nazareth a glorified and spiritualized expression of human identity.

Nestorius (386–431) pushed back, defending both the full humanness of Jesus along with his divinity, but posited that these were almost separate

---

21. Eusebius, *Ecclesiastical History, II.*
22. Arius, *Orations against the Arians.*

entities living in the same body.[23] This duality of persons within a single human did not sit well with most other theologians and pastors, including, particularly, Eutyches (380–456) who spoke vehemently against Nestorius at the Council of Ephesus in 431. Eutyches compensated for Nestorius' somewhat schizophrenic Jesus by pouring both divinity and humanity into a blender that interfused them as a new and different personality altogether.

The Defining Word

It was the Council of Chalcedon (451) that put final boundaries around these debates, condemning the views expressed by Apollonaris, Nestorius, and Eutyches. The outcome was a testimony of Christian Trinitarian faith that eventually became articulated in the Athanasian Creed:[24] Jesus

23. Nestorius, *Bazaar of Heraclides.*

24. "Whosoever will be saved, before all things it is necessary that he hold the catholic faith. Which faith except every one do keep whole and undefiled; without doubt he shall perish everlastingly. And the catholic faith is this: That we worship one God in Trinity, and Trinity in Unity; Neither confounding the Persons; nor dividing the Essence. For there is one Person of the Father; another of the Son; and another of the Holy Ghost. But the Godhead of the Father, of the Son, and of the Holy Ghost, is all one; the Glory equal, the Majesty coeternal. Such as the Father is; such is the Son; and such is the Holy Ghost. The Father uncreated; the Son uncreated; and the Holy Ghost uncreated. The Father unlimited; the Son unlimited; and the Holy Ghost unlimited. The Father eternal; the Son eternal; and the Holy Ghost eternal. And yet they are not three eternals; but one eternal. As also there are not three uncreated; nor three infinites, but one uncreated; and one infinite. So likewise the Father is Almighty; the Son Almighty; and the Holy Ghost Almighty. And yet they are not three Almighties; but one Almighty. So the Father is God; the Son is God; and the Holy Ghost is God. And yet they are not three Gods; but one God. So likewise the Father is Lord; the Son Lord; and the Holy Ghost Lord. And yet not three Lords; but one Lord. For like as we are compelled by the Christian verity; to acknowledge every Person by himself to be God and Lord; So are we forbidden by the catholic religion; to say, There are three Gods, or three Lords. The Father is made of none; neither created, nor begotten. The Son is of the Father alone; not made, nor created; but begotten. The Holy Ghost is of the Father and of the Son; neither made, nor created, nor begotten; but proceeding. So there is one Father, not three Fathers; one Son, not three Sons; one Holy Ghost, not three Holy Ghosts. And in this Trinity none is before, or after another; none is greater, or less than another. But the whole three Persons are coeternal, and coequal. So that in all things, as aforesaid; the Unity in Trinity, and the Trinity in Unity, is to be worshipped. He therefore that will be saved, let him thus think of the Trinity.

"Furthermore, it is necessary to everlasting salvation; that he also believe faithfully the Incarnation of our Lord Jesus Christ. For the right Faith is, that we believe and confess; that our Lord Jesus Christ, the Son of God, is God and Man; God, of the Substance [Essence] of the Father; begotten before the worlds; and Man, of the Substance [Essence] of his Mother, born in the world. Perfect God; and perfect Man, of a reasonable soul and human flesh subsisting. Equal to the Father, as touching his Godhead; and

is fully divine and fully human, neither dual in natures nor confused in personhoods.

Living within these limits of expression has not been easy for the Christian church. Just as the writer of Hebrews is clear in his intent with regard to affirming both Jesus' full divinity and full humanity, yet sometimes appears incapable of stating the exact realities of the relationships of the divine persons without shadow or analogy, so the doctrine of the Trinity has muddled through history. Augustine (354–430) tried to teach it from what has come to be known as the psychological analogy. Emphasizing the oneness of God, Augustine drew out the roles that God enacted fully and completely as each of the three persons of the Trinity. Like a man might be a son to his parents, a husband to his wife, and a father to his children, with all of his personhood caught up in each of these relationships, while remaining a single entity, so Augustine described the Trinitarian identity and emanations, being careful not to come across as modalistic.[25]

Providing an alternative explanation of these things, the great Cappadocians[26] started with the three, Father, Son, and Spirit, explaining how they were uniquely divine and inherently related to one another. Their analogy used the idea of many persons in a room who were each obviously distinct from one another, and yet all and everyone completely and fully human. So with God—there are three persons who are each fully and completely divine, and no others. And these three are each fully and completely divine in their individually unique manners.[27]

The writer of Hebrews seems to anticipate this latter expression of Trinitarian thought. Jesus is fully divine, so he is one with the unnamed "majesty" of heaven. Yet Jesus is also fully human, a person among the people of earth.

---

inferior to the Father as touching his Manhood. Who although he is God and Man; yet he is not two, but one Christ. One; not by conversion of the Godhead into flesh; but by assumption of the Manhood into God. One altogether; not by confusion of Substance [Essence]; but by unity of Person. For as the reasonable soul and flesh is one man; so God and Man is one Christ; Who suffered for our salvation; descended into hell; rose again the third day from the dead. He ascended into heaven, he sitteth on the right hand of God the Father Almighty, from whence he will come to judge the living and the dead. At whose coming all men will rise again with their bodies; And shall give account for their own works. And they that have done good shall go into life everlasting; and they that have done evil, into everlasting fire. This is the catholic faith; which except a man believe truly and firmly, he cannot be saved."

25. Augustine, *The Trinity*.

26. Basil the Great (330–379 AD), bishop of Caesarea; Basil's younger brother Gregory of Nyssa (c.332–395 AD), bishop of Nyssa; and Gregory of Nazianzus (329–389 AD), a close friend of the other two.

27. Basil, *Letters*.

Where Have We Come So Far?

- God has spoken in times past.
    - This is our source of direction and confidence.
    - We know who we are because of the prophets.
- God has recently spoken a stronger, better, and clearer message through Jesus.
    - So when we, who live by the prophetic message, hear Jesus, we had better listen.

Message: Listen!

Chuck Swindoll told of a time when he had been "caught in the undertow of too many commitments in too few days." He says he reacted the way most of us do: snapping at his wife and children, choking down his food at mealtimes, and forcing down irritations when people interrupted his over-scheduled schedule.

But the worst of it, said Swindoll, was that he began to expect that everything around him suddenly had to catch up to his speed. If someone wanted to talk with him, he danced impatiently till she blurted out quickly what she had to say. One evening, as he was rushing out the door, Swindoll's youngest daughter, Colleen, caught him by surprise. Something important had happened to her at school, and she sort of yelled out to him as he breezed by: "Daddy-I-wanna-tell-you-somethin'- and-I'll-tell-you-really-fast."

Suddenly, Chuck realized her frustration and stopped for a moment. "Honey," he said, "you can tell me. And you don't have to tell me really fast; just say it slowly."

Her response cut deeply. "Then," she said, "you have to *listen* slowly."

Into the Quiet

Listen slowly.

That's not a bad command for all of us to remember now and again. Rupert Brooke wrote a powerful poem about catching the meaning of life in the silence, and losing it again in the banging of noisiness. He said:

> *Safe in the magic of my woods*
> *I lay, and watched the dying light.*

Faint in the pale high solitudes,
And washed with rain and veiled by night.
Silver and blue and green were showing.
And dark woods grew darker still;
And birds were hushed; and peace was growing;
And quietness crept up the hill[28]

In that moment, Brooke says, he felt all his puzzlement unfold, as God seemed about to speak to him the key to the mysteries of life. He knew, as he lay there, that in the next moments the meaning of his existence and the depth of his love for one special person would whisper out to him.

"And suddenly," Brooke goes on, "there was an uproar in my woods."[29] Who should it be but his love, "crashing and laughing and blindly going," stomping with her "ignorant feet," dragging the small creatures of the forest to destruction with her "swishing dress," and "profaning the solitudes" with her voice.

"The spell was broken," says Brooke, "the key denied me." His love prances around, "mouthing cheerful clear flat platitudes," and quacking trite noise till the anger welled inside him. "By God," he thought to himself. "I wish—I wish that you were dead."[30]

Strong language, that. And strong sentiments. But maybe we, in our noisy world, need to be moved once in a while to covet the quiet. Does grace always find us in the crowded business of life? Is there no urge within to capture the meaning of our souls again in silence?

Finding the Centering Note

Helen Keller, blind and deaf from early childhood, lived in a world of deep silence. Yet she describes the incredible sensation of "listening" with her hands. She tells of a thrilling moment on February 1, 1924, when the cover was removed from radio speakers, and her hand was placed against the vibrating membrane itself. It was live performance of Beethoven's Ninth Symphony, direct from Carnegie Hall. "I could sense . . . the passion of the rhythm, the pulsation and swell of music," she said. "And the great choir beat sharply against my fingers with its waves and pulses."[31]

---

28. Brooke, "The Voice," 76.
29. Brooke, "The Voice," 76.
30. Brooke, "The Voice," 76.
31. Keller, "My Heart."

Amid the noise and cacophony, to hear the centering stability of things that truly matter is both a miracle and a gift. Lloyd C. Douglas wrote those fascinating novels of an earlier generation, *The Robe* and *The Big Fisherman*. When he went to college, Lloyd boarded in a large house where the owner lived in the basement, and every room on every floor was converted into an income-generating apartment. For some reason (maybe because the landlord himself was a musician), nearly all the tenants were singers or instrumentalists. The place was always filled with music, some of it grand and good, some of it quite hard to take.

Lloyd Douglas had an on-going joke with his landlord. They'd meet on the steps, and Douglas would greet him by saying, "Well, what's the good news today?" Invariably, the man would reach into his pocket, pull out a tuning fork, rap it against his heel, and set it against the wall till the whole stairwell echoed with its sound.

"That's middle C," the landlord would say. "That's the good news today. The soprano in the attic may be singing sharp, and the cellist may be off his music, and the tenor may be flat today, but that's middle C. At least you can count on that."[32]

Abraham Joshua Heschel wrote, in his magisterial appreciation of *The Prophets*,[33] that these ancient messengers of God were pained by language most of us cannot hear. Their ears, said Heschel, were tuned to the piercing voice of heaven, "one octave too high"[34] for the rest of us to perceive. God hammered into their consciences the messages of both grace and judgment that we are too oafish to engage. For them it was a labor of love, as well as a calling that often disrupted and troubled their own personal existences.

In the noisiness of our lives, to have, for a moment, the otherworldliness of the silence that envelops the prophets, and then to hear, with them, God's ringing message that shapes both time and eternity, is a true gift. This is the hope and prayer that opens the treatise of Hebrews.

Leslie Weatherhead once preached a sermon called "The Significance of Silence." "There are two ways of getting through life," he said, "and I think we must decide which we shall follow . . . The first way is to stop thinking. The second way is to stop and think."[35]

Many of us, he said, try the first way. We fill up every hour with rushing, with noise, with earbuds and iPods, with radios and television, with action and reaction. There is no silence, and therefore, there is no real thought.

---

32. Douglas, *Time to Remember*, 9.
33. Heschel, *Prophets*.
34. Heschel, *Prophets*, 9.
35. Weatherhead, "Significance of Silence," 6–7.

But, said Weatherhead, there are some who long for both quiet from these tumultuous times, and a still, small voice that whispers love and meaning. When we stop doing, for a time, and try to find silence, to tune our hearts, to commune with God, we may find more than just rest. We may actually find ourselves. We may find the immensity of creation. We find God.

This is the beginning of Hebrews. The author assumes his readers have learned to hear the voice of God through the prophets of Israel's past generations. But now God has shouted through Jesus, and it is time to listen to a new version of the old message. But we can only listen if we make a conscious choice to get off the speed demon race track and Sabbath for a while. Then we will begin to hear anew the one who is "Lord of the Sabbath."[36]

36. Matt 12:1–8; Mark 2:23–28; and Luke 6:1–5.

Chapter 2

Better Than Angels

The Text: Hebrews 1:5–14

The Son and the Angels

> For to which of the angels did God ever say, "You are my Son;
> today I have begotten you?"[1] Or again, "I will be his Father, and
> he will be my Son"[2]? And again, when he brings the firstborn
> into the world, he says, "Let all God's angels worship him."[3] Of
> the angels he says, "He makes his angels winds, and his servants
> flames of fire."[4] But of the Son he says, "Your throne, O God, is
> forever and ever, and the righteous scepter is the scepter of your
> kingdom. You have loved righteousness and hated wickedness;
> therefore God, your God, has anointed you with the oil of glad-
> ness beyond your companions."[5] And, "In the beginning, Lord,
> you founded the earth, and the heavens are the work of your
> hands; they will perish, but you remain; they will all wear out
> like clothing; like a cloak you will roll them up, and like clothing
> they will be changed. But you are the same, and your years will
> never end."[6] But to which of the angels has he ever said, "Sit at
> my right hand until I make your enemies a footstool for your

1. Ps 2:7.
2. 2 Sam 7:14.
3. Deut 32:43.
4. Ps 104:4.
5. Ps 45:6–7.
6. Ps 102:25–27.

feet"[7]? Are not all angels spirits in the divine service, sent to serve for the sake of those who are to inherit salvation?

Backstory: Angels

The biblical tale of angels feels a bit like a roller coaster ride or a stock portfolio graph. Out of the 108 references to angels in the Old Testament, thirty occur in the Pentateuch, with nearly all of these happening in just two stories—the divine revelatory moments in the life of Abraham,[8] and the maddening recounting of Moabite King Balak's attempt to destroy Israel through the mediation of prophet Balaam.[9] Angel sightings spike again in Judges, especially when Gideon[10] or Samson[11] are around. They float in and out of the histories found in Samuel and Kings, sing some songs in Psalms, and knock on a few doors of the prophets, until one becomes the constant companion of Zechariah.[12]

The spread of angels throughout the New Testament is thicker (165 references in a much shorter collection of writings) and more even (although they group a bit excessively in the birth narratives of Luke's Gospel) until Revelation, where angels pop up on every page—sixty-eight times in total. The terms are consistent: angels are "messengers" (Hebrew *malak* or Greek *angelou*) of God. They show up to communicate something important that we humans might not otherwise pay attention to or understand. Once in a while the message includes a powerful act of deliverance or judgment, but mostly it is in words.

The Old Testament has very little "theology" about angels. Instead, it mostly identifies them as messengers between heaven and earth, between God and humans.[13] The New Testament does not really advance or add significantly to this key idea. In both Testaments there are a number of specific ways by which angels carried out their mandates as messengers:

- Communicating—They helped reveal the law to Moses (Acts 7:52–53), and served as the carriers of much of the material in Daniel and

---

7. Ps 110:1.

8. Gen 16–24.

9. Num 22.

10. Judg 6.

11. Judg 13.

12. Twenty references.

13. There are also a few references to angels simply worshipping God (e.g., Isa 6:1–3; see Rev 4–5 as well).

Revelation. Angels gave instructions to Joseph about the birth of Jesus (Matt 1–2), to the women at the tomb, to Philip (Acts 8:26), and to Cornelius (Acts 10:1–8), and told Paul that everyone on his ship would survive the impending shipwreck (Acts 27:23–25)

- Providing—God has used angels to provide physical needs such as food for Hagar (Gen 21:17–20), Elijah (1 Kgs 19:6), and Jesus after his temptations (Matt 4:11).

- Protecting—Keeping God's people out of physical danger, as in the cases of Daniel and the lions, and his three friends in the fiery furnace (Dan 3 and 6).

- Delivering—Angels released the apostles from prison in Acts 5, and repeated the process for Peter in Acts 12.

- Executioners—An angel brought death to an Assyrian camp (2 Kgs 19:20–34) A destroying angel was sent, but later withheld, to punish David for his vanity in taking a census of the great number of his people (2 Sam 24; 1 Chr 21). At the time of Moses and the Exodus, the Egyptian firstborn where killed by an angel of death (Exod 11–12).

While the New Testament largely echoes the Old Testament in its minimal theology of angels, there was a significant new development in "angelology" between the Testaments that affected many in the Jewish and early Christian communities regarding their perceptions about angels. After the Babylonian exile of the Jews (586–517 BC), "angelology" expanded and diversified, and took on both mystical and apocalyptic qualities. Emerging speculations debated hierarchies, ranks, and supposed key leaders among the angels. Books about spiritual battlegrounds and eternal conflicts became best-sellers,[14] and increasingly developed elaborate perceptions about spiritual battle-

14. Notably the Book of Enoch, parts of which were likely authored in the third century BC, but which probably was edited into its current form in the first century BC. It purported to be a record of visions (hidden for many centuries) received by the mysterious Enoch of Genesis 5:21–24. Enoch supposedly peered into heaven's past and viewed the rebellious angels called "watchers." These watchers challenged God's authority, were defeated and cast out of heaven, and spread sin's pollution to earth during humanity's infancy. The swirling of angelic hosts in constant combat around humankind was thought to be the source of on-going evil intentions among some humans (as picked up by New Testament writer Jude in verses 14–15 of his short but frantic letter) who were as influenced by the fallen ones as others of us are by the good ones. Jude also references (verse 9) the Testament of Moses (sometimes known as the Assumption of Moses) which imagines Moses giving final instructions and reports of visions about the future to Joshua as they wander together up Mount Nebo on Moses' end-of-life journey. Angels, in this document, play a pivotal role in both the rebellion of humans against God, and also in the application of salvation to humankind by God.

fields where unseen angels barely staved off murderous attacks by demons. Even Jesus' close friend Peter (2 Pet 2–3) and his younger brother Jude (Jude 8–16) found this fascinating, and saw this spiritual warfare interrupting and disturbing human history and the composure of the early church.

Spiritual warfare continues to be a deep religious engagement. Popular songs call on angels as warriors for the defense in complex inner struggles.[15] But apocalyptic visions and mystical speculations do not drive the mind of the author of Hebrews, or shape the world as he sees it. Nor is his mind captured by fierce psychological struggles in which angels might lend a winning hand. Instead, the classic messenger role of angels is key to understanding the importance of angels in the early paragraphs of this tome. While angels are mentioned twelve times in Hebrews,[16] ten of those incidents occur in the first two chapters where the message is very clear: in spite of their hugely significant role as divine ambassadors, Jesus, the man who came among us for a time, is vastly superior to the angels.

Where Have We Come So Far?

- God has spoken in times past.
    - This is our source of direction and confidence.
    - We know who we are because of the prophets.
- God has recently spoken a stronger, better, and clearer message through Jesus.
    - So when we, who live by the prophetic message, hear Jesus, we had better listen.
- Jesus is superior to the angels.

Message: Quotations

One of the most traumatic incidents in my life happened when I was teaching at the Reformed Theological College of Nigeria. As was the practice, I

15. Note, for instance, Julia Brennan's powerful prayer "Inner Demons" (https://www.youtube.com/watch?v=3gydcChFnzQ), in which "demons" and "angels" are expressive of elements of self that are both deeply connected to our personal identities, and are also, at the same time, powers that work upon us, and need guidance or taming: "Inner demons don't play by the rules" and "So angels please, please stay here/Take the pain, take the fear."

16. Hebrews 1:4, 5, 6, 7, 13; 2:2, 5, 7, 9, 16; 12:22; 13:2.

assigned the students in my fourth-year Old Testament Prophets class the task of writing an exegesis paper.

An exegesis is an in-depth analysis of a particular passage of Scripture. It examines themes and literary structure, meanings of words, historical context, theological implications, and so forth. In class, we discussed how to write the paper: what resources to use in the library, how to put it together, and what conclusions to draw.

Every day I stopped by the library and saw my students hard at work. They looked up from their books and grinned broadly. They told me their papers were going to be the best papers they had ever written, and that I would be so proud of them.

When the day of reckoning came, my students gleamed with pride. My hopes and expectations ran high. After class, I went straight home and sat down to read.

Plagiarism

Immediately my heart sank. These weren't exegesis papers. These were pages and pages of quotations lifted directly from commentaries—without footnotes or credits. In some cases, the only original word in the paper was the student's name at the top of the first page. I could even detect style changes when a student had switched from copying out of one book to copying out of another.

English was a second language for my students, and they used it quite well. But technical jargon was far beyond them. Yet, technical terms were littered throughout their papers as if they were as common as the greetings we spoke each morning. The students pretended these words and ideas were their own, cheapening the authors' ideas by imitating them.

I went to the principal of the school and unburdened myself. He explained that plagiarism was a perpetual problem; every year he warned students against it, but it never stopped. "Do what you think is best," he advised me.

This is what I did. I took the students' papers to the library. For two days I searched through commentaries, word studies, and other theological resources, finding as many of the passages the students had copied as I could. I wrote the references on their papers. Then I gave an F to all twelve students.

Few experiences have torn me apart as much as this. My decision caused an awful stir at the school. Students from that class came to my door at all hours of the day to protest. "Sir," they said, "you told us to use the commentaries. You told us to read the books. You told us to find out what others were saying."

Nourished by Words

That is the problem, isn't it? There is hardly an original thought in this world. The writer of Ecclesiastes said it generations ago: "There is nothing new under the sun."[17] Whatever is has been before. So my students were caught in a predicament: I wanted them to use the wisdom and knowledge of others, yet at the same time, I wanted them to speak their own thoughts, write their own words, and express their own ideas. After all, that is the only way to truly learn. A photocopier knows nothing. It may process thousands of pictures and billions of words, but it does not have intelligence of its own.

The first several pages of Hebrews seem to weigh heavily as an astounding expression of plagiarism. True, the writer does acknowledge that he is quoting, but he rarely indicates where the quotes are found. In fact, he assumes his readers know the Scriptures as well as he does, so that when he references a passage, they will immediately glom on to both the text and its context.

This style of writing is typical of early Christianity.[18] Paul does much the same in the first chapters of his letter to the Romans, and Matthew includes Old Testament citations thirty-six times, mostly quoted by Jesus, only a few times connecting them specifically with original sources. Peter's first letter is rife with unreferenced Scripture quotations,[19] in a manner very similar to what we find in Hebrews.[20]

But plagiarism is clearly not the intent. Nearly all of these scriptural quotations are acknowledged as such, even if they are rarely attributed to their original books or authors. This is very different from the use of others' words as if they are one's own.

Idea Thieves

A woman once told me of an interesting experience she had one Sunday. At church that morning, she said, her minister preached a sermon based on a

17. Eccl 1:9

18. The fourth edition of the United Bible Societies' Greek Testament (1993) lists 343 Old Testament quotations in the New Testament, as well as no fewer than 2,309 allusions and verbal parallels.

19. Fourteen.

20. Forty-one.

text from one of the Gospels. In the afternoon she went to a friend's church and heard a different minister preach a sermon from a text in the book of Acts.

But the two sermons, she said, were identical. They had the same structure, the same points, the same terminology, and the same conclusion. You may know how this happened—one or both of the ministers was using a sermon prepared by someone else, without making it his own through creative interaction with the text and ideas.

It was probably a good sermon, but under the circumstances, the message was cheapened, wasn't it? The message was not really taken from the Bible texts, for how can one sermon flow from two different passages of Scripture? Nor did it spring from the spiritual struggles of at least one of the ministers, for how can two men, with different personalities and different ministries, preach exactly the same sermon? It cannot be done.

Plagiarism is not right, even when ministers do it—maybe especially then. But there is another side to this coin. Poor is the person who plagiarizes, yet poorer still is the person who has no quotation marks in his life at all: the person who never reads a poem, learns a lesson, memorizes a song, or digs into a book. The person who thinks she can make it through life on her own resources, shaped by her own knowledge. Poor is the person who carries through life few quotation marks from the vast wealth and resources of others.

Shared Foundations

I have always been intrigued by Paul's final comments in his second letter to young Timothy. The letter was written from his final prison cell, and it may be the last thing he wrote before he died. In it, Paul hands Timothy a treasure of fatherly wisdom about pasturing the congregation at Ephesus. He ends by urging Timothy to come visit him and adds, "Bring my scrolls, especially the parchments."[21]

Why were the parchments so important? While we may never be sure of the answer, the request is weighed with meaning. Paul knew that learning was life. He knew that when he stopped reading, he stopped growing. He knew that through education we become richer, deeper, wiser people.

If you were locked up in prison with him, what would you need to survive? Food? Water? An hour of sunlight each day?

What about books? Are there quotation marks in your life—marks that show how broad and deep and wise your heart is becoming?

21. 2 Tim 2:13.

Benjamin Weir, a Presbyterian minister, was a hostage in Lebanon for over a year, much of the time in solitary confinement. How did he survive? How did he keep his wits about him? By calling to mind Scripture passages and reciting verses he had memorized in his younger years. He says he stayed alive only by calling up the quotation marks in his memory.[22]

Enriched by Quotations

Years ago I knew two doctors at a hospital in London, Ontario, Canada—men with extremely busy schedules—who met once a month over coffee to recite a sonnet they had memorized. Poetry was their gift to each other, a treasure they stored in their minds—fourteen lines a month, twelve times a year.

These people knew their inner resources, and they knew that they were nourished by the quotation marks they added to their lives.

Someone once said that the first half of our lives belongs to the extrovert—the person within us who is willing to get out and do things, to make waves, to achieve success in life. But the second half belongs to the introvert—the part of us that sits and thinks and remembers and feeds on the inner resources of our hearts and minds.

If this is true, what would happen if we reached the second half of life and found nothing inside? Listen to the words of Robert Louis Stevenson: "As if a man's soul were not too small to begin with, they have dwarfed and narrowed theirs by a life of all work and no play; until here they are at forty, with a listless attention, a mind vacant of all material of amusement, and not one thought to rub against another, while they wait for the train."[23]

Is Stevenson talking about someone you know? Do you have a treasure of quotation marks in your heart? Have you read the Bible through? Have you memorized the Psalms? Have you read the great classics of literature? Do you know the beauty of poetry?

The novelist Margaret Prescott Montague was blind. One day she realized that her hearing was deteriorating; soon her world would be very small. "How will you cope?" someone asked her. Listen to her answer: "If the world be closed without, I'll sail the hidden seas within."[24]

If your eyes were dimmed and your ears stopped, if your senses no longer brought you news of the world around, how far could you sail on

---

22. Weir, Weir, and Benson, *Hostage Bound.*

23. Madden, Patrick, ed. "An Apology for Idlers." *Robert Lewis Stevenson* (blog) *Quotidiana,* October 21, 2006, http://essays.quotidiana.org/stevenson/apology_for_idlers/.

24. Montague, "Writers of Day," 23–24.

the hidden seas within? Some people's hidden seas are like muddy swamps, shallow and stagnant. But others' are like broad and beautiful oceans. When they leave one port, they have resources to explore new continents and new horizons.

Living in a Bigger World

Years ago someone asked Edgar Frank where he came from. "Goshen," he said.

> *How can you live in Goshen?*
> *Said a friend from afar.*
> *This is a wretched little place*
> *Where people talk about tawdry things*
> *And plant cabbages in the moonlight . . . .*
>
> *But I do not live in Goshen, I answered.*
> *I live in Greece*
> *Where Plato taught and Phidias carved.*
> *I live in Rome*
> *Where Cicero penned immortal lines*
> *And Michelangelo dreamed things of beauty.*
> *Do not think my world is small*
> *Because you find me in a little village.*
> *I have my books, my pictures, my dreams,*
> *Enchantments that transcend Time and Space.*
> *I do not live in Goshen at all,*
> *I live in an unbounded universe*
> *With the great souls of all the ages*
> *For my companions.*[25]

Do you know what Frank was talking about? Are you still going to school— the school of great literature, the school of great music, the school of the Bible? Is yours a life filled with quotation marks?

For the writer of Hebrews, quotations mean everything. They establish common language. They call out recognized idioms. They remind his readers of the theological foundations they share. And they draw attention to cosmological patterns that form the structures of their existences.

25. Edgar Frank, "Goshen," http://poetryexplorer.net/poem.php?id=10060852.

Chapter 3

This Is Important

Text: Hebrews 2:1–4

Angels, Testimony and Miracles

> Therefore we must pay greater attention to what we have heard, so that we do not drift away from it. For if the message declared through angels was valid, and every transgression or disobedience received a just penalty, how can we escape if we neglect so great a salvation? It was declared at first through the Lord, and it was attested to us by those who heard him, while God added his testimony by signs and wonders and various miracles, and by gifts of the Holy Spirit, distributed according to his will.

Backstory: Warning

THIS IS THE FIRST of six warnings issued by the writer of Hebrews. Most warnings are longer than their predecessors, and all grow more detailed in the specifics of what behaviors are challenged:

1. Hebrews 2:1–3—This message is very important, and all who ignore or reject any divinely-given instructions are liable to judgment.

2. Hebrews 3:12–13—All instructions have a time limit for response, and you miss that window of opportunity to your own peril.

3. Hebrews 4:1—God has issued a call for us to enter Sabbath rest, but the door through which we receive it is closing soon.

4. Hebrews 5:11–6:12—Your learning curve seems to be slowing, and I feel like I have to repeat things again and again, but I trust that you will get it now and move along to more complex ideas and challenges.

5. Hebrews 10:19–39—Now that you know the truth, you are responsible for it. Remember the strength of your young faith, years ago? Don't grow weak and disobedient now. Nudge one another along, if you have to.

6. Hebrews 12:1–13:17—The challenge has been laid; keep running toward Jesus in spite of persecution. And live in such a way that those who attack you will notice the godly character of your lives.

These warnings are a natural development from the initial images given in chapter 1. God is speaking, so we had better listen. Because we cannot generally hear the voice of God on our own, or connect with the messages God wishes to communicate without intermediaries, God has provided for us the angels and the prophets. This is the story behind the text, and the writer of Hebrews assumes his readers will immediately catch on, since they have rehearsed often the Passover remembrances of their family.

A New Identity

When the nation of Israel came out of Egypt and met God at Mount Sinai there was a political transaction taking place. Israel had belonged to the Pharaoh of Egypt. Now she belonged to God. God had fought the Pharaoh for the right to own and care for Israel, and he had won. Just as prior to the exodus the Pharaoh had specified the contours of his relationship with Israel, so now God did the same. At the top of Mount Sinai, God and Moses hammered out the political and social and religious covenant that would determine the character of Israel's future existence.

One element of that political landscape included the inescapable clause, "I am the Lord your God who brought you out of Egypt, out of the land of bondage."[1] This was the declaration of sovereign authority. There would be no ruler in Israel except the God of the covenant.

Yet even this God would need mediaries. God would require human spokespersons to translate his glory into Hebrew speech. The greatest of all the spokespersons, of course, was Moses. Moses stood above the common Israeli crowd, an almost superhuman hero, a leader without peers.

1. Exod 20:1.

The First Prophet and Other Voices

Moses stood at the helm of Israel's wandering ship for forty years, bringing her to the lights of Canaan's harbor. Then Moses died, and the navigational sextant was placed in Joshua's hands.[2] Joshua helped Israel claim the new colonial territory on behalf of the kingdom of heaven. And when he died, the lines of authority passed into the care of the "elders" of the people.[3] These older, wiser men were eyewitnesses of many of the great legends that created the nation of Israel.

When they died, the legends grew, but the faith wilted. Israel was adrift at sea, lost in a storm of international intrigue and factional dissension. A few powerful "judges" managed to prevent the confederation from disintegrating all together, but it was obvious that stronger measures of leadership were necessary to bring the nation back to days of self-confidence, and a place of recognition among neighboring kingdoms.

The crisis of the book of Judges precipitated grassroots calls for a king. "Give us a king," they told Samuel.[4] "Give us a king," they prayed to God, so long hidden. The outcome was the monarchy—established by Saul,[5] consolidated by David,[6] expanded by Solomon,[7] ripped apart by Jeroboam,[8] and eventually whimpering into oblivion at the hands of the Assyrian empire (722 BC)[9] and the Babylonian scourge (586 BC).[10]

During the declining centuries of the monarchy, a strange bunch of men wrestled the spiritual leadership of the people from the hands of the political kings, often surrounded by their cultic priests. These "outside-the-system" renegades were known as the prophets. Some bartered their perspectives in the marketplaces. Some became wailing fixtures in the temple precincts. Some were used by kings as ex officio advisors, and some were hunted down as traitors to the political cause.

---

2. See Josh 1.

3. Josh 23. Note how Joshua first handed the direction of Israel's future over to the "elders" of the people, and then followed up by calling all of Israel to a forward-looking covenant renewal ceremony (Josh 24).

4. 1 Sam 8.

5. 1 Sam 9–11.

6. 2 Sam 1–8.

7. 1 Kings 9–10.

8. 1 Kgs 11–12.

9. 2 Kgs 17.

10. 2 Kgs 25.

Growing Concerns

Yet the prophets became the de facto leaders of the people, urging spiritual chastity and calling for restoration of the religious and political and economic order established by the covenant. Elijah was one of the greatest among these.[11] He lived up to his name, which meant "My God is Yahweh."

Although Elijah was able to do many special and seemingly miraculous things, he is never portrayed as a wizard or some kind of superhuman figure. In fact, all of the miracles that happen when Elijah is around point only to God as the one who brings life and promotes healing. Elijah wields no power; rather, he understands what God is all about, what God's goals for the world are, and where to find the imprint of the divine creative and restoring fingers.

Elijah understood the covenant stipulations: when God's people broke faith with God, God would withhold the needed rains until they finally came to their senses. Elijah was well-versed in the promises of God's covenant that the Lord of heaven and earth would make the world blossom for the good of the people when they trusted God. The prophets' prayers were not secret codes that moved the tumblers of heaven's resources' vaults. Rather, they were God's own speech becoming audible again in an age that had forgotten how to listen.

We often want prayer to be our magic potion that will force God to do our bidding. But no one can move the fingers of God until they have first absorbed God's covenant and God's character and God's vision, struggling like the prophets to understand the mind of God and living in a way that has put God's priorities first.

Where Have We Come So Far?

- God has spoken in times past.
  - This is our source of direction and confidence.
  - We know who we are because of the prophets.
- God has recently spoken a stronger, better, and clearer message through Jesus.
  - So when we, who live by the prophetic message, hear Jesus, we had better listen.
- Jesus is superior to the angels.

11. 1 Kgs 17–21.

- The great divine message that formed us came through Moses, but the message itself was delivered to him by angels (Deut 33:2; Acts 7:53).

- Yet Jesus is superior to angels, and therefore delivers a more important prophetic message than that through the great prophet Moses.

- So stick with Jesus, even though you are tempted to turn away from him.

- There is no higher authority or source of connection with God.

- And if our lives are to be connected to God, we turn away from Jesus to our own peril.

Message: Watch Out!

Every parent of young children can identify with this: a little boy was asked his name, and he replied, "John, don't." Sometimes it seems that parents have only no's for their little ones. "No, Sarah"; "You mustn't do that, Matthew"; "John, don't."

It may sound harsh, but when we say "no" to our children it is often a matter of safety, a means of survival. We say it to keep them from falling out of a window or stepping out into a busy street or drinking poison.

Adults need no's in their lives too. But for adults it is not always a matter of safety or survival. Usually it has more to do with self-definition. In order to truly say yes in life, we must also learn to say no.

Defining Character

Think of it. If you can't say no, then you lose the power to say yes. If you are capable of doing anything, if there is nothing you wouldn't do, then you have no character. Character is something we define by drawing lines, by closing off possibilities, by saying, "I am this because I am not that. I cannot be that because I want to be this."

That is really the point of the negatives in the Ten Commandments. God is not trying to play the killjoy. God is dealing with us in grace. "Do not have any other gods before me," God says. "If you do, you will miss the real thing your life is all about. Do not look for happiness in illicit sexual encounters; if you do, you will miss the one greatest joy of your sexuality that you could find in troth. Do not speak an untruth, or you yourself will become a lie."

G. K. Chesterton put it marvelously. He said that art and morality have this in common: they know where to draw the line.[12] That is definition. That is closing some things and shutting other things out. Only when we draw lines can we develop some sense of character, some understanding of personality, some consciousness of identity.

Meandering Journey

Our religious pilgrimage often begins in places and among peoples that know no limits. One day we wake up in the slippery and enticing world where boundaries are gone. We are able to say yes to everything, and in so doing suddenly become a slave of fad and fashion. We don't even know who we are anymore.

That is when the cry of desperation erupts from our lips: "Save me, Lord." Grace works within limits: no to this and yes to that. Any true pilgrim will never crawl to the road toward the kingdom of God until she or he learns the power of the word no, a word that defines the beauty of God's great yes.

The Ugliness of Sin

Oscar Wilde penned a powerful story about behaviors and definitions and justice called *The Picture of Dorian Gray*.[13] Dorian was a handsome young man, a model of physical beauty and moral virtue. People complimented him on his good graces. Parents pointed to him as an example to their youth. One artist even painted an exquisite portrait of him.

Dorian idolized the painting. He woke each morning to admire it. He ended every day with a gaze at his mirrored perfection. Someone so lovely could do no wrong, he began to think, or at least would not be punished for it. In his vanity, he became selfish and indulgent. He sampled the sins of the streets. He debauched himself in the opium dens of London's darker dives.

Of course, Dorian's crimes and carelessness took their toll. Soon the perfect portrait on the wall began to haunt him. The picture of a radiant and wholesome young man gleamed down on his puffy face and diseased body

12. Gilbert Keith Chesterton: "Art, like morality, consists of drawing the line somewhere." In "Our Note Book" by G. K. Chesterton, *Illustrated London News* (May 1928) 780, column 1. London, England.

13. Wilde, *Picture of Dorian Gray*.

and glazed eyes. If only he could look that way again. If only the portrait could absorb the marks of his sin.

Transference

And miraculously, that's what happened. Before long, his youthful glow returned. The more he caroused at night, the healthier and handsomer he became. And on the wall, the painting slowly became etched and lined with the wickedness of Dorian Gray.

What a life. Each day, people marveled at his virtue and eternal youth. And by night he wallowed in every vice, with no recrimination. The now ugly painting on the wall absorbed every evil, and tallied each painful degradation.

Dorian could no longer endure even a casual glance at the horrible picture. He hid it in the attic and only occasionally sneaked up to survey the damage. Over the years, what little resemblance there may have been between young Dorian Gray and the grotesque monster in the painting was all but lost.

But the painting remained a sacramental testimony of his wickedness. It was a haunting conscience, an inviolate judge on the life and times of Dorian Gray. It stood as accuser. It never lied. It drove him mad.

One night he could stand it no longer. Knife in hand, he ascended the stairs to the attic courtroom and attacked the awful witness that spoke silently for the prosecution.

Prosecution

When his servants searched the house the next day, looking for Master Gray, they found only the wretched body of a ghastly old man in the attic, knife through his heart. And on the wall beamed the handsome and virtuous face of the painting of Dorian Gray.

Wilde's story summarizes two themes that linger within each of us. The first is a sense of morality. Dorian knew right from wrong. He realized there was a proper way to live and a style of life that was evil and degrading. God made us with a conscience, says the apostle Paul, and no one is without excuse in matters of morality.

Second, Wilde pointed a finger to justice. Blind justice. Standing there weighing our deeds with her scales, meting out punishments. We would like to be excused. We would like a way out, a miraculous painting that absorbs our punishments and lets us off with only an ugly glance. But we know it will never happen. We get what we deserve, if not now, then when we die. Dorian Gray got his; we will get ours.

Unless someone does something about it. Unless there is a way out of this mess. Unless God might be gracious and transfer the ugliness of our sins to Jesus.

But, of course, if there is such a way, we had better listen to the message of the gospel. Even its warnings.

Chapter 4

Getting into Our Skin

Text: Hebrews 2:5–18

Now God did not subject the coming world, about which we are speaking, to angels. But someone has testified somewhere,

"What are human beings that you are mindful of them,
or mortals, that you care for them?
You have made them for a little while lower than the angels;
you have crowned them with glory and honor,
subjecting all things under their feet."[1]

Now in subjecting all things to them, God left nothing outside their control. As it is, we do not yet see everything in subjection to them, but we do see Jesus, who for a little while was made lower than the angels, now crowned with glory and honor because of the suffering of death, so that by the grace of God he might taste death for everyone.

It was fitting that God, for whom and through whom all things exist, in bringing many children to glory, should make the pioneer of their salvation perfect through sufferings. For the one who sanctifies and those who are sanctified all have one Father. For this reason Jesus is not ashamed to call them brothers and sisters, saying,

"I will proclaim your name to my brothers and sisters,

1. Ps 8:4–6.

in the midst of the congregation I will praise you."[2]

And again,

"I will put my trust in him."[3]

And again,

"Here am I and the children whom God has given me."[4]

Since, therefore, the children share flesh and blood, he himself likewise shared the same things, so that through death he might destroy the one who has the power of death, that is, the devil, and free those who all their lives were held in slavery by the fear of death. For it is clear that he did not come to help angels, but the descendants of Abraham. Therefore he had to become like his brothers and sisters in every respect, so that he might be a merciful and faithful high priest in the service of God, to make a sacrifice of atonement for the sins of the people. Because he himself was tested by what he suffered, he is able to help those who are being tested.

Backstory: A Purposeful Incarnation

The incarnation was a curve ball no one saw coming. As the great story of God's work in ancient Israel (particularly expansive during the reigns of David and Solomon) ignominiously tapered off into oblivion, with the demise of the Northern Kingdom (also called Israel) under the Assyrian onslaught in 922 BC, and the limping into exile of the Southern Kingdom (also called Judah) initiated by the Babylonian captivity finalized in 586 BC, the prophets logged in with an increasingly shrill message: "Here comes the 'Day of the Lord'!"[5]

2. Ps 22:22.

3. Ps 56:3.

4. Isa 8:18.

5. Isa 2:2, 11, 12, 17; 3:18; 4:2, 5; 7:18, 20; 11:11; 13:6, 9, 13; 19:16, 18, 19, 21; 22:5, 12, 25; 24:21; 27:12, 13; 28:5; 30:26; 34:8; 49:8; 51:9; 61:2; Jer 4:9; 5:18; 7:32; 12:3; 16:14, 19; 19:6; 23:5, 7, 20; 25:24, 33; 30:8, 24; 31:6, 27, 31, 33, 38; 33:14; 39:16; 46:10; 47:4; 48:47; 49:26, 39; 50:4, 20, 31; Lam 1:12; 2:1, 22; Ezek 12:23; 13:5; 20:5; 29:21; 30:3; 31:15; 38:18; 39:8, 13, 22; Joel 1:15; 2:1, 11, 31; 3:14, 18; Amos 2:16; 5:18, 20; 8:3; Obad 1:8, 15; Mic 2:4; 4:1; 5:10; Zeph 1:7, 8, 14, 18; 2:2, 3; 3:8; Hag 2:23; Zech 2:11; 3:9, 10; 8:23; 9:16; 12:4, 8; 13:2; 14:3, 13, 20, 21; Mal 3:17; 4:1, 3, 5.

Divine Interruption

This "Day of the Lord" talk was a reflection based first on the divine in-breaking into human history that initiated God's redemptive plan. In its earliest stages, the biblical salvation story was a dialogue between God and the key figures of Abram's[6] family, particularly the great patriarch himself[7] and his notorious grandson Jacob.[8] The real fireworks erupted some five hundred years later, however, when the family had grown very large, but was debilitated through enslavement in Egypt.[9] God forcibly stepped into the days of our lives, fighting against the Pharaoh of Egypt for the right to own and lead Israel to her destiny.[10] Out of this traumatic divine engagement, Israel was born as a nation, shaped at Mount Sinai through a suzerain-vassal covenant,[11] and planted as a witness to the nations in the narrow strip of ter-

6. Known throughout Scripture as "Abraham" after Yahweh changed his name in the covenant-making ceremony of Genesis 17.

7. Gen 12–22.

8. Gen 26–34.

9. Exod 1.

10. Exod 4–15.

11. One of the dominant civilizations of the second millennium was the Hittite kingdom. Somewhat secluded in the mountainous plateaus of Anatolia (eastern Turkey today), the Hittites shaped a vast web of international relations which, at the height of their power in the fourteenth century BC, encompassed most of the ancient Near East. While they were companions of other similar civilizations that shared commonalities of culture and conquests and cities, the Hittites linger in archaeological and historical studies for, among other things, their standardization of a written code used extensively in the normalization of international relations. In order to establish appropriate structures that would spell out the Hittites' on-going interactions with subjected peoples, a prescribed treaty form appears to have been widely used. The parameters of the typical Hittite suzerain-vassal covenant included:

A preamble which declared the identity and power of the ruler responsible for establishing this relationship.

A historical prologue outlining the events leading up to this relationship, so that it could be set into a particular context and shaped by a cultural or religious frame.

Stipulations which specified the responsibilities and actions associated with the relationship.

Curses and blessing that evoked the negative and positive outcomes if this covenant were either breached or embraced by the parties.

Witnesses who were called to affirm the legitimacy of this covenant-making event, and who would then hold the parties accountable.

Document clauses which described ratification ceremonies, specified future public recitations of the treaty, and noted the manner in which the copies of the covenant were to be kept.

What makes this bit of ancient historical trivia so intriguing for biblical scholars is the uncanny correspondence between the elements of this Hittite covenant code and the literature at the heart of Israel's encounter with God at Sinai. Note the following:

ritory called Canaan, bridging three continents and serving as a trade and conquest route for virtually every nation on earth at the time.[12]

As the dark days of Assyrian destructions and Babylonian limitations dominated, Israel's prophets gained regular visions of a coming time when God would again break into human history, this time righting all wrongs, judging nations, cleansing the world, and inaugurating an eternal kingdom

---

When God is first heard to speak from the rumbling mountain, the words are essentially the preamble of a suzerain-vassal covenant: "I am the Lord your God" (Exod 20:1).

Immediately following is a brief historical prologue reminding the people of the events that precipitated this encounter: "who brought you out of the land of Egypt, out of the house of bondage" (Exod 20:2).

Then comes a recitation of stipulations that will shape the ethics, morality, and lifestyle of the community (Exod 20:3–23:19).

Following these are the curses and blessings (Exod 23:20–33) of a typical covenant document. What is unusual in this case is that the order is reversed so that the blessings precede the curses. This provides the same rigors of participatory onus but gives it a freshness of grace and optimism that are often absent from the quick condemnation of the usual ordering.

The witnesses are the elders of the Israelite community (Exod 24:1–2), bringing authentication of this process and these documents into the human realm, when it was often spiritualized in other covenants by listing local gods as moderators of these events.

Finally, there is the document clause (Exod 24:3–18) that spells out the ratification ceremony. It will be followed by a further reflection on the repositories of the covenant document copies once the tabernacle has been built.

The striking resonance between the usual form of the Hittite suzerain-vassal covenant and the essential first speech of Yahweh to Israel at Mount Sinai makes it difficult not to assess the beginnings of conscious Israelite religion in terms other than that of a suzerain (Yahweh) vassal (Israel) covenant-making ceremony. Furthermore, this appears to elucidate the mode and function of the first biblical documents. They were not intended to be origin myths, ancestor hero stories, mere legal or ethical or civil codes, sermons, prophecies, or apocalyptic visions (though all of these would later accrete to the initial writings of the first community encounter with Yahweh); they were initially the written covenant documents formulating the relationship between a nation and the (divine) ruler who earned, in battle, the right to order her world.

This is why the word "covenant" becomes an essential term for all the rest of the literature that will be garnered into the collection eventually known as the Bible. The Bible begins with a covenant-making ceremony that produces certain documents, and then continues to grow as further explications of that covenant relationship are generated. One can read theology or ethics or politics or history out of the Bible, but one cannot do so while ignoring the essential role of the Sinai covenant between Yahweh and Israel. Even the idea of "kingdom," so prevalent and pervasive in the Bible, is predicated on the covenant, for it is by way of the covenant that Israel becomes the dominion of the great King. The kingdom of God is the context for all that is portrayed in the Bible, but the covenant is the administrative document through which the kingdom takes hold and adheres in the human societies which form the front ranks of Yahweh's citizenry.

12. Notice Isaiah's keen sense of this missional purpose for Israel, and the unique role of its geographical location in Isa 2:1–4.

of peace and well-being.[13] The Old Testament ends with these fearful, hopeful, almost wistful expectations,[14] and the Jewish world holds its breath for the big day to arrive.

The Twist No One Saw Coming

Then Jesus comes. John the Baptist ties his arrival to prophetic fulfillment of the "Day of the Lord" prophecies.[15] Jesus himself makes the same connection when he speaks in his hometown synagogue and engages in the healings of the messianic age.[16] Peter clearly affirms exactly this when he preaches to the Pentecost crowds about Jesus using Joel 2 as his text.[17]

Yet it was all a bit of a conundrum. Jesus was supposed to be the central element of this new "Day of the Lord," but his arrival was a lot tamer than the prophets seemed to foretell. Even John the Baptist began to wonder whether he had gotten the message about Jesus wrong.[18]

What nobody had seen coming was that God split the "Day of the Lord," bringing the beginnings of all that was promised in the person of Jesus himself, while delaying the worst of its effects on our world until more might participate in its best. Jesus endured the horrific pains of judgment and punishment on the cross. Jesus called out a remnant community of witness. Jesus displayed the hopeful signs of the coming age through his miracles of healing and life-renewal, and empowered his followers to bring the same touch of eternity into time.

This is what the writer of Hebrews admires about Jesus. It is also why he calls on us to stand back in wonder at the amazing thing God is doing through the Son, who is our true high priest. No other human has ever played such a role. Nor, for that matter, can or could any angel.

Where Have We Come So Far?

- God has spoken in times past.
  - This is our source of direction and confidence.

---

13. Note especially Isa 11–12, 54–64; Jer 31, 33; Ezek 34–48; Zech 9–14; Joel 2.
14. Note the language of Mal 3–4.
15. Matt 3; Luke 1, 3.
16. Luke 4.
17. Acts 2.
18. Matt 11.

- ◆ We know who we are because of the prophets.
- God has recently spoken a stronger, better, and clearer message through Jesus.
  - ◆ So when we, who live by the prophetic message, hear Jesus, we had better listen.
- Jesus is superior to the angels.
  - ◆ The great divine message that formed us came through Moses, but the message itself was delivered to him by angels (Deut 33:2; Acts 7:53).
  - ◆ Yet Jesus is superior to angels, and therefore delivers a more important prophetic message than that through the great prophet Moses.
- So stick with Jesus, even though you are tempted to turn away from him.
  - ◆ There is no higher authority or source of connection with God.
  - ◆ And if our lives are to be connected to God, we turn away from Jesus to our own peril.
- God has made the world subject to Jesus.
  - ◆ God never did this with the angels, so, again, Jesus is superior to them.
  - ◆ But this only happened because Jesus first fully identified with the world.
- Jesus willingly came into the world to fully experience its pain.
- And this is to our benefit for three reasons:
  - ◆ To fully identify with us as sisters and brothers.
  - ◆ To make atonement for our sins (which cause the pain of this world).
  - ◆ To bring us with him fully into the house of God.

Message: He Was One of Us

The story of God's love in the Bible focuses on Jesus, as the writer of Hebrews constantly reminds us. But Jesus did not appear in a vacuum. Throughout the Old Testament, God made it clear that God would send a specially commissioned person to bring healing and forgiveness to the citizens of earth.

As priests, kings, and prophets were anointed with oil at the start of their careers, so this person, too, would be anointed. In fact, this special deliver would be called "the Anointed," a term which comes across in Hebrew as "Messiah" and in Greek as "Christ." This is the idea behind the quotations and reference allusions in the first several chapters of Hebrews.

While God's people remained confident that God was about to do another tremendous redemptive work on planet Earth, the details remained shrouded and misty. It was not at all clear how the looming "Day of the Lord" would emerge from heaven's occluded hiddenness into earth's everyday existence. So when Jesus appeared on the scene, various interpretations about his identity and its relationship to the prophetic "Day of the Lord" quickly developed.

Ebionite "Adoptionism"

One perspective emphasized Jesus' humanity but in a divinely asserted and uniquely empowered role. Seeking continuity with God's saving initiatives in their people's past, Ebionite Christians declared that Jesus was "Savior" and "Messiah" in a similar manner to Moses, Joshua, and Samuel at the great points of crisis and change in Israel's history.[19] Jesus was the Messiah foretold by Israel's prophets, but he was truly and fully human, not divine, empowered by God to bring about deliverance for God's people. In the face of declining Jewish commitments to the ceremonial and legal codes of the Torah, according to the Ebionites, Jesus demanded a stronger fidelity that included heart devotion in addition to external practices. Jesus was killed, said

19. The word *Ebionites* is an anglicized version of an Aramaic term meaning "poor people." Irenaeus first named this group in his *Against Heresies* (I.xxvi.2) without explaining who they were or what they believed. Origen (*Against Celsus* II.1 and *First Principles* IV.i.22) doubly connected the title to poverty, declaring that these resource-challenged folks who were self-presumed Christians were to be considered heretics because of their parallel want of understanding the truth of the gospel (see also Eusebius, *Ecclesiastical History,* III.27). Justin Martyr explained Ebionite beliefs in his *Dialogue with Trypho* (xlvii), where he asserted that there were two groups of Jewish Christians who maintained fidelity with historic Jewish ceremonial practices, the one doing so because it was their custom (similar to Paul's continued expressions that he was a Pharisee well after becoming a missionary of Christ to the gentiles—Acts 23:6), while the other insisting that such practices were necessary for all Christians, even gentiles. This latter group was declared heretical because they denied the virgin birth and divinity of Jesus, continued to hold observance of Mosaic laws as mandatory for salvation, considered Paul a false teacher, and believed only the Gospel of Matthew to be scriptural truth alongside the Law and the Prophets (Irenaeus, *Against Heresies,* I.xxvi.2, III.xxi.2, IV.xxxiii.4, V.i.3; Hippolytus of Rome, *Refutation of All Heresies,* VIII. xxi, X.xviii; Tertullian, *The Flesh of Christ,* xiv.18).

the Ebionites, because the religious leaders of his day found him threatening and unsettling, particularly when he called them hypocrites and invited
the general Jewish population to question their authority. These Ebionites
believed God raised Jesus from the dead to vindicate Jesus' faithful service.
Christians, they said, should respond to Jesus' calls for deep devotion to
God, and serve as his witnesses in the Jewish community, emphasizing the
need for Jews to more fully and faithfully keep the ceremonial practices and
holiness codes. Gentiles might also become Christians, Ebionites admitted,
but only if they first became Jews, and fully invested themselves into Jewish
identity and religious practices.

In effect, Ebionite Christians understood Jesus to be somewhat like a
man wearing a heroic avatar persona. Jesus remained fully human, but due
to God's special dispensation of divine empowerment, he was able to speak
more clearly about the things of heaven, perform miracles, and call God's
people to truer faithfulness. Out of step with most Christians, the Ebionites
would only read Matthew's Gospel as Scripture alongside the Hebrew Bible.
They believed Paul to be a monstrous blasphemer for having adapted so
fully into the non-Jewish Hellenist world of his gentile converts and for vio-
lating true monotheism in his declarations that Jesus is God.

We recognize this Ebionite perspective as it lingers in our current
society. Jesus was a good man, some say, perhaps one of the greatest who
has ever lived. Jesus was an incredible teacher, or a superb moral prophet,
according to others. We have so much to learn from him.

True, but if our appreciation of Jesus stops there, we miss the biblical point. God's work among us is not limited to injecting larger-than-life
leaders into our irredeemable situation now and again, either to wake us up
or get us to cope and survive. God enters our world to address the realities
of sin and evil that threaten and destroy us. And that kind of job requires
someone more than merely human, no matter how good or insightful he or
she might be.

Gnostic "Docetism"

A competing view regarding Jesus in the early church was held by the gnostics. Gnosticism saw the world as cosmologically dualistic. All of physical
reality was bad and degraded, while spiritual dimensions of life were good
and empowering. The ultimate deity was like that of the Greek Stoics—
non-relational, dispassionate, impassive, unchanging, and transcendent.
But since the material world actually existed, an emanation (called the
demiurge) from the transcendent god must have served as a secondary or

subordinate creator. Of course, any god which would bring into being material things was already compromised. So, clearly, the deity of the Jews, the
Creator God of the Old Testament, had to be a bad god. This distinguished
Christianity from Judaism, according to gnostics. Like the demiurge (or
identified with the demiurge), the God of Genesis (and therefore all of the
Hebrew Scriptures) was certainly less than perfect, and may well have been
an ogre with a sadistic mean streak. Human beings, after all, are at best an
evil joke. Many of us (but not all), have a divine spark trapped within our
material shells, imprisoned almost to extinction by the loathsome attach-
ments we have to passion and appetites.

Christianity, however, is the religion of Jesus, the liberator. Obviously, if Jesus is to bring salvation, he needs to transcend the material world,
which is inherently bad. So gnostic forms of Christianity took one of two
approaches when theologizing about Jesus. The docetists (from the Greek
word meaning to "seem" or "appear") believed that Jesus was only a divine
projection into our world (like a hologram), who was not actually human
and did not really interact directly with material substance. It was precisely
because of Jesus' intrinsic difference from us that he was able to speak to our
condition and provide a means of spiritual escape.

The adoptionists, on the other hand, similarly to the Ebionites, believed that Jesus was a very good human being who was then adopted by
God to be used as a temporary transmitter of divine teachings. When Jesus
was baptized by John, the Holy Spirit came upon him, granting to the man
Jesus the ability to see, know, and understand transcendent, spiritual things.
Later, when Jesus was being crucified, he himself acknowledged what had
happened, for he raised his face toward heaven and cried out, "Father, into
your hands I commend my spirit!"[20] This, of course, was the release, or separation, of the divine spirit from the human Jesus. Many of the adoptionist
gnostics believed that God was deeply grateful to Jesus (the man) for his
faithful service and partnership for a time with the divine spirit, and that
after Jesus (the man) died, God raised him up as a new kind of creature. This
resurrected Jesus was the prototype that true Christians should emulate,
and toward which they should aspire.

If we as humans are to gain release from our material prisons and
become truly liberated spirits, we need several things. First, we must gain
the appropriate knowledge. This is the origin of the term Gnosticism,
which is simply taken from the Greek word, γνωσις, meaning "knowing"
or "knowledge." Since we are all trapped in the same material muddle, only
a transcendent divine spirit can communicate this necessary knowledge to

20. Luke 23:46.

us. Jesus' life was all about this, whether as a projection into our experiences who was not himself fully, materially human, or by way of the unique divine insights and abilities granted the man who was adopted by God, and endowed with a special spiritual connection. So we need to learn the teachings of Jesus because these will help us shed the claws of materialism that dig into the divine sparks many of us are beginning to realize that we have. Of course, the sayings and parables of Jesus would be interpreted differently by gnostic teachers than they would by John, the disciple and friend of Jesus, and those who followed in his steps. That was the reason for the controversy which erupted in Gaius's congregation, which triggered the writing of the Johannine Epistles of the New Testament.

Second, we must engage in rituals of purification, through which we learn to transcend our own evil flesh and purify the growing power of our spirits. These may be negations of bodily functions, or solitary mystical reveries. In any case, they are very myopic and self-focused: "I am on a spiritual quest"; "I am seeking truth, which you might not be privy to"; "I cannot be bothered by your needs or concerns, since I have moved into transcendence."

Third, we must release the divine spark within us, ultimately through the death of our physical bodies. This is why, in the gnostic *Gospel of Judas*,[21] for instance, Jesus tells Judas that Judas's planned betrayal of Jesus is of supreme importance and constitutes the most necessary task that any of the disciples could accomplish. Judas is the hero of the story, for Judas alone understands that Jesus cannot be a fully blessed immaterial spirit until his physical flesh and blood dies. Only this will release the divine spark within him. So Judas is praised by Jesus as the one who does the very best thing in having Jesus killed. Physical death is the only guaranteed way to get rid of the material substance that diminishes true human life. Thus, Jesus' death and resurrection are at the center of gnostic theology, but their purposes are strikingly different than expressed in the rest of Christian hope and understanding. For Paul and John and the rest of the New Testament writers, Jesus' death was a scandal and a tragedy, even if it was part of the divine purpose and will. Jesus' resurrection was an affirmation of the goodness of human life restored, precisely in its material state. For gnostics, however, things were exactly the opposite. Jesus' death was the great release, and the resurrected Jesus was fully spiritual, completely separated from physical influence or limitation.

These opposing perspectives about the intended or best expression of human life produced the ethical concerns that the apostle John addresses in

21. Kasser et al., *Gospel of Judas*.

his first letter. Some gnostics evidently believed that since we are powerless to transform our bodies or material substance into anything good, we might as well allow our flesh to enjoy its pitiable quest for passion, and indulge ourselves in any gross sensuality that our bodies might lead us into. After all, our truest beings are not really engaged in these things; it is only our weak and self-destructive bodies that are so inclined. Meanwhile, our spirits are set on higher goals and purposes.

A second element of gnostic behavior, apparently, was that of ignoring the plight of others. Why should we try to alleviate the suffering which others experience in their flesh, since comfort only buttresses the pretense that their bodies have some meaning. We ought not to care for others, because such investments mess us up with material reality. These actions, in turn, only pull us away from our truest spiritual goals, strengthen the capacities and resolve of the material prisons of our bodies which hold our spirits in check, and prevent others, whose flesh is weakening, from gaining more quickly the blessed release that will happen to their spirits when their bodies actually die.

All of this seems to have fostered a kind of gnostic elitism. If some of us know these things, and others do not, we who know are better than those who do not know. We who have true knowledge from Jesus are on the track toward illumination and release, while those others are dumb dodos. Too bad they aren't like us, but there is not a thing we can do about it. We are enlightened; they are not.[22]

Like Ebionite views regarding Jesus, these gnostic perceptions continue to whisper. Jesus is the on-going manifestation of God's presence, appearing now and again to people in need, righting wrongs like Superman, or performing miracles in the unlikeliest of settings.

22. During the second century, a number of gnostic communities sprang up in the Christian church, particularly in its eastern regions. Clement of Alexandria (c. 150–c. 215) and his pupil, Origen (c. 185–254), were among the most articulate spokespersons of gnostic-influenced Christian theology who remained within the Orthodox faith. Irenaeus (c. 140–c. 202), Tertullian (c. 160–c. 220), and Hippolytus of Rome(170–235) all wrote extensively against the heresy of Gnosticism. One notable gnostic leader was Valentinus (c. 100 – c 160), who was born, lived and taught in Alexandria. He went to Rome in 136, expecting to be consecrated as a bishop. But when he was passed over for this promotion, Valentinus settled in Cyprus, further developing and propagating his gnostic ideas over against the teachings of the church he now despised as heretical. Eventually a strong gnostic center would emerge in the secluded safety of Egypt near a settlement today called Nag Hammadi. Here, in 1954, a huge library of "Christian" gnostic writings was discovered.

Immanuel—God with us, God for us

But neither Ebionite adoptionism nor gnostic docetism fit the message of the writer of Hebrews. Jesus is truly God, and that means there is no higher or better or stronger advocate for us (including the angels, esteemed and powerful as they are, who are God's favored creatures). At the same time, Jesus is fully and truly human, sharing with us all of the realities of material and physical life. Because we are struggling in a sin-compromised world, Jesus shared our journey completely with us. But because we need a power-ful Savior who is able to take us out of and beyond the fears and failings and pains of this existence, Jesus is also fully and completely divine.

Walter Wangerin, Jr. powerfully summarized the meaning of Jesus as Messiah in his allegory of the Ragman.[23] Wangerin pictures himself in a city on a Friday morning. A handsome young man comes to town, dragging behind him a cart made of wood. The cart is piled high with new, clean clothes, bright and shiny and freshly pressed.

Wandering through the streets the trader marches, crying out his strange deal: "Rags! New rags for old. Give me your old rags, your tired rags, your torn and soiled rags."

He sees a woman on the back porch of a house. She is old and tired and weary of living. She has a dirty handkerchief pressed to her nose, and she is crying a thousand tears, sobbing over the pains of her life.

The Ragman takes a clean linen handkerchief from his wagon and brings it to the woman. He lays it across her arm. She blinks at him, wonder-ing what he is up to. Gently the young man opens her fingers and releases the old, dirty, soaking handkerchief from her knotted fist.

Then comes the wonder. The Ragman touches the old rag to his own eyes and begins to weep her tears. Meanwhile, behind him on her porch stands the old woman, tears gone, eyes full of peace.

It happens again. "New rags for old," he cries, and he comes to a young girl wearing a bloody bandage on her head. He takes the caked and soiled wrap away and gives her a new bonnet from his cart. Then he wraps the old rags around his head. As he does this, the girl's cuts disappear and her skin turns rosy. She dances away with laughter and returns to her friends to play. But the Ragman begins to moan, and from her rags on his head the blood spills down.

He next meets a man. "Do you have a job?" the Ragman asks. With a sneer the man replies, "Are you kidding?" and holds up his shirtsleeve. There is no arm in it. He cannot work. He is disabled.

23. Paraphrased from Wangerin, Jr., *Ragman*.

But the Ragman says, "Give me your shirt. I'll give you mine."

The man's shirt hangs limp as he takes it off, but the Ragman's shirt hangs firm and full because one of the Ragman's arms is still in the sleeve. It goes with the shirt. When the man puts it on, he has a new arm. But the Ragman walks away with one sleeve dangling.

It happens over and over again. The Ragman takes the clothes from the tired, the hurting, the lost, and the lonely. He gathers them to his own body, and takes the pains into his own heart. Then he gives new clothes to new lives with new purpose and new joy.

Finally, around mid-day, the Ragman finds himself at the center of the city where nothing remains but a stinking garbage heap. It is the accumulated refuse of a society lost to anxiety and torture. On Friday afternoon the Ragman climbs the hill, stumbling as he drags his cart behind him. He is tired and sore and pained and bleeding. He falls on the wooden beams of the cart, alone and dying from the disease and disaster he has garnered from others.

Wangerin wonders at the sight. In exhaustion and uncertainty he falls asleep. He lies dreaming nightmares through all of Saturday, until he is shaken from his fitful slumbers early on Sunday morning. The ground quakes. Wangerin looks up. In surprise he sees the Ragman stand up. He is alive. The sores are gone, though the scars remain. But the Ragman's clothes are new and clean. Death has been swallowed up and transformed by life.

Still worn and troubled in his spirit, Wangerin cries up to the Ragman, "Dress me, Ragman. Give me your clothes to wear. Make me new."

We know the picture. It is Jesus coming into our world to share our sufferings and to bear our shame and guilt. Jesus stands in our place, dying our death so that we might gain a new and renewing relationship with God.

Sure, it is hard to explain. But it is also something, according to the writer of Hebrews, that we cannot live without.

Chapter 5

Better Than Moses

Text: Hebrews 3:1–6

> Therefore, brothers and sisters, holy partners in a heavenly calling, consider that Jesus, the apostle and high priest of our confession, was faithful to the one who appointed him, just as Moses also "was faithful in all God's house."[1] Yet Jesus is worthy of more glory than Moses, just as the builder of a house has more honor than the house itself. (For every house is built by someone, but the builder of all things is God.) Now Moses was faithful in all God's house as a servant, to testify to the things that would be spoken later. Christ, however, was faithful over God's house as a son, and we are his house if we hold firm the confidence and the pride that belong to hope.

Backstory: Moses

MOSES IS A UNIQUE figure in biblical literature. He was miraculously saved from the death sentence imposed by the Pharaoh of Egypt at the time, ending up becoming a member of the royal household. After four decades of wealth, power, and elite training as an Egyptian prince, Moses fled the palaces to begin a second forty-year career as a bedouin shepherd. And then, as if Moses' life was not yet full at eighty, he was called to a third forty-year leadership role, heading the unruly slave population of the Israelites as they broke free from Egyptian bondage and wandered the wildernesses in a

1. Num 12:7.

59

lengthy campout. There has never been another leadership giant like Moses. Even Joshua, whom both Moses and Yahweh declared to be commissioned as Moses' successor, was never the pinnacle figure that Moses asserted (often against his own timid nature) within the community and history of Israel.

Murder and Miracle

Moses' story begins in the struggles of Exodus 1–19. A nasty relationship has developed between the Pharaoh of Egypt and the Israelites, descendants of the family of Joseph, a political superstar who had once saved nearly everyone in the ancient near east from famine.[2] An editorial note declares that "Joseph" has been forgotten,[3] and this small reference forms the bridge that later draws Genesis into an even more broadly extended historical prologue to the Sinai covenant. We find out, by reading backwards, that Joseph was the critical link between the Egyptians and this other ethnic community living within its borders. When the good that Joseph did for both races was forgotten, the dominant Egyptian culture attempted to dehumanize and then destroy these Israelite aliens. An edict was issued to kill all male newborn Israelites by drowning them in the Nile River.[4]

This deadly solution proposed by the Pharaoh as an antidote to the rising population of his slave community may sound harsh, but it was likely a very modest and welcomed political maneuver among his primary subjects. Because there is virtually no rain in Egypt, with most of its territory lying in or on the edge of the great Saharan desert, the Nile is and was the critical source of water that sustained life throughout the region. The Nile "miraculously" ebbed and flowed annually, responding to the rains of central Africa, thousands of miles away. Far removed from Egypt's farmlands and cities, this process was attributed to the gods that nurtured Egyptian civilization. Thus, it was fitting for the people to pay homage to these gods, especially by giving appropriate sacrifices to the power of the Nile. In that manner, having the boy babies of the Hebrews tossed into the Nile's currents would not have been considered genocide, but instead it would be deemed a suitable civic and cultural responsibility. Such a practice provided the Nile god with fittingly dear tribute, and at the same time allowed the bulk of the Egyptian population to save its own babies by substituting those of this surrogate vassal people living within their borders.

---

2. Gen 41–50.

3. Exod 1:6–8.

4. Exod 1:22.

Moses' own name ties him to the royal family of Egypt and its influence (note the frequent occurrence of the letters MSS in the names of Pharaohs of the eighteenth through twentieth dynasties—Thutmoses, Ramses, etc.),[5] and his training in the palace schools would provide him with skills that set him apart from the rest of the Israelites in preparation for his unique leadership responsibilities. Moses' time in the wilderness, on the other hand, made him familiar with bedouin life, and similarly fortified his ability to stand at the head of a wandering community once Israel was released from slavery.

A Burning Commission

In Moses' unique encounter with God at Mount Horeb,[6] he experienced the power of the forgotten deity of Israel, and learned a name by which this divinity would soon become known again to the people. "Yahweh" (יהוה)is a variation on the Hebrew verb of existence, and that is why translators bring it into English with terms like "I am" or "I will be." Furthermore, through the voice from the burning bush, this God immediately connected the current events with a specific past through a historical recitation that would later be explicated at length in the extended Genesis historical prologue to the Sinai covenant: Yahweh is the God of Abraham, Isaac, and Jacob. Because of the promises made to that family, Moses is now to become the agent through whom the Israelites will be returned to the land promised to their ancestors. Of course, this is what triggered the battle for control of the nation, and eventually set the stage for Yahweh to claim suzerainty over Israel at Mount Sinai.

The conflict intensifies when Moses makes his first dramatic appearance back in Egypt.[7] The Pharaoh's initial reaction is disdain; why should

---

5. The meaning of Moses' name is derived from the ancient Egyptian word describing the action of "emerging" or being "drawn from," which connects Moses to the story of his discovery by the Pharaoh's daughter (Exod 2:10). But it also links Moses to the royal family of his era. Several generations before Moses' birth, *Aakheperkare* (1520–1492) established a dynasty that ruled for nearly a century, with three successive males in the leadership line identifying themselves as "*Thutmose*." This name meant "draw from" or "born out of *Thot*," one of the more important gods of the ancient Egyptian pantheon. Greater still was *Ra*, the sun god, for whom *Thot* acted as a primary guardian or emissary, and whose identity the pharaohs of Moses' own day took upon themselves: *Menpehtire Ramses*—"drawn from" or "born out of *Ra*" (1292–1290) and *Usermaatre-setpenre Ramses* (*Ramses* II or *Ramses* "The Great," 1279–1213).

6. Exod 3–4.

7. Exod 5:1—6:12.

he listen to the apocalyptic ravings of a wilderness wild man, even if he seems unusually aware of Egyptian language and protocol?[8]

At this point the famous plagues enter the story.[9] While these miracles of divine judgment make for great Hollywood screenplay, the reason for this extended weird display of divine power is not always apparent to those of us who live in very different cultural contexts, especially when it is interspersed with notes that Pharaoh's heart was hardened, sometimes, in fact, seemingly as an act of Yahweh. Could not Yahweh have provided a less destructive and deadly exit strategy for Israel?

Battle of the Superpowers

The plagues begin to make sense when they are viewed in reference to Egypt's climate and culture. After the initial sparring between Moses and the Pharaoh's sorcerers,[10] with snakes to show magical skills, the stakes are raised far beyond human ability merely to manipulate the natural order. First the waters are turned to blood, making the Nile a source of death rather than life.[11] Then the marshes send out a massive, unwelcome pilgrimage of frogs that carried the death expressed through the first plague from the Nile, creeping beyond its banks and into every Egyptian home and workplace.[12] Next the dust is beat into gnats which make the good earth an itching torment,[13] soon to be followed by even peskier flies;[14] subsequently the livestock gets sick from the dust,[15] and this illness then spreads to human life in the form of boils and open sores.[16] Penultimately, the heavens send down mortar shells of hail,[17] transport in a foreign army of locusts,[18] and then withhold the light of the sun.[19] Finally, in an awful culmination, the firstborn humans and animals across Egypt die suddenly.[20]

8. Exod 5.
9. Exod 7–12.
10. Exod 7:10–13.
11. Exod 7:14–25.
12. Exod 8:1–15.
13. Exod 8:16–19.
14. Exod 8:20–32.
15. Exod 9:1–7.
16. Exod 9:8–12.
17. Exod 9:13–35.
18. Exod 10:1–20.
19. Exod 10:21–29.
20. Exod 11:1–12:32.

Strange. But not quite as much when seen in three successive group-ings. Among the many deities worshipped in ancient Egypt, none super-seded a triumvirate composed by the Nile, the good earth, and the heavens which were the home of the sun. So, it was that the initial plagues of bloody water and frogs both turned the Nile against the Egyptians, and showed the dominance of Yahweh over this critical source of national life.

The ante was then upped when Yahweh took on the farmland of Egypt, one of the great breadbaskets of the world. Instead of producing crops, Mo-ses showed, by way of plagues three through six, how Yahweh could cause these fertile alluvial plains to generate all manner of irritating and deadly pestilence, making it an enemy instead of a friend. Finally, in the third stage of plagues, the heavens themselves became menacing. Rather than provid-ing the sheltering confidence of benign sameness, one day the heavens at-tacked with the hailstone mortar fire of an unseen enemy. Next, these same heavens served as the highway of an invading army of locusts. Then old friend *Ra* (the sun), the crowning deity of Egyptian religion, simply van-ished for three days. The gloom that terrified the Egyptians was no mere fear of darkness but rather the ominous trepidation that their primary deity had been bested by the God of the Israelites.

All of this culminated in the final foray of this cosmic battle, when the link of life between generations and human connectedness with ultimate reality was severed through the killing of Egypt's firstborn. The Egyptians believed that the firstborn carried the cultural significance of each family and species, so in a sudden and dramatic moment the very chain of life was destroyed. Furthermore, since the Pharaohs themselves were presumed to be deity incarnate, descending directly from the sun by way of firstborn inheritance, cutting this link eviscerated the life-potency of the Egyptian civilization not only for the present but also for the future. It was a true cultural, religious, political, and social knockout punch.

Changing Allegiance

This explains why the plagues originally served not as gory illustration ma-terial for modern Sunday school papers but rather as the divine initiatives in an escalating battle between Yahweh and the Pharaoh of Egypt over claims on the people of Israel. The plagues were a necessary prologue to the Sinai covenant because they displayed and substantiated the sovereignty of Yah-weh as suzerain not only over Israel but also over other contenders. Israel belongs to Yahweh both because of historic promises made to Abraham, and also by way of chivalrous combat in which Yahweh won back the prize of lover and human companion from the usurper who had stolen her away from the divine heart. Furthermore, Yahweh accomplished this act *without* the help of Israel's own resources (no armies, no resistance movements, no terrorist tactics, no great escape plans), and in a decisive manner that announced the limitations of the Egyptian religious and cultural resources.

This is why the final plague is paired with the institution of the Passover festival.[21] The annual festival would become an on-going reminder that Israel was bought back by way of a blood-price redemption, and that the nation owed its very existence to the love and fighting jealousy of its divine champion. In one momentous confrontation, Egypt lost its firstborn and its cultural heritage, while Israel became Yahweh's firstborn and rightful inheritance.

These things are further confirmed in the reiteration of the importance of circumcision.[22] The rite of circumcision was practiced by most peoples of the ancient Near East,[23] but invariably as either a mark of elitism (only those of a particular class in the community were circumcised)[24] or as a rite of passage (boys or young men who did heroic deeds in battle or the hunt would be circumcised to show that they had become part of the adult warrior caste).[25] What is unique about the commands regarding circumcision for Israel is that it is egalitarian (all males are to be circumcised, and through them all females gain the right to be called the people of Yahweh), and that it is to be done typically on babies or young boys prior to any efforts on their part to perform deeds of valor. This transforms a regional practice that had been identified primarily as a badge of honor earned, into a mark of ownership given, as expressed in the patriarchal antecedent found in Genesis 17. It is through this lens that the New Testament practices of baptism must also be viewed; John's baptism (along with many purification rituals among, e.g., the Essenes and Pharisees) carried with it the flavor of a ritual of passage leading to earning the colors of heightened spiritual maturity, while

---

21. Exod 12:1–28.

22. Exod 13:1–16.

23. As Herodotus traveled and received reports regarding the practices and lifestyles of many civilizations in his world, he stated that the Egyptians, Colchians, and Ethiopians, from very early times, were circumcised, and that he knew also of this practice among the Phoenicians and Syrians of Palestine (his term for the Jews), *History*, II, 104.

24. E.g., the priests of Egypt; the Aztec and Celebes tribes. See Bancroft, *Native Races*, 439–40.

25. Frazer, *Golden Bough*, 691–701; Wilcken, Keil, and Dick, "Traditional Male Circumcision."

the use of baptism in the church followed the ownership markings of Israel's practice of circumcision.[26]

Related to this divinely-initiated ownership theme is the miraculous deliverance of Israel through the Red Sea, coupled with the annihilation of the Egyptian army and its national military prowess in the same incidents. While Exodus 14 narrates the episode in the nail-biting urgency of a documentary, chapter 15 is given over largely to the ancient song of Moses, which unmistakably identifies the entire exodus event as divine combat against Pharaoh over the possession of Israel. Furthermore, the victory ballad also clearly anticipates the effect of this battle on the other Near Eastern nations, with the result that Yahweh is able to march the Israelites through many hostile territories, and eventually settle the nation in Canaan as an on-going testimony to Yahweh's rightful prestige. So it is that the exodus itself is not the divine goal, but only the first stage toward something else.

A House for God

What this further divine intention might be is then illumined by the singular event which follows from the covenant-making ceremony of Exodus 20–24: the construction of the tabernacle. The narrative of Exodus 25–40 has three major sections. In chapters 25–31, preparations for the tabernacle are made, and detailed plans are formulated. Then comes the intruding and jarring incident of the golden calf (chapters 32–34), in which not only Israel's loyalty to Yahweh but also Yahweh's loyalty to Israel are tested. Finally, the architectural initiatives of Exodus 25–31 are resumed in the actual construction of the tabernacle and its dedication,[27] almost as if the dark blot of the interlude had never happened.

Why all of this emphasis on building the tent-like tabernacle? Why invest in a movable shrine rather than rally around some sacred hilltop (Mount Sinai, for instance)? The answer is intrinsically related to the covenant-making event itself. If Israel is now the (reclaimed) possession of Yahweh, then Yahweh must take up visible residence among the people. The tabernacle is not a strange phenomenon of the natural order, like an unfailing spring or a volcanic vent or a residual meteor rock. Instead, it is the fabrication of a civilization that is intentionally on a journey, guided by an in-residence deity who travels with them. These people do not make pilgrimage to a shrine and then return to their homes; rather they move

26. See, for instance, Jesus' command regarding baptism in Matt 28:18–20 and Paul's connection of baptism and circumcision in Col 2:11–12.

27. Exod 35–40.

about in consort with the source of their identity actually residing within the center of their unwieldy sprawl.

Testimony of this is contained within the very architectural plans for the tabernacle. Although parts of the facility will be off-limits to most of the people (and thereby somewhat mysteriously remote), the basic design is virtually identical to that of the typical Israelite portable residence and the living space that surrounds it. First, the cooking fire of any family unit was found out in front of the tent. Second, there would be vessels for washing located near the door of the tent. Third, while many meals might be taken around the fire, some were more ordered and formal, and occurred in the initial spaces within the tent. These required atmospheric accoutrements like dishes, lamps for lighting, and the aromatic wafting of incense. Finally, the privacy of the intimate acts of marriage and family were reserved for the hidden recesses of the tent where visitors were not allowed.

Emmanuel—God with Us

This, then, became the plan for the tabernacle. Its courtyard was public space for meals with God and others of the community around the altar of burnt offering.[28] The laver or bronze basin held waters for washing and bodily purification. In the closest part of the tabernacle itself the hospitality area was found where Yahweh figuratively dined more formally with guests at the table, in the soft ambience created by the lamp and altar of incense. To the rear of the tabernacle Yahweh reserved private space, yet had it fashioned with all of the symbolism of royalty. The ark of the covenant was essentially a portable throne upon which Yahweh was carried with the people, for its uppermost side was designated as the mercy seat. Furthermore, this throne was under the guard of two representative heavenly creatures simply called "cherubim." In a manner akin to the sentries posted at the garden of Eden in Genesis 3, these beings stood watch to ensure that the holiness of the deity was protected.

Thus the tabernacle existed uniquely in its world, representing the physical home of the community's deity as a residence within its own spatial and temporal context. Israel was not a people who needed to create representations of powers that it then idolized; instead, the very society in which it lived emanated from the identity of the chief citizen who lived at its heart.

It is in this context that the golden calf incident of Exodus 32–34 must be understood. Moses' delay on the mountain, talking with Yahweh on behalf of the people, bred frustration and anxiety within the community. So

---

28. See Lev 1–7.

they begged Aaron for symbols around which to rally, and what emerged was a bull calf made of gold. The Israelites were probably not seeking to worship something other than the God who brought them out of Egypt so recently; rather they were trying to find a representation of that God within their cultural frame of reference, so that they could cajole (or manipulate) this deity into further meaningful actions, rather than wasting time in the seeming stall of their current lethargy. Since the bull calf was revered among the Egyptians for its ability to portray the liveliness of sentient power, it could well serve the Israelites in their quest to display national adolescent brash energy.

The problem for Yahweh, however, was twofold. First, the calf was an *Egyptian* symbol, and thus essentially blasphemous in light of Yahweh's recent decisive victory over all aspects of Egyptian power and civilization. Second, the calf reflected brute strength in the natural order, and of a kind that could be controlled by human will. A bull was meant to be yoked and harnessed and guided by whips and goads. True, it was more powerful than its human driver, but at the same time it became a tool in service to the human will. For Yahweh to be represented in this manner undermined the significance of the divine defeat of Egypt and its culture, and appeared to turn Yahweh into a mighty, albeit controllable, source of energy serving the Israelite will.

"Faithful in All God's House"

Under Moses' leadership, his own tribe, the Levites, rallied to avenge Yahweh's disgrace. Because of that action they were appointed to the honored position of keepers of the house of God. Meanwhile, Yahweh himself wished to break covenant with Israel and instead start over with Moses' family; after all, Moses and Yahweh had become great partners and almost friends over the past few years, and especially through their time on the mountain. Moses argued against this divine turnabout, however, for two reasons. First, he reminded the great one that Yahweh had sealed this suzerain-vassal covenant with Israel, and it could not so easily be discarded or broken. Yahweh had deliberately invested Yahweh's own destiny into this people, and while they might wrestle with the chafing fit of the new relationship, Yahweh no longer had a right to deny it. Second, Moses raised the card of shame. What would the nations say if Yahweh quit this project now? The peoples of the ancient Near East had begun to tremble because of Yahweh's decisive victory over Pharaoh; if the God of Israel was able so clearly and convincingly to topple the deities of Egypt and their power in both the natural and supernatural realms, what hope could there be for any other mere national interest or powers? But if Yahweh now suddenly left the Israelites to die in the wilderness, the nations around would see that this god was no more than a flash-bang, a one-hit wonder, a dog with more bark than bite. Moses used Yahweh's own covenant to make the deity toe the line and get back into bed with Israel on this honeymoon night.

All of this is affirmed in various ways through the text of these chapters. For instance, prior to the construction of the tabernacle Moses sought to commune with Yahweh not only on the mountain but also in a small structure called the "Tent of Meeting," which was located slightly outside the camp.[29] Once the tabernacle had been built, however, this designation of the "Tent of Meeting" was transferred to that newer edifice.[30] Furthermore, the term used to describe the grander "Tent of Meeting" is *mishkan*, which means place of dwelling. The same root is also found in the Hebrew term *shakhen*, which means neighbor (so the significance of Yahweh moving into the neighborhood), and again in the *shekina* ("presence") cloud of glory that settled on the tabernacle as its divine occupant moved in.

Similarly, Moses was to chisel out two tablets of stone[31] on which Yahweh would inscribe the summary of the covenant stipulations,[32] which were identified as the Ten Commandments.[33] Most of our representations of the Ten Commandments today picture them as too large to fit on one stone surface, so two tablets are needed to contain all the words. Furthermore, since the first four commandments seem to focus on our relationship with God while the last six have the human social arena in purview, the Ten Commandments are typically arranged on the two stone tablets to reflect this division. This is not the intention of the ancient text, however. There were always two copies made of a suzerain-vassal covenant: one to remain with the subjected people in their homeland and the other to take up residence in the distant palace library of the king. What is unique about Israel's situation is that the two copies of the covenant were to be kept in the very same place—within the ark of the covenant. While we might miss the significance of this because of our lack of sensitivity to the ancient customs, the impact on the Israelites would be nothing short of astounding—the king was planning to live in the same place as his people. Both copies of the

---

29. Exod 33:7–11.

30. See Exod 40:6–7, 22, 24, 29–30, 34–35; Lev 1:1; 24:3; Num 1:1; 31:54; Deut 31:14–15; Josh 18:1; 19:51; 1 Sam 2:22; 1 Kgs 8:4; 1 Chr 6:32; 9:21; 2 Chr 1:3.

31. Exod 34:1, 4.

32. Exod 34:27.

33. Exod 34:28.

covenant could be kept in the same receptacle (which also functioned as the king's throne) because Israel's monarch was not a distant absentee landlord. As went the fortunes of Israel, so went the identity of Yahweh, for Yahweh covenantally committed the divine mission to the fate of this nation.

This is why the tabernacle was more than a religious shrine for Israel. It was different than a mere ceremonial place for offerings. It was, in fact, the home of Yahweh at the center of the Israelite community. When the sun settled behind the horizon and the cooking fires were banked to save wood as the people traveled through the wilderness, one tent continued to have a light on all night. In the heart of the camp the lamp glowed in the fellowship hall of the tabernacle; Yahweh kept vigil while the community slept. In the morning and evening, a meal could be taken with Yahweh (the sacrifices, burnt so that Yahweh might consume the divine portion by way of inhaling the smoke), and constantly the feasting room was made ready for the King to meet with his subjects.

What happened at Mount Sinai? God formally claimed Israel as partner in whatever the divine mission was for planet Earth. Israel, in turn, owned Yahweh as divine King and suzerain. In effect, Yahweh and Israel were married, and their starter home was built at the center of the camp. And Moses was God's servant who made it all happen.

Yet recently, according to the writer of Hebrews, a new thing is taking place. Moses may have been faithful in the house of God, but he did not *own* the house. The writer of Hebrews references an incident recorded in Numbers 12, where Moses' older siblings, Miriam and Aaron, make a play for being considered the proper stewards of the recently built tabernacle, since Moses is only their little brother (he is in is early eighties while they are in their late eighties or early nineties.) God makes it very clear, through some dramatic public displays, that Moses is God's first choice of house master, and the best person to function in that role.

Still, Moses is not the owner of the house. God is. And the theology of Hebrews affirms, again and again, that Jesus is God. Therefore, the tabernacle, and later the temple, belong to Jesus. He is the only one who can open the doors to let us in. He is the only one who can give us access to all rooms in the house, including the very throne room of the most high. Moses might be great—greater, in fact, than all other humans who ever lived. Until now. Because Jesus supersedes Moses.

Why would this be such a big deal? It is strange, really, since within Orthodox Judaism, this is considered heresy.

Yes, the people who are first receiving this document are Christians, and within Christianity, Jesus' supremacy is assumed. So what's the big deal? Why is this so important?

Evidently this community is Christian, but still cares deeply about Jewish theology and worldview perspectives. It is also struggling with whether Christian theology and perspectives can or should supersede Jewish theology and perspectives. In other words, this community is torn between Moses and Jesus when it comes to figuring who is supposed to be in charge of God's house.

Where Have We Come So Far?

- God has spoken in times past.
  - This is our source of direction and confidence.
  - We know who we are because of the prophets.
- God has recently spoken a stronger, better, and clearer message through Jesus.
  - So when we, who live by the prophetic message, hear Jesus, we had better listen.
- Jesus is superior to the angels.
  - The great divine message that formed us came through Moses, but the message itself was delivered to him by angels (Deut 33:2; Acts 7:53).
  - Yet Jesus is superior to angels, and therefore delivers a more important prophetic message than that through the great prophet Moses.
- So stick with Jesus, even though you are tempted to turn away from him.
  - There is no higher authority or source of connection with God.
  - And if our lives are to be connected to God, we turn away from Jesus to our own peril.
- God has made the world subject to Jesus.
  - God never did this with the angels, so, again, Jesus is superior to them.
  - But this only happened because Jesus first fully identified with the world.
- Jesus willingly came into the world to fully experience its pain.
- And this is to our benefit for three reasons:

      • To fully identify with us as sisters and brothers.

      • To make atonement for our sins (which cause the pain of this world).

      • To bring us with him fully into the house of God.

- So Jesus is greater than (over) the angels, but Jesus is also greater than (over) Moses.

Message: A Better Housekeeper

Homes come in all shapes and sizes. The Biltmore in Asheville, North Carolina, for instance, boasts 250 rooms and claims to be the largest private home in the world. More on the weird and wacky side, the home of Sarah Winchester in San Jose, California is an architectural monstrosity. After her husband and her only child died, Mrs. Winchester believed spirits were telling her that she should buy a particular seventeen-room house, then under construction, and that she would continue to live so long as she kept building it. She did manage to survive another thirty-eight years, dwelling in solitude as the construction continued on around her. But even the builders couldn't keep death from going in to visit her one night. Her house is now one of the strangest curiosities in the world.

But certainly, one of the most unusual stories of house-building happened in Detroit, Michigan. Henry Ford erected a marvelous home called "Fairlane" on the upper slopes of the River Rouge. It is a masterpiece of craftsmanship and artistic design. Ford had learned early in life that he could never fully count on anyone else, so he spent an extra $200,000, already back in 1917, to put in his own electric power plant for the whole estate.

In all his years at Fairlane, the power plant served faithfully, lighting and heating his impressive home, even when power outages threatened his neighbors from time to time. Only one time did Henry Ford's security fail: in early April of 1947, torrential rains lashed the Detroit area. The River Rouge rose from its banks, and on the night of April 7, the floods entered the Fairlane boiler room, smothering the fires and causing the steam pressure to drop. That night the lights went out at Fairlane. And that's also the night Henry Ford died in his bed at the age of eighty-seven.

Houses and Homes

It is an interesting parable, isn't it? Here was a man who put North America on wheels, who invented one gadget after another to make life less tedious and more enjoyable, who helped to usher in our modern technological society. Here was a staunchly independent man, one who took care of himself and did not owe anybody anything. Here was a man who even managed to separate his wiring grid from that of the public utilities. And yet, the very night he dies, forces beyond his control snatch away his source of power and minimize his abilities to own his dwelling and maintain his household protections.

It reminds us of Jesus' parable about a rich man who built bigger barns.[34] Wealth, said Jesus, was not the issue. Self-sufficiency was. We can each build our own houses, rich or poor, luxurious or humble, extravagant or miserly, but we are not entirely the masters of our circumstances, nor completely lords of our castles. More than that, only love can turn a house into a home.

Of course, love is the business of the greatest home builder of all time. In fact, the house of the greatest builder is a central feature throughout the Bible. First, God builds a home for Adam and Eve, and they spend time together each day at afternoon tea. Then they are ejected from the house because they failed to live by its values and rules. So they leave home, and build cities with no heart in them. Yet God does not wish to leave them homeless, so God comes again to spend time in Abraham's tent, as an honored guest and a welcome friend. Their conversations lead to plans for a future journey together, one in which God's new house, the tabernacle, will be at the center of the community of faith. Later, when David, a "man after God's own heart," desires to refurbish the tabernacle, and turn it into a permanent home, God says that David's son is the man for the job. Indeed, Solomon builds one of the greatest structures ever to grace planet Earth. When it was dedicated, all heaven poured into its marvelous magnificence.

A Tragic Story

Of course, that temple no longer exists. In fact, its failure is closely related to the story behind this book of Hebrews. Jesus' kingship and kingdom are rooted directly in the covenant Yahweh made with David in 2 Samuel 7. In that passage, the themes of God's house and David's house came together in powerful symmetry. David wished to build a house for God, since Israel was

34. Luke 12:13–21.

now settled in the promised land. While God appreciated this appropriate desire on David's part, through the prophet Nathan, God communicated that it would be David's son, a man of peace, who would take up that honor and responsibility. But because David's heart and desires were in the right place, God made a return commitment to him. God would build a royal "house" out of David's descendants, and there would always be one of his sons ruling as king over God's people.

This promise began well, with the amazingly successful reign of Solomon. The great temple was built, the borders of the kingdom were expanded from Mesopotamia to Egypt, the economy soared, and people flooded to Jerusalem from all over the world to hear the wisdom of Solomon and experience the blessings of Yahweh. Then it all began to falter. Solomon's massive empire was split at his death (922 BC), and the family successors who ruled the truncated kingdom from Jerusalem were a mixed lot with varying degrees of success in both politics and religion. By the end of the Old Testament history, merely a remnant of the people remained to be deported in the cataclysmic Babylonian exile. Fewer still returned to Jerusalem later, under Persian rule, and they were not permitted to reinstall David's descendants to a self-governing throne. Only shortly before Jesus' birth, through the Maccabean revolt, had a measure of Jewish self-determination been regained. But David's family was not on the throne.

The Return of the Homeowner

Gospel writer Matthew makes it clear that the miraculously-born deliverer Jesus is, indeed, the one who will fulfill, both at this time and forever, God's commitment to David. Matthew communicated this forcefully in the opening chapter of his Gospel, when he linked Jesus to David, and again in chapter 2 when the Magi questioned King Herod's authority as the "King of the Jews." But the biggest statement of Jesus' kingly status takes place a bit later in the Gospel, when Matthew narrates Jesus' entry into Jerusalem.[35]

Upon Jesus' arrival at the capital city of ancient Israel and modern Judea, he is welcomed as king. The crowds immediately and publicly connect Jesus to David's royal family,[36] and give him a royal salute. Furthermore, when Jesus enters the city, he moves directly to the temple. This, of course, was "God's House," the dwelling of Yahweh on earth. It was the permanent replication of what the tabernacle had been throughout Israel's wilderness wanderings. Just as when that portable structure had been dedicated by Mo-

35. Matt 21.
36. Matt 21:9.

ses, and the glory of God swooshed in as Yahweh took up residence,[37] so the same had happened while Solomon dedicated the first temple.[38] But a vision later recorded by the prophet Ezekiel announced the awful portent that the glory of God was leaving the temple and that God had gone back to heaven, moving out of Israel's neighborhood.[39]

It was Yahweh leaving "God's House" that precipitated the Babylonian destruction of Jerusalem and the temple and initiated the years of Jewish exile and captivity. When Cyrus of the Persians issued an edict sending the exiles back to Jerusalem, they rebuilt the temple on a small scale with their modest resources. But the glory of God never returned to the rebuilt temple. During the times of the prophet Malachi, around 400 BC, the people were still pleading with God to return and take up residence with them again.[40]

It is this history that Matthew draws upon, as he marks the steps of Jesus entering Jerusalem. Jesus goes directly to the temple, the house of God, and by implication, his own house *as* God. He cleans the place, a task which only the owner of the house can authorize.[41] There, Jesus receives his kingdom citizens who need royal favors—the blind and the lame.[42] While Jesus is holding royal court, he is also presented with an impromptu concert from the most trusting stakeholders in his realm: the children.[43] When the "chief priests" (i.e., those who have been left in charge of God's house) chide Jesus for inappropriately seeming to take over, Jesus quotes Psalm 8, as if it were his own, to verify the correctness of these happenings.[44] Jesus is King. Jesus is the eternal ruler who has a right to sit on the throne of David, fulfilling the covenant Yahweh made with him. Jesus is the obvious resident of Israel's royal palace.

Competing Loyalties

But these tenants have no use for Jesus and do not want him to disturb their hold on power and territory. A few verses later, Jesus' authority is directly questioned[45] within the very temple courts themselves. In response, Jesus

37. Exod 40.

38. 1 Kgs 8.

39. Ezek 9–10.

40. Mal 3–4.

41. Matt 21:12–13.

42. Matt 21:14.

43. Matt 21:15.

44. Matt 21:16.

45. Matt 21:23–27.

tells two parables,[46] each of which declares the horrible things that are about to happen because the tenants reject the royal claims of the Creator's family. Jesus is King, but this rule will not be won easily. It will be gotten only through the horrible death that Jesus is about to endure.

Matthew never relents from this central message that Jesus is the last and greatest and eternal son of David. Before the crucifixion, Jesus is identified openly as King at least four different times.[47] When Jesus dies, the curtain of the temple, which marked Yahweh's hidden quarters and separated God from the people, is torn away, so that the place becomes ceremonially dysfunctional[48] and Israel's ruler must move out of this particular residence. Even the earth itself heaves and groans in the seismic religious shift that is taking place between the Old and New forms of the covenant mission of Yahweh.[49]

But the picture is clear. God prepares a home for us. When we leave that home because of our own willful tendencies, God comes back, pursues us, until God finds a way to "tabernacle" with us.[50] In the long run, however, it is God who creates a new dwelling for us and calls us back home. This is the home that truly matters and the one which stands as the archetype of all our other homes and places of residence. Most importantly, there is no question as to who is the true master of this house. It is not Adam. It is not Eve. It is not Abraham, nor Noah, nor even Moses. This house belongs to God. And the one, as we read here in Hebrews, who truly serves as steward and host of God's house is Jesus.

Jesus' House

A friend once explained it like this: in a dream, he saw a marvelous apparatus of yellow silk billowing in the breezes next to a cliff. It was a transportation device of some kind, though he couldn't see either engines or supports. Like a magical tent, it floated in space.

Inside was a man whose face seemed so familiar and friendly that my friend knew immediately this was an intimate acquaintance. However, he could not seem to remember how they were associated, nor the man's name. The man, with a smile of warmth, invited him to step off the cliff into the contrivance and be carried on a delightful journey in the yellow tent.

46. Matt 21:28–46.
47. Matt 27:1–44.
48. Matt 27:51.
49. Matt 27:52.
50. See John 1:14.

But my friend was so intrigued by the device itself that he wanted to try it on his own. *He* wanted to pilot the magical airship. So, when he entered the craft he fought the man for control and pushed him out onto the cliff. Unfortunately, just as my friend felt the power of flight swell in his commanding grasp, the entire yellow tent began to collapse in on itself and plummet to disaster below. No matter what he did, my friend could not make the "machine" fly. He cried out for help and suddenly the man he had pushed out reappeared at his side. In that exact moment, the airship began to billow and slow its freefall. Soon they were soaring together.

Without a further thought my friend knew that the strangely familiar man was Jesus. He also knew why Jesus said to him, "Don't you know that the power to fly is not found in the 'machine' nor in your skills as a pilot but in me?"

None of us begins to soar in life until we meet Jesus. As the writer of Hebrews makes clear, and as the whole Bible echoes, it is all about Jesus.

Chapter 6

Back to School

Text: Hebrews 3:7–19

Therefore, as the Holy Spirit says,

> "Today, if you hear his voice,
> do not harden your hearts as in the rebellion,
> as on the day of testing in the wilderness,
> where your ancestors put me to the test,
> though they had seen my works for forty years.
> Therefore I was angry with that generation,
> and I said, 'They always go astray in their hearts,
> and they have not known my ways.'
> As in my anger I swore,
> 'They will not enter my rest.'"[1]

Take care, brothers and sisters, that none of you may have an evil, unbelieving heart that turns away from the living God. But exhort one another every day, as long as it is called "today," so that none of you may be hardened by the deceitfulness of sin. For we have become partners of Christ, if only we hold our first confidence firm to the end. As it is said,

> "Today, if you hear his voice,

---

1. Ps 95:7b–11.

do not harden your hearts as in the rebellion."[2]

Now who were they who heard and yet were rebellious? Was it not all those who left Egypt under the leadership of Moses? But with whom was he angry forty years? Was it not those who sinned, whose bodies fell in the wilderness? And to whom did he swear that they would not enter his rest, if not to those who were disobedient? So we see that they were unable to enter because of unbelief.

Backstory: Learning from the Past

The writer of Hebrews knows his Bible very well. It is likely that he is entering all of these Old Testament quotes into his running teaching on the fly, from memory.

While this is extraordinary in itself, even more astounding are the intricacy and fittedness of each quotation. Here, for instance, the writer wishes to show a parallel between the current situation of his readers and a similar challenging time in the history of their forebears. He chooses a particular set of events (the rebellions of ancient Israel against Moses and Yahweh, as told in the book of Numbers) within a context (the forty years of wilderness wanderings following the great revelation of God to the people at Mount Sinai). The points of connection mount up, even if they are not all specifically noted:

- Both times were periods of great stress for God's people.
- Both occasions happened in the wake of a tremendous new revelation from God.
- Both situations challenged God's people's faith deeply.
- Both developments caused many to doubt and lose hope.
- Both traumas involved calls from a commanding leader to remain true, strong, and faithful to the promises, in anticipation of salvation and shalom.

The only difference between the times of Israel in the book of Numbers and the current experiences of God's people to whom Hebrews is being written is that these contemporaries who are reading the teachings in Hebrews know the outcome to the Numbers' stories: all were suffering, all were tempted to give up, but only some actually did so. And that is exactly what the writer of Hebrews is playing on. The details of the seemingly overwhelming events

2. Ps 95:7b-8a.

for God's people in both ancient and recent times are extremely similar. But in the history lesson, God came through for God's people and brought them into the promised land. These modern folks are still in the "wilderness" pressures with only God's promises to hang on to.

And that is where the quick quotation from Psalm 95 comes in. Rather than pulling lengthy passages from the book of Numbers as object lessons, the writer of Hebrews taps his finger elsewhere. He knows the theme and central elements of Psalm 95. These capture the heart of the Numbers' wrestlings powerfully, so he throws in a few of its poignant verses[3] (requoting the key opening warning for emphasis[4]), providing a kind of brief memory jogger couched in the tones of warning and judgment used by the psalmist. Immediately his readers will recall and review the eleven murmurings and rebellions[5] found in Numbers' fifteen core chapters.[6]

Most notably, the writer of Hebrews includes the reference to "today" found in Psalm 95:7b. The psalmist had already decided to tie his strong call to worship[7] to an equally strong warning not to be like the rebellious ancient Israelites, who, five hundred years earlier, had allowed their lack of trust in God to keep them from the promised outcome of entering into the "rest" of homegoing into Canaan. Whatever was taking place in Jerusalem during

---

3. Ps 95: 7b-11.

4. Ps 95: 7b-8a.

5. As soon as the Sinai covenant has been declared and instituted, a series of challenges to its structures and authority takes place, outlined in varying details in the book of Numbers:

General complaining is punished by divine fire (11:1–3).

Lack of meat is answered by quail gluttony (11:4–34).

Moses' leadership is challenged by his siblings (12:1–15).

The wisdom of Yahweh in choosing Canaan as Israel's homeland is denied (13:1–14:45).

A Sabbath-breaker is condemned (15:32–36).

Moses' leadership is challenged by others from his tribe (16:1–40).

Moses' and Aaron's leadership is challenged by the rest of the nation (16:41–17:13).

Lack of water is answered by a gushing rock (20:1–13).

General grumbling is punished by venomous snakes (21:4–9).

The Amorites challenge Yahweh's authority and are defeated (21:21–35).

The Moabites challenge Israel's identity and are defeated (22:1–25:18).

Each challenge is answered with Yahweh proving himself to be both Israel's true sovereign and the world's true Creator God. Furthermore, as Yahweh declared in Leviticus 26:44–45—"I will not reject them or abhor them so as to destroy them completely, breaking my covenant with them. I am the Lord their God. But for their sake I will remember the covenant with their ancestors whom I brought out of Egypt in the sight of the nations to be their God. I am the Lord."

6. Num 11–25.

7. Ps 95:1–7.

the psalmist's time required both a massive invitation to re-engage with God and a similarly awesome challenge to stay true in faith, not repeating the devastating falling away of their ancestors.

It is precisely this urgency of "today" that the writer of Hebrews grasps as he pulls together the Numbers' conjoined divine promises and devastating human rebellions, and the psalmist's almost frightening hazard warnings elicited from them. Hebrews wedges these past failures and critical cautions into his current "today" of the first century AD.

We expect this kind of rhetoric in the religious exhortations of Scripture. Yet the stridency expressed in Hebrews, as these warnings are picked up, also tells us something about the conditions in which these readers live:

- They are Jews shaped deeply by the prophetic revelations and calls of Hebrew Scripture.

- They are Christians living under mounting social pressures that weaken their faith.

- These challenges seem to shake their trust in Jesus more than their commitments to Jewish ceremonial practices.

- So the critical choice appears not to be whether to believe in God as Jews, but whether to trust in Jesus, recently arrived on the scene, as Messiah.

The writer of Hebrews has now made two points about this: (1) Jesus is superior to the angels who deliver God's messages to humans, and (2) Jesus is superior to Moses, through whom the whole of Jewish life and practices were received and shaped. As a result, we are beginning to understand that those receiving Hebrews originally were Jewish Christians who were not in danger of losing their religion generally, but appear to have been tempted to give up on the new thing added to their faith in the person of Jesus. In other words, they remained deeply devout to God, but the pressures of their times caused them to question whether Jesus was, in fact, the promised Messiah.

This, then, becomes the major next point to be raised by the writer of Hebrews. By connecting the "rest" which ancient Israel hoped for when entering the promised land (after the challenges of wilderness struggles) with the "rest" promised to followers of Jesus when he returns (after the challenges of persecutions now), these readers are called, challenged, and cajoled to stick with Jesus through current difficult times, knowing what awaits them.

Where Have We Come So Far?

- God has spoken in times past.
    - This is our source of direction and confidence.
    - We know who we are because of the prophets.
- God has recently spoken a stronger, better, and clearer message through Jesus.
    - So when we, who live by the prophetic message, hear Jesus, we had better listen.
- Jesus is superior to the angels.
    - The great divine message that formed us came through Moses, but the message itself was delivered to him by angels (Deut 33:2; Acts 7:53).
    - Yet Jesus is superior to angels, and therefore delivers a more important prophetic message than that through the great prophet Moses.
- So stick with Jesus, even though you are tempted to turn away from him.
    - There is no higher authority or source of connection with God.
    - And if our lives are to be connected to God, we turn away from Jesus to our own peril.
- God has made the world subject to Jesus.
    - God never did this with the angels, so, again, Jesus is superior to them.
    - But this only happened because Jesus first fully identified with the world.
- Jesus willingly came into the world to fully experience its pain.
- And this is to our benefit for three reasons:
    - To fully identify with us as sisters and brothers.
    - To make atonement for our sins (which cause the pain of this world).
    - To bring us with him fully into the house of God.
- So Jesus is greater than (over) the angels, but Jesus is also greater than (over) Moses.

- Therefore, be careful that you don't disconnect from Jesus (who is God):

    ◆ Remember how those in our past who disconnected from God came under punishment.

    ◆ The same can happen to you if you do not stay true and committed to Jesus.

Message: Altar Call #1

British researchers once discovered that 42 percent of the church-goers in that country fall asleep during the sermon. The numbers may be astounding, but the habit is as old as Eutychus's fatal nap in Acts 20.

Even the great eighteenth-century evangelist John Wesley noticed that a number of people in his congregation were fast asleep. Without a warning, he suddenly broke his train of homiletic thought, and yelled out at the top of his voice, "Fire! Fire!"

Startled, the sleepers jumped to their feet, now quite awake. "Where's the fire?" they shouted, glancing around the room.

"In hell," replied Wesley. "For those who sleep under the preaching of the Word."

Slumbers Interrupted

Wesley's homiletic drama may be overplayed, but it is related to the rather strident warning issued by the writer of Hebrews. It is also connected to the urgency of both the message of Hebrews and the broader New Testament passionate calls to faith because of the coming of Jesus.

This came home to me in a powerful manner one night when I was working the sign-off show at a radio station during my seminary days. It was just after 11:30 one night when the telephone rang. A sleepy voice at the other end asked, "Is this that religious radio station?"

"Yes," I said.

"Well I'm dialing all over the place on my radio," she told me, "and I can't find your music."

So I gave her the frequency of our signal, and then tried to engage her in a little more conversation. She sounded like she needed someone to talk with as much as she needed the music.

During the next twenty-five minutes her story spilled out. Much of it was an awkward tale of bad choices and bad times, more recently etched with both physical and relational pains. That night, in the dark and lonely places of her world, it all began to seem too much for Betty and she decided to end her life. She took a bunch of pills and now was trying to find the right kind of music on her radio. Then she would slip away exchanging my music for that of the angels. Or so she told me.

I tried to get Betty's address so that I could call the police. I tried to get her telephone number, but she would not let anything slip out.

At midnight, I had to give a station ID along with headline news and the weather forecast before switching to a recorded program. It would all take about three minutes. I told Betty to stay on the line, and that I would be back with her as quickly as I could. But when I picked up the receiver again there was no one at the other end.

I went home that night torn inside. Who was Betty? What had happened to her? Why was she all alone? Would she survive till morning?

Midnight Confessions

It was four nights later that my roommates shook me awake at 1:30 a.m. There was a woman on the telephone. She had the number at our apartment but she didn't know why. When I picked up the receiver I knew immediately that it was Betty. Once again, the world had gotten very small and dark for her, and down in her dungeon Betty needed God. Mostly, Betty needed God with skin on. And that is why, when she found a scrap of paper with a strange telephone number written on it, she called our number trying to find God. And in the confessions of our second late-night phone chat Betty did find God.

Betty knew personally the thing that we all have to face: we become followers of Jesus only with a sob of our souls when we no longer believe the lie of society. We hear it every day in its subtle forms: "Things are really getting better and better all the time"; "Everyone has an equal opportunity in life"; "Education will conquer all our ills"; "If you just try hard enough, you can make it on your own."

The advertisements tell us that we are really pretty good, and that the world itself is a rather pleasant and harmless place when we dress right, smell right, eat right, exercise right, and drive the right cars or invest in the right companies. Everything will work out well for the nice people.

But the way of the disciple takes its first step with the jolt of crisis. She cries for help. He confesses that he cannot make it on his own. This was the call and invitation of the writer of Hebrews which chants in urgency, the first hint of dawn calling to minds newly awakening from the twisted darkness of the world in which they are trapped: the advertiser who claims to know what I need and what I want and who can make everything better with just a single credit card; the entertainer who promises me a quick fix, a cheap trick, a sensuous fling that really *is* love; the politician who has my best interests at stake, and who will make me ruler with him if I just give him my vote; the psychiatrist who will help me achieve gain without pain by lowering my standards to the mud around me.

Cry for Help

Those who follow Jesus see the world through different eyes and begin the journey of faith with a cry of repentance. It is then, and then alone, that dawns a ray of hope. The journey begins in that moment, just as Bill W. testified in *The Big Book* of Alcoholics Anonymous. It starts at the bottom.

The Bible is full of calls for repentance, precisely because none of us will take the journey to God on our own. It is not until we come to our senses, down in the hog wallows of our lives, that we begin to cry in agony for the grace of deliverance.

When repentance comes, it can be a devastating thing. I will never forget the torment in my own soul the afternoon that my life collapsed around me and I lay face down on the carpet of a dark room, pounding the floor with my fist, painting my cheeks with my tears, and crying out in the anguish of my soul, "I need you, God. I need you, God. I need you, God."

It is not the same for everybody, of course. But this I know—I have yet to meet a person in life with true spiritual depth who has not come through some agonizing moment of inner turning: turning from this to that; turning from one set of values to another; turning from lesser gods to someone far more profound. This, in the Bible, is the meaning of repentance. It means the turning of our inner selves from one direction to another.

Jolted back to Jesus

This, obviously, goes against the consumer mentality that has gripped our society. We have been drugged into believing that we are okay on our own, that we have all the means and resources necessary to see us through any jam in life's river. That is why, in a culture guided by consumption, we are not really on the way to anywhere. We do not need to repent, according to pop psychology, but only to obtain. We do not need to change our ways, only our strategies. We do not need some outside power to help us, only to encourage us. We can do just fine on our own, thank you. So as the writer of Hebrews knows well, this call to discipleship and pilgrimage often dies before it gets a good response from our lips or a faithful commitment in our actions.

Still, "the longest journey begins with the first step," as the Chinese philosopher Lao Tzu put it.[8] And repentance is the first step on the road to healing. Grace has no place in the self-satisfaction of a do-it-yourself religion. Jesus himself said that he did not come to gather the so-called righteous (i.e., the ones who are satisfied with where they are at), but *sinners* to repentance.[9]

The Bad that Leads to Good

Madeline L'Engle once explained to a conference gathering how she came to understand the meaning of her life. At the time, she was the "writer in residence" at the Cathedral of St. John the Divine on Fifth Avenue in New York City. She met regularly with the rest of the staff at the church and developed a fast friendship with the cathedral bishop.

One day the two of them were talking about the times in their lives when they felt they had grown the most in terms of inner graces and spiritual depth. It did not take long for each to realize that the most creative energies had come to life only at the end of periods of great struggle, often filled with agonizing mental and emotional torment. In fact, said Madeline L'Engle, the best of her books were written just after the worst times of her life.

As they talked, each experienced the growing realization of what poet and hymn-writer Margaret Clarkson identified when she penned *Grace Grows Best in Winter*.[10] More than that, they also found that the turning point leading out of the dark night of the soul was, for each of them, always a moment of repentance.

After some tender moments of further sharing, the bishop got up to leave. At the door, said L'Engle, he stopped for a moment and then turned around to face her. "Madeline," he said to her, "I don't know how to say this, but have a *bad* day."

He was the best kind of friend, Madeline told us, for he truly cared about her. He did not wish for her to experience the nastiness of life. Yet he did wish for her to find the grace of God that only emerges with power out of the repentance that comes to those who realize the insufficient, incomplete,

8. Lao Tzu, *Tao Te Ching*, chapter 64.

9. Matt 9:12–13.

10. Eerdmans, 1984.

inept, and inconsistent state of their hearts. Only a very kind and truly great friend could see that sometimes what we need most is a bad day that will help us turn our hearts toward home.

Crawling Home

There is a familiar gospel song that breathes with both the pain and the urgency of the writer of Hebrews' pleading challenge in these verses. Thomas Dorsey was born in 1899 with music in his soul. He was known as "Georgia Tom," entertainer and blues singer. When he became a Christian, his music took on more depth as Dorsey explored the profound spiritual blues of scripture.

In 1938, Dorsey was scheduled to be the lead singer at a series of revival meetings in St. Louis, Missouri. His wife was pregnant, and Dorsey grew more hesitant to leave her as the due date approached. But she knew the impact of his ministry and urged her husband to keep his musical commitments for the sake of those who were seeking God. So, he traveled the long road from Chicago to St. Louis.

On the first night of the revival, while Dorsey was already on the platform and the service was in progress, a telegram came. Dorsey's wife had died in a sudden and serious childbirth. Dorsey left for Chicago immediately and found his infant son barely hanging onto life. The child died a few hours later. In a moving funeral service, Thomas Dorsey buried his beloved wife and tiny son in the same casket.

Despondency set in. The great blues singer wandered in a depression that seemed to know no limits. A friend took him in for a while, just to care for his physical needs. One evening Dorsey wandered over to a piano and began to improvise on the keyboard. A melody gradually emerged, and the words soon followed. It sings in the heart of every person who has started the steps of faith that begin at the point where the resources of self prove insufficient:

> *Precious Lord, take my hand,*
> *Lead me on, help me stand,*
> *I am tired, I am weak, I am worn.*
> *Through the storm, through the night,*
> *Lead me on to the light.*
>   *Take my hand, precious Lord; lead me home.*

When my way grows drear,
Precious Lord, linger near—
   When my life is almost gone.
Hear my cry, hear my call,
Hold my hand lest I fall—
   Take my hand, precious Lord; lead me home.

When the darkness appears,
And the night draws near,
   And the day is past and gone,
At the river I stand,
Guide my feet, hold my hand,
   Take my hand, precious Lord; lead me home.[11]

11. "Take my Hand, Precious Lord," gospel song. Written by Thomas A. Dorsey in August 1932.

Chapter 7

Sabbath Rest

Text: Hebrews 4:1–13

Therefore, while the promise of entering his rest is still open,
let us take care that none of you should seem to have failed to
reach it. For indeed the good news came to us just as to them;
but the message they heard did not benefit them, because they
were not united by faith with those who listened. For we who
have believed enter that rest, just as God has said,

"As in my anger I swore,
'They shall not enter my rest,'"[1]

though his works were finished at the foundation of the world.
For in one place it speaks about the seventh day as follows, "And
God rested on the seventh day from all his works."[2] And again
in this place it says, "They shall not enter my rest."[3] Since therefore it remains open for some to enter it, and those who formerly
received the good news failed to enter because of disobedience,
again he sets a certain day—"today"—saying through David
much later, in the words already quoted,

"Today, if you hear his voice,
do not harden your hearts."[4]

1. Ps 95:11.
2. Gen 2:2.
3. Ps 95:11.
4. Ps 95:7b-8a.

For if Joshua had given them rest, God would not speak later about another day. So then, a sabbath rest still remains for the people of God; for those who enter God's rest also cease from their labors as God did from his. Let us therefore make every effort to enter that rest, so that no one may fall through such disobedience as theirs.

Indeed, the word of God is living and active, sharper than any two-edged sword, piercing until it divides soul from spirit, joints from marrow; it is able to judge the thoughts and intentions of the heart. And before him no creature is hidden, but all are naked and laid bare to the eyes of the one to whom we must render an account.

Backstory: Rhythm, Rest and Reiteration

The concept of "sabbath" is unique to ancient Israelite culture, although it carries on, to a degree, within the Jewish and Christian traditions which emerge from it. Egyptian time flowed around a ten-day week, with work cessation only for some craftsmen, but not for slaves or general workers, on the last two days. This was the routine Israel knew during its centuries of slavery.

Living by a New Calendar

With liberation under the renewed leadership of Yahweh, the God of their ancestors and the Creator of all, came a new calendar to manage their national and personal times.[5] Time itself was reoriented and reinterpreted for Israel so that each marker would remind the nation of its unique identity and purpose. Daily sacrifices connected the people and their God in a

---

5. Exod 23:10–19; Lev 1–7, 16, 23–24, 25; Num 28–29; Deut 15–16.

meal-like setting.[6] Weekly sabbaths echoed the rhythm of creation,[7] with its goal of confirming the meaningfulness of labor in reflection and worship. Months were marked by celebratory trumpet salutes.[8] The year itself was stepped forward by a number of festivals:

- Passover—a reminder of original deliverance and identity (spring).

- Feast of Weeks/Harvest/Firstfruits—a celebration of divine provision, both during the wilderness wanderings and also from year to year in agriculture generally (late spring/early summer).

- Rosh Hashanah (New Year)—a recognition of the orderly progression of time in the creation of God (late summer).

- Day of Atonement—annual spiritual cleansing and renewal (early fall).

- Feast of Tabernacles/Booths—the great Harvest Celebration commemorating God's care through the wilderness, continuing right to the present time (late fall).

6. There are five types of offerings specified in Leviticus 1–7:

1) *Burnt offering* (Lev 1): animal offerings only, totally consumed (no meat for priests or offerers); purpose: to provide regular renewal with God.

2) *Cereal/grain offerings* (Lev 2): either raw grain or baked loaf, token part burned, rest for priests/Levites; purpose: indicates thankfulness.

3) *Peace offerings* (Lev 3): animal offerings only, only certain organs and fat burned; purpose: the rest appears to be available to eat as a symbol of relationships restored.

4) *Sin offerings* (Lev 4:1–5:13): animal offerings only, only certain organs and fat burned; purpose: atones for wrong actions in social contexts.

5) *Guilt offerings* (Lev 5:14–6:7): animal offerings only, only certain organs and fat burned; purpose: atones for wrong actions in specifically cultic religious contexts.

The first of these, the burnt offering, are to take place daily in late afternoon and again around mid-morning (Num 28:1–8), at essentially the same times as meals were taken by the Israelites. Moreover, the set-up of the tabernacle imitated the general format of Israelite tents and family use of space during the years of wilderness wanderings: there was an outdoor arena for public life and daily meals in front of the tent, a forward area within the tent for private meetings and meals and hospitality with friends and family, and a rear portion of the tent reserved for intimacy and sleep. With its similar layout, the tabernacle portrayed Yahweh's life among God's people in parallel proportions. Hence, the daily sacrifices, along with the special offerings, were to happen in the public space commonly used for meals and community conversations. Note also that most of these sacrifices involved both people eating meat or grain from the cooked offering, and also God receiving benefit (through the burning process, with smells and residual matter in the form of smoke rising to heaven). The offering of ancient Israel were essential meal times between God and God's people.

7. Gen 2:2–3; Exod 20:8–11, 23:12, 35:1–3; Lev 23:3.

8. Num 10:10, 28:11–15. Interestingly, the blowing of trumpets was either a call to arms or to celebration (Num 10:1–10), but always in the context of a remembrance the Yahweh was master of Israelite identity.

And finally, there were the two massive events that shepherded the larger arcs of life:

- Sabbath Years—occurring every seventh calendar revolution, canceling debts, freeing slaves, and restoring family properties[9]
- The Jubilee Year—happening every fiftieth year (essentially once in a lifetime), bringing all of the best remaining festivals together for a full year celebration right after the seventh Sabbath Year of that cycle[10]

The Meaning of the Sabbath

All of these, though, were essentially anticipations, reflections, echoes, and amplifications of the Sabbath. Daily rest looked forward to the weekly work pause to regain bearings. Monthly trumpet blasts celebrated the movement of time in the freedom of those who were sabbatically self-determining, rather than slaves of others. Yearly festivals reminded the people that God's care superseded the output of even the best of laborers, and invited relaxed community engagement with one another in the context of God living among them. And the Sabbath years, coupled with the lifetime Jubilee event, brought all of this into a macro expression of trust and celebration. Biblical Israel was shaped by the Sabbath.

The Sabbath itself connoted several things. First, it was a reflection that time and life were determined by the Creator and came to best expression within the context of God's plans and designs. This is clearly spelled out in the fourth of the Ten Commandments,[11] establishing the Sabbath as symbiotic harmony attuned to the divine rhythm of life, thus rooted in creation.

Second, the Sabbath was key to understanding the meaning of human life itself. Moses notes this as he connects the fourth command in his final testimony to Israel, the book of Deuteronomy, to Israel's release from slavery.[12] Not only is the Sabbath resonating with the rhythm of creation, but it also testifies to the different values at work within the Israelite worldview, expressed in the early chapters of Genesis.

---

9. Exod 23:10–11; Lev 25:1–7, 20–22; 26:33–35; Deut 15:1–6; 31:10–13.
10. Lev 25.
11. Exod 20:8–11.
12. Deut 5:12–15.

A Different Worldview

The cosmological origins myths of Genesis 1–11 are apologetic devices that announce a very different worldview than that available among and within the cultures which surrounded Israel. The two dominant cosmogonies in the ancient Near East were established by the civilizations of Mesopotamia (filtered largely through Babylonian recitations) and Egypt. These cosmogonic myths described the origins of the world as each group of peoples understood it, providing a paradigm by which to analyze and interpret contemporary events.

Distilled from the various records that are available to us, the generalized creation story of ancient Egypt emerged roughly like this.[13] *Nun* was the chaos power pervading the primeval waters. *Atum* was the creative force which lived on *Benben*, a pyramidical hill rising out of the primeval waters. *Atum* split to form the elemental gods *Shu* (air) and *Tefnut* (moisture). *Tefnut* bore two children: *Geb* (god of earth) and *Nut* (goddess of the skies). These, in turn gave birth to lesser gods who differentiated among themselves and came to rule various dimensions of the world as we now know it. Humanity was a final and unplanned outcome, with these newly produced weaklings useful only to do the work that the gods no longer wished to do, and to feed the gods by way of burning animal flesh in order to make it accessible.

Similar, and yet uniquely nuanced, are the cosmogonies of ancient Mesopotamia.[14] The name *Mesopotamia* literally means "between the waters." It denotes that region of the Near East encompassed by the combined watersheds of the Tigris and Euphrates rivers. Early civilizations here, enveloped by a somewhat different climatic environment than that found in Egypt, reflected this uniqueness in their origin myths. *Apsu* was the chaos power resident in the primeval waters. *Tiamat* was the bitter sea within the primeval waters upon which earth floated. *Lhamu* and *Lahamu* were gods of silt (at the edges of earth) created from the interaction of the primeval waters and the bitter seas. The horizons, *Anshar* and *Kishar*, were separated from one another by the birth of their child *Anu* (sky). *Anu* engendered *Ea-Nudimmud*, the god of earth and wisdom. All of these gods were filled with pent-up energy and this caused them to fight constantly. Since they existed within the belly of *Tiamat*, *Apsu* got indigestion and made plans to destroy all his restless and noisy children (i.e., the rest of the gods). In order to survive, *Ea* cast a spell which put *Apsu* to sleep. Then *Ea* killed *Apsu*, but his remains formed new gods, all of which were now in bitter struggle

13. Leeming, *Creation Myths*; Hart, *Egyptian Myths*.
14. See Dalley, *Myths from Mesopotamia*.

with each other and with their older relatives. Among the gods, *Marduk* rose as champion, quelling the fights and resurrecting order. To celebrate his success, *Marduk* created Babylon, which thus became the center of the universe and the source of all human civilization. These late-on-the-scene beings were created from the spilled blood of the gods, and they were deliberately fashioned as slaves who would do the work that the gods no longer wished to do.

Vision for Human Blessedness

When placed alongside these other cosmogonic myths, the Genesis creation story is very spare and poetically balanced. In brief testimony, it declares that God existed before the world that is apprehended by our senses was brought into being. It also asserts that creation happened by way of divine speech rather than through the sexual interaction of deities, or as the animation of guts and gore left over and emerging out of their conflicts. Moreover, creation was an intentional act that took place by way of orderly progression:

- Day 1: Arenas for light and darkness[15]
- Day 2: Arenas for sky and sea[16]
- Day 3: Arenas for Earth's dominant surfaces[17]
- Day 4: Inhabitants of light and darkness[18]
- Day 5: Inhabitants of sky and sea[19]
- Day 6: Inhabitants of Earth[20]

In the balanced rhythm of poetic prose, the Genesis creation story shows how divine planning and purpose brought the world into being specifically as a home for humanity. These creatures are not the byproduct of restless fighting among the gods. Nor are they a slave race produced in order to give the gods more leisure. In fact, according to the Genesis account, human beings are the only creatures made in the image of God, thus sharing the best of divine qualities.

---

15. Gen 1:3–5.
16. Gen 1:6–8.
17. Gen 1:9–13.
18. Gen 1:14–19.
19. Gen 1:20–23.
20. Gen 1:24–31.

It is obvious from the careful structuring of the Genesis creation account that it is neither a journalistic description of sequential events, nor the scientific report of an unfolding lab experiment. "Light" is the first "creation," cutting through and overturning the power of darkness and chaos which otherwise precluded meaningful existence. Yet the sources of light that actually make illumination happen in our world do not begin to exist until the fourth "day" of creation. What is going on? Why are things about creation expressed in this manner?

The answer seems to be a combination of contrast and organization. All other ancient stories of cosmological beginnings also start with chaos, but none of them ever fully emerges from it. Elements of random functionality may present themselves at times in or out from chaos, but behind, above, and around such moments of meaningful structure the cosmos remains a chaotic entity. In some civilizations, competing forces within chaos (such as *yin* and *yang*) may actually balance one another enough to provide temporary stability and even creative energy. Yet they remain the restless tentacles of chaos which pervades everything.

The Genesis cosmological myth sees the world very differently. Before existence and chaos, there is/was God. Existence itself is not the roiling of quasi-independent powers, but the expression of thoughtful divine intent. The manner in which things came into being had purpose and organizational structuring from the start.

If, as the literature itself requires, the creation stories of Genesis 1–2 are part of a lengthy historical prologue to the meeting of Yahweh and Israel at Mount Sinai, these cosmogonic myths are not to be read as the end product of scientific or historical analysis. They are designed to place Israel in an entirely different worldview context than that which shaped their neighbors. Humanity's place in this natural realm is one of intimacy with God, rather than fear and slavery. The human race exists in harmony with nature, not as its bitter opponent or only a helpless minor element. Women and men together share creative responsibility with God over animals and plants. In other words, the Sabbath is symbolic of the essential identity and character of human existence.

Parallel Lives, Parallel Hopes, Parallel Warnings

This, then, brings us to one more feature of the writer of Hebrew's use of the Sabbath concept. If the Sabbath is the intended expression of human life at its best, we are too much kept from it by the evil at work in these times.

Sabbath rest is illusory because we can never fully attain it. The Sabbath itself whets our appetite for a feast we have never actually tasted.

With that in mind, the writer of Hebrews shows Israel seeking a fuller expression of sabbath living once it gets into the promised land of Canaan. But the path to the promised land of sabbath rest is charged with many obstacles, much discomfort, and challenges that often caused the people of God to lose heart and give up. Many who set out to the promised land never got there. In fact, according to the book of Numbers, an entire generation of doubters died in the misery of the wilderness without reaching that beckoning hope.

Here, the parallel hits the writer of Hebrews' contemporary readers. The argument has several parts:

1. The time of Israel, guided by God's word deliver by prophets, has been superseded by this new age in which Jesus himself is the living divine Word, better than angels or even Moses.

2. While the Israelites lived their existence in a manner common to all of humankind, what pulled them forward was the promise of the land of rest, the land of fulfillment, the land of hope.

3. But the way to the promised land went through the wilderness, where famine, peril, enemy armies, drought, and suffering were the daily norm.

4. These challenges caused many to lose hope and give up. They murmured against God and lost confidence in the divine promises.

5. So too today (in the contemporary setting of the writing of Hebrews), those who have heard the voice and message of Jesus believe he has finished the redemptive process and has gone away for a time but will soon return to make all things new.

6. Yet these times are getting long, Jesus is delaying, and many challenges are multiplying. Most significant among these is direct opposition to Christian testimony, leading to confiscation of Christians' property, jailing of Christian leaders, and, more recently, threats of harm and death to Christians themselves.

7. Many recent converts to Christianity from within the Jewish community are giving up. They are renouncing Jesus and rejecting Christian hopes.

These, according to the writer of Hebrews, are dying in a new wilderness, just short of reaching the promised land. How unfortunate.

Where Have We Come So Far?

- God has spoken in times past.
    - This is our source of direction and confidence.
    - We know who we are because of the prophets.
- God has recently spoken a stronger, better, and clearer message through Jesus.
    - So when we, who live by the prophetic message, hear Jesus, we had better listen.
- Jesus is superior to the angels.
    - The great divine message that formed us came through Moses, but the message itself was delivered to him by angels (Deut 33:2; Acts 7:53).
    - Yet Jesus is superior to angels, and therefore delivers a more important prophetic message than that through the great prophet Moses.
- So stick with Jesus, even though you are tempted to turn away from him.
    - There is no higher authority or source of connection with God.
    - And if our lives are to be connected to God, we turn away from Jesus to our own peril.
- God has made the world subject to Jesus.
    - God never did this with the angels, so, again, Jesus is superior to them.
    - But this only happened because Jesus first fully identified with the world.
- Jesus willingly came into the world to fully experience its pain.
- And this is to our benefit for three reasons:
    - To fully identify with us as sisters and brothers.
    - To make atonement for our sins (which cause the pain of this world).
    - To bring us with him fully into the house of God.
- So Jesus is greater than (over) the angels, but Jesus is also greater than (over) Moses.

- Therefore, be careful that you don't disconnect from Jesus (who is God):

  ◆ Remember how those in our past who disconnected from God came under punishment.

  ◆ The same can happen to you if you do not stay true and committed to Jesus.

- Let God's people in the earlier redemptive sequence be your instructors:

  ◆ Like us, they were saved and led to their "(sabbath) rest" in the promised land.

    ▪ But they failed to stay connected to God by way of the word of the prophet (Moses) and died before reading "rest."

  ◆ Now God has promised us a coming "rest" (i.e., "heaven" when we die).

    ▪ But we will receive it only if we remain connected to God by way of the word of the prophet (Jesus) and live faithfully through these trials.

Message: A Lesson from the Past

Charles Eliot was president of Harvard University for forty years at the turn of the twentieth century. One evening, colleagues at the school were honoring him with a dinner and toasting his accomplishments. One fellow raised his glass and said, "Since you became president, Harvard has become a storehouse of knowledge."

Eliot modestly replied, "What you say is true, but I can claim little credit for it. It is simply that the first year students bring so much, and the graduates take so little away."

In a similar way, early Amherst College president George Harris lamented, in his opening speech of the school year, "Ah, I intended to give you some advice, but now I remember how much is left over from last year unused."

Precious Commodity

Education is a precious thing, and the writer of Hebrews makes his point well. "Those who cannot remember history are condemned to repeat it,"[21] said philosopher George Santayana, and it was in this frame of mind that Hebrews continually presents lessons from the past. Good schools and continuing skill development on the job are important in our lives generally, but even more so in our walk of faith. Like Eliot and Harris, we rightly tend to pity those who have opportunities to grow and learn but fail to take advantage. In their context, the original readers of Hebrews needed prodding to go back to school, so that they would not lose touch with the essential foundation of their trust in God.

Watching an infant mature through the stages of life is an awesome thing. The size of the body changes, although the torso and limbs grow much more rapidly than the head. That doesn't mean, however, that little is happening in the slow-growing skull. The opposite is, in fact, the case. Our brains are almost like sponges, taking in information as fast as our senses can process it.

What is most striking about the way that we mature, however, is its global integration. Muscles tone, coordination develops, the will becomes stronger, facts are memorized, and analogies unfold that make it possible for us to apply old learning to new situations. Growth is a never-ending process of insight deepened through experience and applied to expression. It is difficult to track the process of maturation but easy to tell when it is missing. No one complains about children being childlike, but the childishness of adults is nearly always panned.

Practices of Faith

So too in the Christian life there is a child-like exuberance that energizes every room where a new child of God enters. We delight in the amazing grace of the faith-birthing process and are thrilled with the stories of change and transformation that happen when God comes home to live in a life of one of his children.

But the stories of conversion are not enough to sustain faith or to explore the wonder of life in the promised land. Faith needs to grow. Horizons need to expand. Insights need to connect and skills of service need to be put to use. Most of all, dependence on God needs to multiply.

---

21. Santayana, *Life of Reason*, 284.

Yet, as the old hymn put it, "Change and decay in all around I see."[22] The changing face of life creates a kind of mist in which we can wander aimlessly or become silly in our self-importance. So, to grow well means that we have to reach for those things that truly matter. Too often the changing days and decaying months sap from us what Harry Emerson Fosdick called "the power to see it through."[23] Rarely do we lose hope and courage in an hour. Instead, our passions leak away over time like a dripping faucet, and we drain our emotional resources a nickel and a dime at a time. As the poet put it:

> East and west will pinch the heart
> That cannot keep them pushed apart;
> And he whose soul is flat—the sky
> Will cave in on him by and by.[24]

Charles Darwin, for instance, who grew up in a devoutly Christian home, wrote in his diaries that he never lost his faith through scientific challenge or intellectual argument. Instead, he said, belief slipped away over time until it didn't really matter anymore.[25] His story is rewritten a thousand times each generation by others who have simply "lost" faith and felt their souls flatten.

What can broaden and deep and empower our souls enough to help us live lives of significance in this new millennium? Years ago, a friend in Israel pointed me to the writings of the great mystic of modern Judaism, Abraham Joshua Heschel. For hours on end I sat in the library of Hebrew University in Jerusalem poring over his sensitive inspiration. Heschel said this: "In the tempestuous ocean of time and toil there are islands of stillness where a man may enter a harbor and reclaim his dignity."[26]

Homecoming Port

Everyone looks at one time or another for places like that, especially those who experience the trials of life that James predicts. Yet where would the tested soul find these islands? Heschel went on: "The Sabbath is the island, the port, the place of detachment from the practical and attachment to the spirit." He pictured us in mad motion: "Rushing hither and thither time

22. Henry Francis Lyte. "Abide With Me," Christian hymn. Written in 1847. Composed in 1861.

23. Fosdick, *Power*.

24. Millay, "Renascence," 1.

25. Darwin, *Autobiography*.

26. Heschel, *Sabbath*, 29.

becomes soiled and degraded." That's why, he said, we need the Sabbath. It is God's gift, allowing us "the opportunity to cleanse time."

The Sabbath is a biblical concept that helps us step out of our own lives in order to see things again from God's perspective. The Sabbath allows us to worship, gaining a harbor for the soul where we can find again our bearings in a sea of lost horizons and wintry winds. Those who move through the wilderness, like ancient Israel, will need to know well the value of the Sabbath.

Yet there is more to the Sabbath than simply a day of pause each week. The larger picture of Hebrews is that the rhythm of our calendar sabbaths is intended to remind us both of the degradation and challenge of life, and also of that which lingers just off our radar screens, beckoning us toward a hope that is larger than our current experiences.

H. G. Wells pictured it powerfully in his short story "The Door in the Wall."[27] A boy, five years old, wanders down a street and sees a green door in a white wall. Fascinated and intrigued, the boy pushes at the door and stumbles into a land of enchantment where two great black panthers greet him, yet he is not afraid. The world around him scintillates, pulsing with freshness and vibrancy. The blue sky is bluer, the flowers almost radiate reds and golds and violets. Animals abound, of every type, many of which he has never encountered and doesn't know their names, and yet all are familiar to him, and he tumbles and plays with each in delirious fun. People surround him too, folks of all ages. They seem to know him, and boys gather him quickly into their games. Food, smells, tastes, and the air itself are rich and energizing. A woman even takes him on her lap to read a book, which turns out to be the story of his own life, right up to the point where he stepped through the green door.

And then it is time to leave. The boy doesn't know how or why, but he moves back through the green door and finds himself again in the world of time and normalcy. Only now, everything seems very drab. The colors all look rather grayish. Sounds are more noisy. People rush by, not caring about each other. The experiences of life are harsh and cold, intimidating and unfriendly.

The boy grows to be a man, now telling his story to a trusted friend. Yet he is haunted by the world he once knew behind that green door. He tries to find it again but cannot. More than anything else, he seeks to bring something of that world into the lifeless meanderings of his existence here. The hope of that world keeps him going through the challenges of these times.

27. Wells, *Door in the Wall*.

So it is for Hebrews readers. Worn down by life at its worst, beaten by crises and cares too numerous to recall, and daily in danger of giving up since nothing seems to matter, they are beckoned on by the Sabbath. Not just the break from work that comes at the end of the week, but by the door in the wall sabbath. The future world sabbath. The taste of things better than we can imagine sabbath.

Our hearts strengthen and our minds renew even as our bodies falter. We reach again for the hands of those who pilgrim with us, and we sing the song of Bernard of Cluny:

> Oh, sweet and blessed country,
> The home of God's elect!
> Oh, sweet and blessed country
> That eager hearts expect!
> In mercy, Jesus, bring us
> To that dear land of rest!
> You are, with God the Father
> And spirit, ever blest.[28]

---

28. "Jerusalem the Golden" is a nineteenth-century Christian hymn by John Mason Neale. The text is from Neale's translation of a section of Bernard of Cluny's Latin verse *De Contemptu Mundi*.

Chapter 8

New Age Cosmology

Text: Hebrews 4:14–5:10

Since, then, we have a great high priest who has passed through the heavens, Jesus, the Son of God, let us hold fast to our confession. For we do not have a high priest who is unable to sympathize with our weaknesses, but we have one who in every respect has been tested as we are, yet without sin. Let us therefore approach the throne of grace with boldness, so that we may receive mercy and find grace to help in time of need.

Every high priest chosen from among mortals is put in charge of things pertaining to God on their behalf, to offer gifts and sacrifices for sins. He is able to deal gently with the ignorant and wayward, since he himself is subject to weakness; and because of this he must offer sacrifice for his own sins as well as for those of the people. And one does not presume to take this honor, but takes it only when called by God, just as Aaron was.

So also Christ did not glorify himself in becoming a high priest, but was appointed by the one who said to him,

"You are my Son,
today I have begotten you";[1]

as he says also in another place,

"You are a priest forever,

1. Ps 2:7.

according to the order of Melchizedek."[2]

In the days of his flesh, Jesus offered up prayers and supplications, with loud cries and tears, to the one who was able to save him from death, and he was heard because of his reverent submission. Although he was a Son, he learned obedience through what he suffered; and having been made perfect, he became the source of eternal salvation for all who obey him, having been designated by God a high priest according to the order of Melchizedek.

Backstory: Seeing Earth in a New Way

The writer of Hebrews mentions the tabernacle of ancient Israel on ten occasions,[3] and alludes to it almost as many times.[4] It is obvious that both he and his readers know what the tabernacle means for their faith and can visualize its structure, even though it was destroyed over a thousand years before when Solomon's grand temple replaced it.

In earlier allusions to the tabernacle,[5] the author described the relationship between Moses, the excellent *steward over* the house of God, and Jesus, the more excellent *owner of* the house of God. Now, however, the focus changes. Since Jesus, as God, is the owner of God's house, Jesus is also the only one who can provide full hospitality in God's house. In order to appreciate how the writer of Hebrews develops this, it is important to understand what God's house was all about.

Honeymoon Home

One third of the book of Exodus is given to explaining the meaning and construction of the tabernacle. The divine intention for this structure follows from the covenant-making ceremony of Exodus 20–24, which establishes the unique relationship between Yahweh and Israel. Exodus 25–40 has three major sections. In chapters 25–31, preparations for the tabernacle are made, and detailed plans are formulated. Then comes the intruding and jarring incident of the golden calf,[6] in which not only Israel's loyalty to Yahweh but also Yahweh's loyalty to Israel are tested. Finally, the architectural

---

2. Ps 110:4.

3. Heb 8:2, 5; 9:2, 3, 6, 8, 11, 21; 11:9; 13:10.

4. Heb 3:2, 3, 4, 5, 6; 10:21; 13:11.

5. Heb 3:2–6.

6. Exod 32–34.

initiatives of Exodus 25–31 are resumed in the actual construction of the tabernacle and its dedication,[7] almost as if the dark blot of the interlude had never happened.

Why all of this emphasis on building the tent-like tabernacle? Why invest in a movable shrine rather than rally around some sacred hill-top (Mount Sinai, for instance)? The answer is intrinsically related to the covenant-making event itself. If Israel is now the (reclaimed) possession of Yahweh, then Yahweh must take up visible residence among the people. The tabernacle is not a strange phenomenon of the natural order like an unfailing spring, a volcanic vent, or a residual meteor rock. Instead, it is the fabrication of a civilization that is intentionally on a journey, guided by an in-residence deity who travels with them. These people do not make pilgrimage to a shrine and then return to their homes; rather they move about in consort with the source of their identity actually residing within the center of their unwieldy sprawl.

Testimony of this is contained within the very architectural plans for the tabernacle. Although parts of the facility will be off-limits to most of the people (and thereby somewhat mysteriously remote), the basic design is virtually identical to that of the typical Israelite portable residence and the living space that surrounds it. First, the cooking fire of any family unit was found out in front of the tent. Second, there would be vessels for washing located near the door of the tent. Third, while many meals might be taken around the fire, some were more ordered and formal, and occurred in the initial spaces within the tent. These required atmospheric accoutrements like dishes, lamps for lighting, and the aromatic wafting of incense. Finally, the privacy of the intimate acts of marriage and family were reserved for the hidden recesses of the tent where visitors were not allowed.

Such is the theology behind both the tabernacle and its later expression as the temple. Both were different from mere cultic shrines. They were the resident of Israel's true bridegroom and master. The destinies of God and Israel were inextricably intertwined.

Back to Hebrews

At this point, the genius of the writer of Hebrews blazes again. He visualizes the movement of God's people from the outer distances of the world and the camp toward intimate and personal contact with God. He then applies this same journeying imagery more specifically to his readers in their new and Christian context.

7. Exod 35–40.

How did this psychological and spiritual and physical moving toward God take place in the tabernacle days? There were a number of successive steps:

- People recognized the central place of God in their existences and sought to commune with God.

- So they came to God's house with gifts.

- At the entrance to God's house, those entrusted with its care washed themselves so that they might be ready to receive these gifts on behalf of God.

- The gifts were quickly turned into meals that God and God's people shared together in front of the tent.

- The keepers of God's house would regularly enter the front section of God's tent to express rituals of deepening hospitality symbolically:

  - A table was set there, always ready, indicating a God's delight in sharing a meal with God's people.

  - The lamp was lit, providing light in these more intimate and darker places.

  - An altar of incense softened the mood and scented the air for deep companionship.

- And then, once a year, a representative who stood for both God and God's people (the high priest), communed deeply with God in the sacred private space (the holy of holies) where God's merciful throne (the ark of the covenant) stood.

This is the dance of movements between God and God's people that the writer of Hebrews now broadens, deepens, and richly symbolizes. Since Jesus is the owner of God's house and Jesus has the right to provide hospitality for those he wished in God's house, and since Jesus is God residing with the "Majesty in heaven,"[8] Jesus is the only one who can meet us at the door of God's house, receive the gifts we bring, lead us into and through God's house, and bring us to the very throne of God.

The writer of Hebrews takes the topographical locations of the tabernacle and its surroundings and sets the whole map on end so that it begins in this world and ends in heaven. The scattered peoples of earth, including Jews, need to find and approach their loving Creator. But God is not to be found in any earthly building today. Instead, God resides in heaven, ruling

8. Heb 1:3.

from the mercy seat.[9] And only Jesus, who is God, can come from that place to lead us back to that place.

Where Have We Come So Far?

- God has spoken in times past.
    - This is our source of direction and confidence.
    - We know who we are because of the prophets.
- God has recently spoken a stronger, better, and clearer message through Jesus.
    - So when we, who live by the prophetic message, hear Jesus, we had better listen.
- Jesus is superior to the angels.
    - The great divine message that formed us came through Moses, but the message itself was delivered to him by angels (Deut 33:2; Acts 7:53).
    - Yet Jesus is superior to angels, and therefore delivers a more important prophetic message than that through the great prophet Moses.
- So stick with Jesus, even though you are tempted to turn away from him.
    - There is no higher authority or source of connection with God.
    - And if our lives are to be connected to God, we turn away from Jesus to our own peril.
- God has made the world subject to Jesus.
    - God never did this with the angels, so, again, Jesus is superior to them.
    - But this only happened because Jesus first fully identified with the world.
- Jesus willingly came into the world to fully experience its pain.
- And this is to our benefit for three reasons:
    - To fully identify with us as sisters and brothers.

9. See Heb 10:19–22.

- To make atonement for our sins (which cause the pain of this world).

- To bring us with him fully into the house of God.

- So Jesus is greater than (over) the angels, but Jesus is also greater than (over) Moses.

- Therefore, be careful that you don't disconnect from Jesus (who is God):

  - Remember how those in our past who disconnected from God came under punishment.

  - The same can happen to you if you do not stay true and committed to Jesus.

- Let God's people in the earlier redemptive sequence be your instructors:

  - Like us, they were saved and led to their "(sabbath) rest" in the promised land.

    - But they failed to stay connected to God by way of the word of the prophet (Moses) and died before reading "rest."

  - Now God has promised us a coming "rest" (i.e., "heaven" when we die).

    - But we will receive it only if we remain connected to God by way of the word of the prophet (Jesus) and live faithfully through these trials.

- And, again, the only one who can keep you connected to God is Jesus:

  - He is our true high priest who will take us boldly to God's merciful throne through his actions on our behalf on the Day of Atonement. He is fully human, so he completely understands the struggles of our lives and sympathizes deeply, to the point of anguished cries.

- In fact, he is as fully committed to fulfilling the mandate and responsibilities of his priestly order as are others.

  - They in their "Aaronic/Levitical priestly order."

  - He in his "Melchizedek priestly order."

Message: Dual Citizenship

One fellow tells of his work as a hospital volunteer. He couldn't believe the pain and suffering he saw there. Burn victims. Deformities. Terminal cancer. He watched the little ones cry. Some were so lonely: their parents couldn't take the trauma, so they never came to see their own children. How horrible.

He decided to get a clown's nose and a pair of oversized shoes. Then he painted his face and pulled on a wig. When he went to work dressed like that the next day, some of the children were scared, some were captivated, and some even showed hints of a smile for the first time in ages.

But others couldn't stop wailing. They were consumed by agony. What could he do for them? The next day the clown brought along some popcorn. When he came to the side of a crying child, he took a kernel of popcorn, placed it against the child's cheek, and soaked up the cascading tears with its fluff. Then he popped that kernel into his mouth and ate it.

It was a stroke of genius. The only time some of those children stopped crying was the moment they knew that somebody else cared enough to swallow their tears.

Double Homeland

According to the writer of Hebrews, Jesus brings us to a place like that. He takes us, at the end of our journey, into the "sanctuary" of God, the holy of holies, where we approach the mercy seat of God's throne with awe and caution, but also thankfulness and delight. Even though our daily walk is often in painful places, Jesus brings us through the house of God right into God's merciful and protective presence. "Sanctuary" is refuge, fortress, safe house, security, arms of love, a place where someone cares enough to swallow our tears and protect us from the worst that could harm us.

And the reason that Jesus can do this is because he holds dual citizenship. On the one hand, he is a "high priest selected from among men"[10] who "is able to deal gently with those who are ignorant and are going astray,"[11] because he "has been tempted in every way, just as we are,"[12] and is "himself subject to weakness."[13] He "offered up prayers and petitions with loud

---

10. Heb 5:1.
11. Heb 5:2.
12. Heb 4:15.
13. Heb 5:2.

cries and tears"[14] and "suffered"[15] all the way to death. Jesus is fully human, completely like us, aware totally of our needs and concerns, our tears and suffering.

Yet on the other hand, Jesus is "the Son of God"[16] who "has gone through the heavens,"[17] the "perfect"[18] one who "became the source of eternal salvation."[19] Jesus is fully God, with all of the capabilities of divinity and its power. Because of that he is able to deliver us from the spooky and scary things that go bump in the night.

In other words, Jesus has dual citizenship. He belongs fully to the world of humanity, sharing its sorrows, woes, pains, crises, and tears. But Jesus is also one of the only three who holds permanent and eternal citizenship in heaven, the deity who is absolutely and completely God, Son of the Father, and participant in all things divine from before time began.

Dance in the Desert

Madeleine L'Engle paints a picture of this very human deity, or very divine human, in one of her children's books,[20] a parable of the Gospel record about Jesus. L'Engle tells of a young couple on a desert journey through wilderness in a rough caravan. They're on their way to Egypt. Someone is after them; someone wants to kill their little boy.

The journey is a rugged one. The desert is alive with ferocious beasts. All eyes cast about uneasily as darkness settles. There'll be little sleep in the camp tonight. They build a great fire to drive back the shadows and keep away the world that belongs to monsters with glowing eyes. Suddenly they start in terror; a great lion appears at the bonfire. The mother reaches for her child, desperately trying to draw him to safety.

But the child stands and laughs. He opens his arms wide to the lion. The lion lifts his front paws and hops around on his hind legs. He's dancing! And then, from the desert, come running several little mice and two donkeys and a snake and a couple of clumsy ostriches. Three great eagles swoop in from the purple skies. From the other side of the camp a unicorn emerges, a pelican, and even two dragons.

14. Heb 5:7.
15. Heb 5:8.
16. Heb 4:14.
17. Heb 4:14.
18. Heb 5:9.
19. Heb 5:9.
20. L'Engle, *Dance in Desert.*

They all bow before the child and then dance together, round and round him. He stands at the center of their great circle, laughing in delight. It's a dance in the desert, as L'Engle calls it. In essence, it's the sum and substance of our worship here on earth, pilgrims passing through the wilderness of ghastly beasties and mournful hurts.

Like those to whom Hebrews was written, the first coming of Jesus has brought us very near to the fullness of the kingdom of God. Eternity and the renewed creation seem close, but we are not there yet. We still spend time in the dark alongside those who wrestle with demons and shadows and beasties. Yet because of our confidence in the incarnation, we see the light, and clap our hands in celebration of the child who comes to dance around our fires.

He swallows our tears and fears, even as they keep recurring. And in his dance between earth and heaven, we are protected by the walls of grace that close the mouths of lions and cause Leviathan to frolic in the deeps.

Living in Two Worlds

This inherently dual identity of Jesus becomes a source for our own transformations. Once Jesus connects with us, living in our very scary human world, he also makes us participants in the safety and refuge of God's divine home. We, too, gain a type of dual citizenship, when Jesus takes us by his high priestly hand and walks us through the house of God.

A true parable comes to mind. One of the German army prison camps during World War II was divided into two sections. In order to keep tighter control of captured allied soldiers, British and Commonwealth internees were segregated from American captives. A fence and out-of-bounds territory on either side of it marked a no-man's-land where machine gun fire would kill those who strayed suspiciously close to one another.

But one time each day, right at noon, the ranking officer from either group was allowed to approach his counterpart at the fence. Armed German soldiers stood close, monitoring every word spoken. After a brief and formal conference, the two leaders would march back to their groups, and the dull routine of prison life would continue.

The situation appeared hopeless. Still, the ranking officers figured out that they both knew enough of the Gaelic language to use it for passing messages that they didn't want the Germans to comprehend. They rarely used Gaelic, of course, saving it for times of greatest urgency—perhaps an escape attempt, or the like.

Things changed when a recently captured soldier managed to smuggle in the parts of a crystal radio set. Each morning it was hidden by scattering the pieces throughout a variety of secret recesses in the barracks. Each night it was rebuilt, and the world outside floated in over the airwaves.

Then came the day that news of the D-Day invasion at Normandy entered the camp. The excitement of the prison soldiers on one side of the fence had to be transmitted to those on the other side. That noon, the ranking officers met for the usual formal interchange. A few words were spoken in Gaelic, with no expression twitching either dutiful face. Then the officers turned stiffly from one another. With no show of emotion, they marched under guard back to their respective companies.

The Germans were more than a little curious, however, when the barracks on one side of the camp suddenly erupted with cheers and shouting. They themselves knew nothing of the invasion. Hitler's propaganda machine creatively rewrote world events for them.

For three more months, the camp carried on a comical inversion of reality. The guards, with their guns and their superior status, were prisoners of ignorance and the coming defeat. Those who cowered in the barracks, on the other hand, were certain of their eventual freedom. They wore prison clothes. They ate prison food. They smelled the stench of prison life around them. But because they knew the outcome, their confidence soared. In their hearts, they were free.

The former captives who were part of that incredible experience have never stopped telling others of the feelings that filled their spirits during those three months. They were a lot like the thoughts and emotions that drove the writer of Hebrews as his brings home his point: hounded by enemies, we might be, yet we are also vindicated and released through the great work of our high priest. We experience the pain of deadly struggles, yet we know the confidence of God's deliverance. The present demands all our attention, but we live in the hope of the future.

This is the good news about Jesus, dual citizen and great high priest over the house of God.

Chapter 9

Coach's Challenge

Text: Hebrews 5:11–6:12

About this we have much to say that is hard to explain, since you have become dull in understanding. For though by this time you ought to be teachers, you need someone to teach you again the basic elements of the oracles of God. You need milk, not solid food; for everyone who lives on milk, being still an infant, is unskilled in the word of righteousness. But solid food is for the mature, for those whose faculties have been trained by practice to distinguish good from evil.

Therefore let us go on toward perfection, leaving behind the basic teaching about Christ, and not laying again the foundation: repentance from dead works and faith toward God, instruction about baptisms, laying on of hands, resurrection of the dead, and eternal judgment. And we will do this, if God permits.

For it is impossible to restore again to repentance those who have once been enlightened, and have tasted the heavenly gift, and have shared in the Holy Spirit, and have tasted the goodness of the word of God and the powers of the age to come, and then have fallen away, since on their own they are crucifying again the Son of God and are holding him up to contempt. Ground that drinks up the rain falling on it repeatedly, and that produces a crop useful to those for whom it is cultivated, receives a blessing from God. But if it produces thorns and thistles, it is worthless and on the verge of being cursed; its end is to be burned over.

Even though we speak in this way, beloved, we are confident of better things in your case, things that belong to salvation. For God is not unjust; he will not overlook your work and the love that you showed for his sake in serving the saints, as you still do. And we want each one of you to show the same diligence so as to realize the full assurance of hope to the very end, so that you may not become sluggish, but imitators of those who through faith and patience inherit the promises.

Backstory: Back to School

THERE IS A DEEP connection between this short passage and the sermon spoken by Peter at Pentecost in Acts 2. Similarly, the testimony of Paul regarding his conversion to Christianity, narrated initially in Acts 9 and then retold again in both Acts 22 and 26, resonates with the writer's message in these verses. Jesus and all of his disciples were Jews. More than that, they were devout Jews who bathed in Scripture (the Hebrew Bible or the Old Testament), and breathed its language as if oxygen itself. They were never in danger of losing their faith in God. Still, the massive corner-turning event of Jesus' coming as Messiah made some of them seriously question whether Jesus was the one they should trust, and, if so, what this meant for their religion.

Getting to Know These People

It is for this reason that the writer of Hebrews chides his readers about their timidity, their hesitancy, their seeming inability to dig in and live boldly by the gospel of Jesus. As these notes of admonition sound a staccato warning beat, we are able to learn more about the community to whom Hebrews is written. Among many other things:

- These people have been Christians for a fairly long time, long enough, according to the writer, to have adopted the centrality of Jesus as irrefutable and undeniable within their religion.

- Yet, at the same time, they are becoming resistant about having anyone telling them what they should be doing or not doing.

- Moreover, as they "mature" within their faith community, they are actually forgetting what attracted them and excited them about Christianity in the first place, what originally drew them in.

For these reasons, the writer of Hebrews feels the need to go back to early conversations they had at the beginning of their Christian journey. He needs to remind these people of things that brought them to faith in Jesus at the start.

In this context, the writer of Hebrews hints at things he considers the foundational teachings that they first needed to own and profess in their initial transition into the Christian community.

- They needed to repent from dead works.

- They needed to express faith toward God.

- They needed to be baptized since this was the Trinitarian mark of God identifying the community of on-going Israelite faith now processed through the divine Messiah Jesus.

- They needed to recall the empowerment of the Holy Spirit, received at first when the apostles laid hands on them in the Christian ceremony of anointing.

- They needed to understand that resurrection was not merely a future possibility at the end of time, but the confirmation of Jesus' unique identity and work, initiating the new age of mission and eschatological expectation.

- They needed to recall Jesus' teachings about the judgment day which is looming, and get back to the business of the church's witness to all nations about Jesus, even if (and perhaps more specifically because of) persecutions were growing.

The admonition is clear. But couched in its challenges and warnings is a caricature of this community. It is very akin to what we think about regarding Paul before his conversion from aggressively pious historic Judaism to assertively transformative Jesus-oriented Christianity. And, it is very much in tune with Peter's Christian sermon preached to devout Jews at Pentecost, urging them not to give up their faith but boldly to take hold of the next and amazing phase of it as revealed in Jesus.

What we might distill, about this community, from these hints looks like this. Those receiving Hebrews initially:

- were likely Jews who did not find the symbolic practices of Judaism to be fulfilling once they heard the dynamic message about Jesus.

- needed to repent because they recognized that the sins and contaminations of their lives could only find divine expiation through the recent atoning death of Jesus.

- learned that they should trust in Jesus as the promised Messiah foretold by the prophets, since he was their new avenue of faith to God.

- were baptized (either in the name of Jesus, or in the Trinitarian name) as a sign of belonging to the Christian community, but had recently begun to wonder whether this baptism had any efficacy in their current tortured situation.

- received the empowerment of the Holy Spirit when others laid hands on them, but no longer experienced either its exhilaration or its emboldening.

- began to understand the "resurrection of the dead" in a new way, not just something that might happen at the end of time but recently having happened already for Jesus, and about to happen again when very soon Jesus would return to raise the current fallen dead.

These are Jewish Christians who once were extremely excited that the messianic age had arrived. They had believed in Jesus as the promised Messiah, which was confirmed for them when he rose from the dead. They understood that Jesus left for a while, so that his disciples could tell as many people as possible that the end of times, with its unsettling divine judgment, was very near. They believed that when Jesus returned, very shortly, the hammer would fall and those who did not believe in Jesus would be doomed to divine punishment. But they had been steadfastly confident that all could come to faith in Jesus and experience the joys of the future peaceable kingdom, escaping the wrath of punishment.

Recently, however, their trust in Jesus had slipped. Instead of striding boldly in the confidence of Jesus' Spirit-empowered disciples, they had begun to slip back into corners of timid Jewish practices, seeking to hide from the world rather than evangelize it. The preachers of Christ had to go back to school. Even more, these Jews needed to find again their Messiah.

A Strategically Motivating Homily

The manner in which the writer of Hebrews attempts to reschool these folks is through a series of rhetorical moves. First comes a discouraging word.[1] Those who walk away from a great gift cannot expect to retain or recover that gift. Once it has been rejected, it is no longer available to them. This community had, in fact, received such a present. Indeed, it was overwhelming in its size and shape:

---

1. Heb 6:4–6.

- They had been "enlightened." That is, they had come out of the darkness of ignorance and superstition into face-to-face knowledge and insight of the grace and plans of God almighty.

- They had tasted the divine nectar when the Holy Spirit came on them in power. It was an intoxication that stimulated every aspect of their beings, without any negative side effects. Through the Holy Spirit they had come to be more fully what God had always intended for them.

- They had reached into eternity and found the rarified air of its bracing beauty. Suddenly the habits and experiences of time seemed tedious and the surroundings of sensuality appeared nauseating. These people had reached beyond the gossamer vail hiding the spiritual world from everyday existence, and they could never view ordinary life as sufficient.

Moreover, the only source of this transforming vision was Jesus. So if they now would say that Jesus was not the only way into the marvelous kingdom of God, or if they thought they could gain the experiences of that kingdom through a different channel, they were not merely ignoring Jesus or sidestepping him; they were actually accomplices in his horrible death. They had become the mocking voices of the Jewish leaders. They were wielding the hammers of the Roman soldiers. They were spitting in the very face of God.

Second, this heart-breaking challenge is coupled with a powerful agricultural illustration.[2] The soils of the earth cannot help but grow plants. Bring the rain, bring the sun, and even the deserts bloom. There is, however, a difference between what emerges from fields that have been cultivated and those which are left to their own devices. Where a farmer takes the time to till the ground, restrain the weeds, plant good soil, and provide organic nourishment, gardens and acreages ought to sprout with vegetables, grains, fruit trees, and vineyards. Yes, the weeds will come, but they will be in the minority and will not overwhelm the good things that were planted and tended. So if a field suddenly produces no beneficial vegetation, and springs up with a nasty overgrowth of thorns and thistles, the farmer will abandon his homestead, or set the nasty weeds ablaze and then tear the earth apart with plows until it submits to his intents.

Third, the writer ends this brief homily with a loving note of encouragement.[3] We do not believe these warnings are needed, sisters and brothers,

2. Heb 6:7–8.
3. Heb 6:9–10.

he notes, for we "are confident of better things in your case."[4] The author of Hebrews stakes his surety on one thing: God is still in control. God began a good work in you and God will see things through.[5]

This leads, fourth, to expectation.[6] Our words to you, says the author, are intended to nudge you from sluggishness into action, from fear into boldness, from reticence into assertiveness about your faith.[7] Regain what you have let slip, and recover your energy for the central elements of the gospel. You are enlightened. You have tasted the food of heaven. You have reached into eternity and found a place to stand.

So be the good soil you know you are, and carry on as you started. Get over the slump, the sluggishness. Don't become lazy just when fortitude is needed.

Divine Election or Human Choice?

Of course, this passage has caused a lot of theological discussion over the centuries, regarding the nature of election and the perseverance of the saints of God. Is it possible for the elect to fall away? Can God's work in our lives be rejected? Are we "once saved, always saved," or is it better to admit that sometimes we feel like we are in the grip of grace and other times we know we are falling and fallen?

The Greek text of Hebrews is incredibly learned and polished, and each word is carefully chosen. With the precision provided by the writer, some of these conundrums are resolved while others are deepened. Here is a list of the key terms and their meanings as dictated by the exact form chosen by the author:

- "impossible" (Heb 6:4): Ἀδύνατον. When applied to people, this term has the force of incapacity; when spoken of things or events, it brings the idea of impossibility. Overall, it initiates the sense of something taking place that is not possible.

- "to restore" (Heb 6:4): γευσαμένους. This is a present, active, infinitive, expressing an action of the subject that is suspended in its relation time. In other words, there is no presumption that fallenness has taken place or that restoration is needed. This is merely a declaration of causal relationships.

4. Heb 6:9.

5. See, in this regard, Phil 1:6.

6. Heb 6:11–12.

7. See, again, Phil 2:12–13.

- "have once been enlightened" and "have shared in the Holy Spirit" (Heb 6:4): φωτισθέντας and μετόχους γενηθέντας πνεύματοςάγίου. These are both aorist passive participle which connote actions that definitively ceased their on-going work, but not by the active choice or will of the subjects. These people had been caused by God to be enlightened and they had experienced the energizing of the Holy Spirit. Neither of these actions of God was a result of the individuals' own initiatives and any cessation of these things was not attributed to them either.

- "have tasted" (twice, once in Heb 6:4 and again in Heb 6:5): γευσαμένους. The form is aorist middle participle and it declares that the action of the subject, which has either benefited it or suffered it, has ceased. What was once experienced is no longer taking place.

- "have fallen away" (Heb 6:6): παραπεσόντας. Here, the form is aorist active participle, meaning that an action which has definitively ceased its on-going work by the explicit choice of the subject.

- "crucifying" and "holding him up to contempt" (Heb 6:6): ἀνασταυροῦντας and παραδειγματίζοντα. Both are present active participle, giving the force of on-going action by the subjects in the present moment.

In choosing his words carefully, the writer of Hebrews has expressed that God's initiatives in bringing enlightenment and the empowering Spirit into the lives of these people was a matter beyond their control. God initiated insight and salvation, and they were not able to counter this divine work through human stubbornness or sinfulness.

At the same time, the human responses of holding onto God's promises and acting upon them does lie within the domain of personal development. We become responsible for our use and nurturing of the gift which God initiates. We can neglect it, or we can hone and shape it. The origin of salvation is in the hands of God, but its effectiveness in our lives is, at least in part, a matter of our own volition.

This is where the illustration of the soils becomes fruitful. Ground that is tilled and farmed has no choice to decide what it is or where it is. Still, the land is expected to produce a crop, not thorns and thistles. When the former happens, God blesses the land for its response. And where the earth supports the endeavors of the latter, God rightly judges and burns and punishes.

Similarly, according to the author, God still recognizes and responds to the work of the saints. It is precisely this divine recognition and response that gives hope and provides the energy for perseverance to the very end. Thus, it is actually the compliment of human wishful struggles coupling with divine redemptive activity that will help avoid apostasy and nurture faithfulness through uncertainty.

When analyzed carefully, both divine election and human responsibility are affirmed and safeguarded in the writer of Hebrews' deliberately chosen words and their grammatical forms. This encouragement will be reiterated again in several ways in the coming chapters[8] and the expectation drawn out will emerge at least twice more in rather lengthy "altar calls."[9]

Where Have We Come So Far?

- God has spoken in times past.

    - This is our source of direction and confidence.

    - We know who we are because of the prophets.

- God has recently spoken a stronger, better, and clearer message through Jesus.

    - So when we, who live by the prophetic message, hear Jesus, we had better listen.

- Jesus is superior to the angels.

    - The great divine message that formed us came through Moses, but the message itself was delivered to him by angels (Deut 33:2; Acts 7:53).

    - Yet Jesus is superior to angels, and therefore delivers a more important prophetic message than that through the great prophet Moses.

- So stick with Jesus, even though you are tempted to turn away from him.

    - There is no higher authority or source of connection with God.

    - And if our lives are to be connected to God, we turn away from Jesus to our own peril.

- God has made the world subject to Jesus.

    - God never did this with the angels, so, again, Jesus is superior to them.

8. Notably Heb 10:19–25 and 12:14–29.
9. Especially Heb 10:26–39 and 13:1–19.

- ◆ But this only happened because Jesus first fully identified with the world.
- Jesus willingly came into the world to fully experience its pain.
- And this is to our benefit for three reasons:
  - ◆ To fully identify with us as sisters and brothers.
  - ◆ To make atonement for our sins (which cause the pain of this world).
  - ◆ To bring us with him fully into the house of God.
- So Jesus is greater than (over) the angels, but Jesus is also greater than (over) Moses.
- Therefore, be careful that you don't disconnect from Jesus (who is God):
  - ◆ Remember how those in our past who disconnected from God came under punishment.
  - ◆ The same can happen to you if you do not stay true and committed to Jesus.
- Let God's people in the earlier redemptive sequence be your instructors:
  - ◆ Like us, they were saved and led to their "(sabbath) rest" in the promised land.
    - ▪ But they failed to stay connected to God by way of the word of the prophet (Moses) and died before reading "rest."
  - ◆ Now God has promised us a coming "rest" (i.e., "heaven" when we die).
    - ▪ But we will receive it only if we remain connected to God by way of the word of the prophet (Jesus) and live faithfully through these trials.
- And, again, the only one who can keep you connected to God is Jesus:
  - ◆ He is our true high priest, who will take us boldly to God's merciful throne through his actions on our behalf on the Day of Atonement. He is fully human, so he completely understands the struggles of our lives and sympathizes deeply, to the point of anguished cries.
- In fact, he is as fully committed to fulfilling the mandate and responsibilities of his priestly order as are others.

♦ They in their "Aaronic/Levitical priestly order."

♦ He in his "Melchizedek priestly order."

- I wish you were getting this. You should be mature enough to teach others, but it seems you have lost your passion for Jesus and are trying only to protect yourselves

    ♦ Though I write strong words, I am confident that you will continue in our faith in Jesus.

Message: Altar Call #2

When Vince Lombardi was hired as head coach of the Green Bay Packers in 1958, the team was in dismal shape. A single win in season play the year before had socked the club solidly into the basement of the NFL and sportscasters everywhere used it as the butt of loser jokes. But Lombardi picked and pulled and prodded and trained the players into become a winning team. They were NFL champions for three consecutive seasons and took the game honors for the first two Super Bowls.

Lombardi was a drill sergeant and a strategist, finding and developing the best in each of his players individually and then crafting a team community that could visualize the prize. "Winning isn't everything," he was often quoted as saying, "It's the only thing."[10] His Packers proved him true, time and again.

Where's the Team?

Coaching is nothing without a team that responds. Leaders are merely overblown egos if there is no one who will follow. During the tumultuous French Revolution of 1789 mobs and madmen rushed through Paris streets. One journalist reported a wide-eyed, wild-haired wastrel lumbering along one day, feverishly demanding from all he saw, "Where is the crowd? I must find them. I am their leader."

This is the problem that the author of Hebrews pointedly addresses in his short homily, tucked in between all of his other deep theological instructions. God is the greatest coach, but this team seems unwilling to follow.

---

10. Lombardi was actually quoting UCLA Bruins football coach Henry Russell ("Red") Sanders, who is documented as having spoken at least two different versions of the quotation in the late 1940s.

Because of that, people mill about or wander aimlessly, losing their way and muting the testimony of the church.

It is a bit like England, prior to Churchill—only a patchwork of competing ideologies, stymied at the crossroads of the twentieth century's critical international events. Or, think again of India before Gandhi: lacking cohesive identity and playing games of competitive kowtowing to expatriate authorities, and only turned around when the "Great Soul" helped inspire a national common cause. But of course, even more tragic is the situation in the church when God's people skirt from the light in embarrassment or timidity or simply tiredness.

The problem, as the writer of Hebrews puts it, is that the great leader has recently come but those who are sub-coaches now think they can play the game without the head coach. They use a different play book and try to win minor trophies that will gather dust on their mantles, rather than looking for the winning season that would honor the owner.

Whose Fault Is It?

Among the religious discussions of the nascent church there was a similar confusion of identities. For some, evil was inherent in the system like yin's twin yang. For others, humans had incurred the wrath of the gods and were punished through the spread of vices that flowed out of Pandora's mythical box. Others still believed divine perfection was trapped by a mean-spirited Creator into the corrupt and forgetful stuff of human flesh, waiting magical gnostic liberation.

The author of Hebrews provides a quick reminder about the origins of good and evil. God is good, creation is good, and human alienation from the good is a late introduction brought about by our sinful choices. For the readers of Hebrews, the message communicated was that all of humanity had the same opportunities to remain in fellowship with the Creator and all are equally responsible for their distance from God.

But the writer also couched the story in swaddling folds of never-ending grace. Time after time God initiated a restoration of relationships with humanity. All are welcome to be part of the team. As part of our latter days, in fact, God sent in Jesus to spur the team to new spiritual victories. Jesus is the expression of God's righteousness inserted recently into our world and the means by which we are attached to the eternal righteous endeavors of God. Jesus is the glue that binds the team together and keeps us connected both to the owner and the game.

Jesus has clearly expressed his divine power and wisdom. Enough so, in fact, that winning the real game of life means playing by a set of rules that has not been used for a long time on planet Earth. It is like the "deep magic" of Aslan in C. S. Lewis' great tale, *The Lion, the Witch and the Wardrobe*.[11] Most don't understand it, but without it the game becomes a never-ending cycle of violence in which there are only losers.

Forging a New Team

For that reason, the writer gives a brief exhortation, reminding his readers about the process that led them to come onto the Jesus team in the first place. It is not self-preservation but service that counts. It is not superiority but selflessness that wins points. It is not stridency but sacrifice that finds recognition from the owner of the club. Jesus is building a team that will change the world. Unfortunately, on that day, too few people seemed willing to show up at the try-outs.

There is a scene in J. R. R. Tolkien's *The Fellowship of the Ring*[12] where a partnership is forged among those who would accompany Frodo on his journey to destroy the ring of power, the symbol and driving force of all that is evil. The movie version makes for a very gripping visual illustration and the original literary text is equally as moving. What comes through as the bond that unites these creatures is a sense of selflessness. Each subsumes his will to the greater cause, and trusts an unseen and transcendent good for an outcome that will bless all of Middle Earth, even if the trek itself causes the demise of any or all of the compatriots.

So it is Jesus' small glimpse of the mission of God echoed in these verses. In a world turned cold to its Creator, in an age riddled by Delphic oracles and temple prostitutes and emperors claiming divinity, in a little corner of geography where messianic hopes ran high, God called together a strange team to make its mark by playing a different game. These folks are part of a great divine mission of transformation. Still, many are losing nerve, getting weak-kneed, and slipping back from the light of grace into the shadows of fear and alienation. They need a great pep talk from the coach, and it resonates through the voice of the author of Hebrews. "Come on, people. You started brilliantly. But you have lost heart, and you're losing the game. Remember who you are. Remember whose you are! Get back in, and let's see this thing through. You are winners, but you have to play the game."

---

11. Lewis, *Lion, Witch*.

12. Tolkien, *Fellowship of Ring*.

Walter Wangerin, Jr., in his great allegory, *The Book of the Dun Cow*[13] (along with its wonderful sequel, *The Book of Sorrows*[14]), captures both the scope of the divine mission as well as the underrated character of the team. If the focus remains on the team, apart from the mission, the point is lost. God is reclaiming God's creation but does so through human agency. The game is fierce and the playing field is rough. Only those who can tear up their personal score sheets in order get into God's game will make the team. Only they are truly called. Only they are equipped to serve and follow and play on the greatest winning team of all time.

Jesus took the road to the cross, and now he calls others to join him in that same pilgrimage. The cost of discipleship,[15] as Dietrich Bonhoeffer noted, is self-denial. The words of the writer of Hebrews are a strong call to that vocation, not as an end in itself or as a means to a self-help goal (like dieting), but rather as a counter-cultural missional testimony. Those who travel this road do not get to Easter without first enduring Good Friday; they do not presume a glorious outcome that gathers the media like paparazzi vultures, but sense that the journey of service brings light in darkness, hope in despair, healing for pain, and faith where power corrupts and destroys.

Have you entered the cause?

---

13. Wangerin, Jr., *Dun Cow*.
14. Wangerin, Jr., *Sorrows*.
15. Bonhoeffer, *Cost of Discipleship*.

Chapter 10

Where the Story Begins

Text: Hebrews 6:13–20

When God made a promise to Abraham, because he had no one greater by whom to swear, he swore by himself, saying, "I will surely bless you and multiply you."[1] And thus Abraham, having patiently endured, obtained the promise. Human beings, of course, swear by someone greater than themselves, and an oath given as confirmation puts an end to all dispute. In the same way, when God desired to show even more clearly to the heirs of the promise the unchangeable character of his purpose, he guaranteed it by an oath, so that through two unchangeable things, in which it is impossible that God would prove false, we who have taken refuge might be strongly encouraged to seize the hope set before us. We have this hope, a sure and steadfast anchor of the soul, a hope that enters the inner shrine behind the curtain, where Jesus, a forerunner on our behalf, has entered, having become a high priest forever according to the order of Melchizedek.

Backstory: Abraham

ABRAM WAS AN ARAMAEAN from the heart of Mesopotamia. His father Terah began a journey westward, which he continued upon his father's death. Whatever Terah's reasons might have been for moving from the old

---

1. Gen 22:17.

family village—restlessness, treasure-seeking, displacement, wanderlust—
Genesis 12 informs us that Abram's continuation of the trek was motivated
by a divine call to seek a land which would become his by providential appointment. This is the first of four similar divine declarations that occur in
quick succession in chapters 12, 13, 15, and 17. Such repetition cues us to
the importance of these theophanies, but it ought also cause us to look more
closely at the forms in which the promises to Abram are made.

In brief, Abram's first three encounters with God are shaped literarily
as royal grants. Only in Genesis 17 does the language of the dialogue change
and elements are added to give it the flavor of a suzerain-vassal covenant.
This is very significant. When Abram received royal grant promises of land
or a son, he seemed to treat these divine offerings with a mixture of indif-
ference and skepticism. He immediately left the land of promise in Genesis
12, and connived with his wife, Sarai, and her handmaid, Hagar, to obtain
an heir through reasonably reliable human means in Genesis 16. Even in
the stories of Genesis 13–14, where Abram remained in the land but fought
with others to regain his nephew Lot from them after local skirmishes and
kidnappings, Abram turned his thankfulness toward a local expression of
religious devotion through the mystical figure of Melchizedek (Gen 14:18–
20). Only when God changed the language of covenant discourse, bringing
Abram into the partnership of a suzerain-vassal bond, did *Abraham* enter
fidelity and commitment to this new world, new purpose, and new journey.

Genesis 12—Royal grant: Land	Abram's response: Leave the land
Genesis 13—Royal grant: Land	Abram's response: Fight over the land
Genesis 15—Royal grant: Son	Abram's response: Connive to get Ishmael as son
Genesis 17—Suzerain-vassal: Land, son; renaming, circumcision	Abraham's response: Faith and trust (see chapter 22)

For Israel, standing at Mount Sinai in the context of a suzerain-vassal
covenant-making ceremony, the implications of this story in their forma-
tive heritage would be striking. First of all, the nation would see itself as
the unique and miraculously born child fulfilling a divine promise. Israel
could not exist were it not for God's unusual efforts at getting Abram to
make Sarai pregnant in a way that was humanly impossible. Second, the
people were the descendants of a man on a divine pilgrimage. Not only was
Abram *en route* to a land of promise, but he was also the instrument of God
for the blessing of all the nations of the earth. In other words, Israel was
born with a mandate and it was globally encompassing. Third, while these

tribes had recently emerged from Egypt as a despised social underclass of disenfranchised slaves, they were actually landowners. Canaan was theirs for the taking because they already owned it. They would not enter the land by stealth but through the front door; they would claim the land, not by surreptitious means or mere battlefield bloodshed, but as rightful owners going home. This would greatly affect their common psyche: They were the long-lost heirs of a kingdom, returning to claim their royal privilege and possessions. Fourth, there was a selection in the process of creating their identity. They were children of Abraham, but so were a number of area tribes and nations descending from Ishmael. What made them special was the uniqueness of their lineage through Isaac, the miraculously born child of Abram and Sarai's old age. Israel had international kinship relations, but she also retained a unique identity fostered by the divine distinctions between branches of the family. Fifth, in the progression of the dialogue between Yahweh and Abram, there was a call to participation in the mission of God. As the story of Abram unfolded, it was clear that his commitment to God's plans was minimal at best until the change from royal grants to the suzerain-vassal covenant of chapter 17. Each time Abram was given a gift, he seemingly threw it away, tried to take it by force, or manipulated his circumstances so that he controlled his destiny; only when God took formal ownership of both Abram and the situation through the suzerain-vassal covenant of Genesis 17 was there a marked change in Abram's participation in the divine initiative. The renaming of Abram and Sarai to Abraham and Sarah was only partly significant for the meaning of the names; mostly, they were a deliberate and public declaration that God owned them. To name meant to have power over, just as was the case when a divine word created the elements of the universe in Genesis 1 and when Adam named the animals in Genesis 2. Furthermore, in the call to circumcise all the males of the family, God transformed a widely used social rite-of-passage symbol into a visible mark of belonging, now no longer tied to personal achievements like battlefield wins or hunting success but merely to the gracious goodness of God and participation in the divine mission.

The power of the fourth covenant for Abraham cannot be overstated. This is clearly what the writer of Hebrews has in mind as he rehearses briefly these events. He talks about God's oath-making and quotes from the "binding of Isaac" story in Genesis 22. It is precisely when God makes oaths that we gain absolute confidence in God's follow-through.

The initial incident recounted in Genesis 22 is identified as a test of Abraham's faith. In light of his failing responses to earlier royal grant promises, Abraham is now called to declare his loyalty to the God who has ratified a suzerain-vassal covenant with him.

Although the test may seem overly demanding, there are mitigating factors that help us understand it more fully within its own framework.

First, it was not out of the ordinary for people at that time to believe that deities required human sacrifice. The unusual twist in this story is that Yahweh, by stopping the bloodshed of Isaac, chooses deliberately to distance himself from these other deities and shows that he does not delight in human sacrifice. Second, Yahweh provides an alternative offering, a ram divinely placed on the scene. Third, the place is named "Moriah," which can ambiguously mean either "Yahweh sees" or "Yahweh will be seen," both of which are correct, thus illuminating the idea presented in the text that "Yahweh provides" the sacrifice. Fourth, this idea is further confirmed by later references to the location of the site. In 2 Chronicles 3:1, this mountain is specified as the future location of Solomon's Temple. Such a designation would tie the animal sacrifice to the temple rituals of a later century. It would also put the events of Genesis 22 on the very spot where Jesus would be crucified some twenty centuries hence, in another intense Father/Son engagement.

This is only the second time that Abraham is mentioned in Hebrews, but here, for the first time, the focus is directly on events from the man's life. The language clearly refers to the covenant-making ceremony of Genesis 22 which is built upon the four-fold covenant ceremonies of Genesis 12, 13, 15, and 17. The references to oath-making are designed to affirm surety for the readers of Hebrews. People want to be trusted, so they make promises, but because people cannot always be trusted, they swear oaths in order to confirm their own truthfulness. A double affirmation makes for strong commitments.

So also with God, according to the author of Hebrews. God made an oath to Abraham, but since there is no one higher or more powerful than God, God swears by God's own self. This is the double affirmation that God will do the right thing and follow through on God's promises.

So, the logic flows, our hope is secure. It is double-anchored. And then comes another interesting twist. Where is the anchor of our hope lodged? In the "inner shrine, behind the curtain." This, of course, is a reference to the "holy of holies," the most sacred and secure place in God's house, the tabernacle.

But how did our hope get lodged there? Because God's house is Jesus' home. Jesus is the master (high priest) of the tabernacle.

Now the plot thickens. But how can the tabernacle be the home of Jesus as a high priest when Jesus was not a Levite or Aaronic high priest? Only because Jesus' priestly order (that of Melchizedek) is of a higher level.

In quick succession, the writer of Hebrews moves from the story of Abraham wrestling with his faith, to God's sure promises, sealed in a double oath, to Jesus anchoring these same divine promises for us in the inner room of the tabernacle. The next main topic will be a reminder as to why Jesus, a non-Levite, and thus not eligible for the priesthood, becomes the best high priest ever. It has to do with a mysterious figure who moves in and out of Scripture only three times. His name is Melchizedek.

Where Have We Come So Far?

- God has spoken in times past.
    - This is our source of direction and confidence.
    - We know who we are because of the prophets.
- God has recently spoken a stronger, better, and clearer message through Jesus.
    - So when we, who live by the prophetic message, hear Jesus, we had better listen.
- Jesus is superior to the angels.
    - The great divine message that formed us came through Moses, but the message itself was delivered to him by angels (Deut 33:2; Acts 7:53).
    - Yet Jesus is superior to angels, and therefore delivers a more important prophetic message than that through the great prophet Moses.
- So stick with Jesus, even though you are tempted to turn away from him.
    - There is no higher authority or source of connection with God.
    - And if our lives are to be connected to God, we turn away from Jesus to our own peril.
- God has made the world subject to Jesus.
    - God never did this with the angels, so, again, Jesus is superior to them.
    - But this only happened because Jesus first fully identified with the world.
- Jesus willingly came into the world to fully experience its pain.

- And this is to our benefit for three reasons:
  - ♦ To fully identify with us as sisters and brothers.
  - ♦ To make atonement for our sins (which cause the pain of this world).
  - ♦ To bring us with him fully into the house of God.
- So Jesus is greater than (over) the angels, but Jesus is also greater than (over) Moses.
- Therefore, be careful that you don't disconnect from Jesus (who is God):
  - ♦ Remember how those in our past who disconnected from God came under punishment.
  - ♦ The same can happen to you if you do not stay true and committed to Jesus.
- Let God's people in the earlier redemptive sequence be your instructors:
  - ♦ Like us, they were saved and led to their "(sabbath) rest" in the promised land.
    - ▪ But they failed to stay connected to God by way of the word of the prophet (Moses) and died before reading "rest."
  - ♦ Now God has promised us a coming "rest" (i.e., "heaven" when we die).
    - ▪ But we will receive it only if we remain connected to God by way of the word of the prophet (Jesus) and live faithfully through these trials.
- And, again, the only one who can keep you connected to God is Jesus:
  - ♦ He is our true high priest, who will take us boldly to God's merciful throne through his actions on our behalf on the Day of Atonement. He is fully human, so he completely understands the struggles of our lives and sympathizes deeply, to the point of anguished cries
- In fact, he is as fully committed to fulfilling the mandate and responsibilities of his priestly order as are others.
  - ♦ They in their "Aaronic/Levitical priestly order."
  - ♦ He in his "Melchizedek priestly order."

- I wish you were getting this. You should be mature enough to teach others, but it seems you have lost your passion for Jesus and are trying only to protect yourselves.

  - Though I write strong words, I am confident that you will continue in our faith in Jesus.

  - After all, God has made absolute promises of care toward us that are our hope.

  - And Jesus is the only anchor we have today to ensure that we will receive what was promised.

Message: A Promise Sustains Everything

Psychiatrist Viktor Frankl often wrote about the meaninglessness of his patients' lives. He was able to sympathize with them in a powerful way, since he spent part of World War II in a German concentration camp. He remembered the dark weeks of 1944 vividly. The numbness of the gray days, the cold sameness of every dreary morning.

And then, suddenly, like a bolt of bright colors, came the stunning whisper that the Allies had landed at Normandy. The push was on. The Germans were running. The tide of the war had turned. "By Christmas we'll be released." they told each other.

Promises, Promises

Frankl recalled the changes that took place in the camp: every day the workers went out to their same jobs, but their hearts were lighter and the work seemed a bit easier. Each mealtime they peered into the same cauldron of slop but somehow it seemed less difficult to swallow since every bite was a countdown to freedom. The stress in each barracks community was the same: people fighting for a little privacy; jealousies and dislikes aired in spicy retorts. Yet forgiveness came a little easier these days, for the ups and downs of the present dimmed as the future became a closer and closer reality.

It was interesting, said Frankl. Fewer people died in those months. Even the weakest ones began to cling tenaciously to life. But Christmas 1944 passed, and the Allied troops never came. There were setbacks and defeats, and the bits of news smuggled into the camp made no more promises.

And then, wrote Frankl, the people began to die. No new diseases came into the camp. Rations remained the same. There was no change in working conditions. But the people began to die one after the other, as if some terrible plague had struck.

The Plague of Hopelessness

And, indeed, it had. It was the plague of hopelessness, the epidemic of despair. Studies show that we can live forty to sixty days without food, eight to twelve days without water, and maybe three minutes without oxygen. But without hope, we can't survive even a moment. Without hope, we die. Without hope, there is no reason to wake up in the morning.

Those who first read Hebrews knew that. They had endured testings and social ostracism in the past. Now the persecutions were ramping up again, and it seemed, for many of them, that they needed to step back from their religious commitments in order to recover hope and safety. In the past, Christianity has been perceived by the Roman government as a subset of Judaism, a branch of that old and established religion. More recently, however, officials were distinguishing between Christianity and Judaism, affirming the validity of the latter while becoming more antagonistic with the former. So the key issue at stake in this oppressive world was whether these Jewish Christians should stick with Jesus and be killed, or give up on Jesus (blending back into the safety of the religious community that had first given them identity and morality) and thus live. For some, hope was gone, life had turned cruel, and the future was only a blank wall. They stopped believing in Jesus, choosing instead to find safety in mere morality and the old ceremonial ways. But precisely then, says the writer of Hebrews, there is only one way to carry on. "Remember God's promises," he cries. God may seem distant and silent, but God has spoken loudly and firmly in the past. Remember God's promise to our father Abraham.

This may seem like a call to give up on Jesus and confirm a return to pre-messianic Judaism. But not so. The writer of Hebrews takes this link to the past in a whole new direction. In the actions of our ancient Father Abraham, the bigness and tremendous significance of Jesus is actually confirmed. For Abraham found strength of character and moral fiber not in the rituals which would emerge from his family later as the rites of the Levitical priesthood and the ceremonies found in tabernacle offerings. Instead, even the great patriarch of all Judaism would reach for a mediator outside of the family. He would fall down and worship God at the feet of Melchizedek.

Only a priest like Melchizedek could manage the full religious needs of Abraham. And thus, through Abraham, only a priest after the order of Melchizedek could serve the true condition of those who came from the monumental head of the family. Only someone like Melchizedek could stand against the challenge of hopelessness in a very troubling time.

Testimony

Years ago, Dr. Arthur Gossip preached a sermon titled, "When Life Tumbles In, What Then?" He brought that message to his congregation on the Sunday after his beloved wife suddenly died. In the powerful closing lines he said, with his own testimony of experience,

> Our hearts are very frail, and there are places where the road is very steep and very lonely. Standing in the roaring Jordan, cold with its dreadful chill and very conscious of its terror, of its rushing, I . . . call back to you who one day will have your turn to cross it, "Be of good cheer, my brother, for I feel the bottom and it is sound!"

This is at the heart of Hebrews 6. With a brief nod, the writer points to that great testimony of Abraham. He was a great old man, probably 125 or so, when the scene took place. God had come to him in the past in strange and wonderful ways. When Abraham wore a younger man's clothes, the VOICE had called him on a journey with no fixed destination. But the beckoning was always one of blessing: "I will give you land beyond measure. I will make sure you have a child, old as you are, Your descendants will populate these hills and valleys like rain."

The promises started coming true, to a degree. The land sort of took him in, not as a permanent owner, but at least as a long-term occupant. And then, after some fits and starts, Abraham and Sarai did get a child. By the time the stories of Genesis 22 came about, Abraham's pension plan was still far from clear, even though his life in these later years was peaceful and prosperous. After all, there was Isaac. His boy's name meant "laughter," and that certainly was what he brought Abraham. Life had turned out okay.

A Darker Chapter

But now the VOICE came to him again. Could it really the same VOICE? "Sacrifice your son Isaac on the altar to me," it said. What kind of God was this? Or was it perhaps a demon's mocking mimic? "Kill your boy. Choke out the laughter." God forbid. Please, God, let it not be so.

There would be no sleep that night. Abraham's mind whirled while his old bones crawled in pain. *Get the servants . . . Get the transportation . . . Get provisions . . . Get wood . . . Get the son . . .*

Three days travel they went, with every step harder than the last. Isaac chattered his usual banter, laughter echoing in Abraham's freezing heart. Reluctantly, Abraham finally spied the high place. The mountain of doom. The plateau of death.

Strangely gruff, Abraham ordered the servants to stay. "The boy and I will go it alone from here." Two on a murderous mission. Only one would return. The father-son hike soured even more when Isaac's laughter lilted a deadly, chilly question: "Where's the lamb, father?"

Mockery

What could Abraham say? Should he tell Isaac the truth: "Son, the God who said he loved me enough to give you to your mother and me now says he wants you back, and I've got to do the dirty work"? How does one lie with a straight face, when heaven is ripped apart by hell? Is it a spiteful retort, spat out in unholy jest, that finally clears his throat, "My son, God will provide"?

So here they were, clearing, building, and preparing. And then the end crept with horror into Isaac's eyes. His father bound him. His father thrust him on the wood. His father stood over him with a glinting knife. And the laughter dies . . .

But not yet. In a miraculous moment, time stopped and grace pointed to another sacrifice. The son is free and faith is affirmed. And Abraham called the place Moriah.

Moriah is one of those delightfully ambiguous names that can mean several things at once. It probably has to do with seeing at this point, or knowing. Where God sees, God will be seen. Something like that.

A Strange Vision

But what is it that God sees on a mountain called Moriah? For one thing, God sees a man. A weak man. A stumbler on the earth. A business man who got ahead in life. A husband who cheated on his wife. A father who knew the joy of bringing new life into being.

Even more than that God sees a man who was willing to put it all on the line. Here was someone who counted his relationship with the God of the VOICE to be the one thing that mattered, the one thing that put everything else together, the one thing that could raise even heaven out of this stench of hell.

Probably the most important thing about the moment of seeing is not only that God sees Abraham there on Mount Moriah. In some mysterious way, God is also seen by Abraham.

A geography lesson tells the rest of the story. On this same barren spot of ground, centuries later, David would urge Solomon to build the temple of God. It would stand as a doorway between earth and eternity. And then, in the mysterious design of the ages, one day another Father would walk these slopes with another Son. That Son, too, would raise his voice to his Father, and the Father for a time would be silent. The wood of the offering would be prepared, and the Son would be lifted as a sacrifice. On what the world would later call "Good Friday" this other Father would shed tears of pain as his child died—this time with no escape.

Somehow history would repeat itself and more with a vengeance. Yet this Lamb would also be chosen by God for the altar. And laughter would be silenced for three days while all the world looked on in wonder.

The Language of Faith

Abraham found his faith that day on Mount Moriah, but it cost God his Son on the same spot. The mystery of life is found now not in a faith that pretends laughter, but in a promise that God knows pain. Because God has walked a mile in Abraham's shoes and ours, God will never leave us. God will never forsake us. This is the power of the promise that the writer of Hebrews brings to his readers. Keep trusting God, even in these difficult times.

The poet Gordon Jensen put it powerfully:

> Often you wondered why tears came into your eyes
> And burdens seem to be much more than you can stand.
> But God is standing near; he sees your falling tears.
> Tears are a language God understands!
>> God sees the tears of a broken-hearted soul.
>> He sees your tears, and hears them when they fall.
>> God weeps along with man, and takes him by the hand.
>> Tears are a language God understands!

Chapter 11

Melchizedek

Text: Hebrews 7:1–28

This "King Melchizedek of Salem, priest of the Most High God, met Abraham as he was returning from defeating the kings and blessed him"; and to him Abraham apportioned "one-tenth of everything."

His name, in the first place, means "king of righteousness"; next he is also king of Salem, that is, "king of peace." Without father, without mother, without genealogy, having neither beginning of days nor end of life, but resembling the Son of God, he remains a priest forever.

See how great he is! Even Abraham the patriarch gave him a tenth of the spoils. And those descendants of Levi who receive the priestly office have a commandment in the law to collect tithes from the people, that is, from their kindred, though these also are descended from Abraham. But this man, who does not belong to their ancestry, collected tithes from Abraham and blessed him who had received the promises. It is beyond dispute that the inferior is blessed by the superior. In the one case, tithes are received by those who are mortal; in the other, by one of whom it is testified that he lives. One might even say that Levi himself, who receives tithes, paid tithes through Abraham, for he was still in the loins of his ancestor when Melchizedek met him.

Now if perfection had been attainable through the levitical priesthood—for the people received the law under this priesthood—what further need would there have been to speak of another priest arising according to the order of Melchizedek, rather than one according to the order of Aaron? For when there is a change in the priesthood, there is necessarily a change in the law as well. Now the one of whom these things are spoken belonged to another tribe, from which no one has ever served at the altar. For it is evident that our Lord was descended from Judah, and in connection with that tribe Moses said nothing about priests.

It is even more obvious when another priest arises, resembling Melchizedek, one who has become a priest, not through a legal requirement concerning physical descent, but through the power of an indestructible life. For it is attested of him,

"You are a priest forever,
according to the order of Melchizedek."

There is, on the one hand, the abrogation of an earlier commandment because it was weak and ineffectual (for the law made nothing perfect); there is, on the other hand, the introduction of a better hope, through which we approach God.

This was confirmed with an oath; for others who became priests took their office without an oath, but this one became a priest with an oath, because of the one who said to him,

"The Lord has sworn
and will not change his mind,
'You are a priest forever.'"

Accordingly Jesus has also become the guarantee of a better covenant.

Furthermore, the former priests were many in number, because they were prevented by death from continuing in office; but he holds his priesthood permanently, because he continues forever. Consequently he is able for all time to save those who approach God through him, since he always lives to make intercession for them.

For it was fitting that we should have such a high priest, holy, blameless, undefiled, separated from sinners, and exalted above the heavens. Unlike the other high priests, he has no need to offer sacrifices day after day, first for his own sins, and then for those of the people; this he did once for all when he offered himself. For the law appoints as high priests those who are subject to weakness, but the word of the oath, which came later than the law, appoints a Son who has been made perfect forever.

Backstory: Superhero

MELCHIZEDEK IS A SHADOWY figure who only emerges three times in the Bible. First, there is a brief mention of Abram's encounter with Melchizedek in Genesis 14:18–20. Abram meets the "king of Salem" and "priest of God Most High" after rescuing Lot from neighboring warlords who had raided their compound, stolen cattle and goods, and made off with some in the camp who were to become slaves. Abram routed his enemies and was on his way back to their residence when Salem loomed as a welcome rest stop. The king of the city provided the travelers some much appreciated hospitality. Evidently, during these conversations, Abram discovered that King Melchizedek was also a devout spiritual mediator. So, Abram asked Melchizedek to officiate at a sacrifice of thanksgiving for the rescue and deliverance that had been provided. Because Abram already had a unique relationship with God, and yet also received a divine blessing from Melchizedek, he then honored this king and priest by giving a tenth of his goods. Through this set of rituals, Melchizedek gained distinction as standing above Abraham (and therefore also all of his descendants) in spiritual authority.

In summary, we are told five things about Melchizedek in Genesis 14:18–20:

- He was king of Salem (the town name means "peace," and it was probably the early stage development of what would eventually become Jerusalem).
- He was "priest of God Most High."
- He brought a light meal to restore the strength of Abram and his men.
- He blessed Abram.
- Abram tithed the spoils of battle to Melchizedek (gave him one-tenth of the captured booty).

A New Class of Leadership

Second, this heightened sense of Melchizedek's mediatorial role is next played out in Psalm 110. Attributed to David, Psalm 110 might be David's response to the promise made by God in 2 Samuel 7: that one of David's descendants will always be king over God's people. David knew that he and his family, from the tribe of Judah, came to a unique place of leadership in Israel through a side door. The designated tribe for national guidance, from Israel's national beginnings in Exodus, was Levi, the tribe of Moses and Aaron. Moses' unique role could not be duplicated, but its lingering impact was institutionalized through divine appointment of the Levites as the perpetual keepers of the tabernacle and mediators of the Sinai covenant. Because of God's unique selection and commissioning of both David and his family to permanent leadership within the nation, David looked for another reference point to confirm this divine endorsement. He found it in Melchizedek. Melchizedek appeared also to be divinely commissioned outside of the Mosaic/Aaronic family appointments. So when David experienced his unique ordination to Israel's leadership role, he reached to the brief, obscure reference about another outsider who blessed the people of God in a different age. In a moment of inspired genius, he dubs the whole enterprise the "Order of Melchizedek."

Third, the writer of Hebrews conflates these two minimal references to Melchizedek and then develops a deeper, more profound outcome. The writer selects tiny bits of information from the Genesis story and the reflections of David in Psalm 110, and also the lack of other testimony about Melchizedek, making both useful in connecting the ancient king and priest to the recently ascended Messiah.

In a number of ways, the writer of Hebrews enhances the significance of the Genesis 14 story. For one thing, he emphasizes the meaning of Melchizedek's personal name and role as well as his city's name. These, he makes clear, are names that fit well with Jesus also. The writer of Hebrews then goes on to extrapolate what would otherwise appear to be unwarranted conclusions from missing information. Since Melchizedek's parents and family are not mentioned in Genesis 14, the writer of Hebrews draws an analogy between Melchizedek and Jesus, presuming that both are eternal, without beginning or end.

His conclusion is: "See how great he (Melchizedek) was," and that is exactly where the allegorical link to Jesus grows deeper. One of the key indications of Melchizedek's greatness is that the greatest figure in Israelite history, founding father Abraham, used the priestly services of Melchizedek to mediate between himself and God. For this reason, according to the writer of Hebrews, Melchizedek must be greater than Abraham.

A Genetic Participation

But wait. There's more. Since the complete roster of Abraham's descendants are theoretically resident in the biological systems of Abraham (after all, every one of the Israelites will be descended from him), the nation of Israel itself, through Abraham's actions, actually bowed before Melchizedek and used him as its mediatorial priest. This included, by implication, even Moses and all of the Levites. Thus, the very Levitical priesthood is subservient to the priestly ministration of ancient King Melchizedek. Because of what father Abraham did, all of the Levitical priests, including those who served as high priest throughout the generations since, have paid tithes to Melchizedek and have acknowledged that he is their superior, their priest, their intercessor.

In point summary, the argument looks like this:

- The "greater" blesses the "lesser" (Melchizedek blessed Abram, and so also the Levites within him).
- The "lesser" tithes to and through the "greater" (Abram, and thus also the Levites within him, tithe to Melchizedek).

So the Levitical priests, including the great high priest, needed an outside priest to mediate between them and God. And now, like Melchizedek, Jesus stands outside the ordinary priestly system of Israel and therefore can function in a unique way as a mediator. The outcome is clear: Jesus is God's chosen method for bringing full spiritual cleansing to God's people. While the mediation of the priests, including the appointed high priest, has been a tremendously helpful and central element of biblical religion, it cannot meet the ultimate demands of permanent cleansing and spiritual renewal. Those who stick with the Levitical priesthood life in a state of perpetual temporariness and sacrificial incompleteness. Only Jesus, like Melchizedek of Old, can initiate a permanently secure mediation with God. Only Jesus can bring us home to the very throne of God.

Where Have We Come So Far?

- God has spoken in times past.
  - This is our source of direction and confidence.
  - We know who we are because of the prophets.
- God has recently spoken a stronger, better, and clearer message through Jesus.
  - So when we, who live by the prophetic message, hear Jesus, we had better listen.
- Jesus is superior to the angels.

- ◆ The great divine message that formed us came through Moses, but the message itself was delivered to him by angels (Deut 33:2; Acts 7:53).

- ◆ Yet Jesus is superior to angels, and therefore delivers a more important prophetic message than that through the great prophet Moses.

- So stick with Jesus, even though you are tempted to turn away from him.

  - ◆ There is no higher authority or source of connection with God.

  - ◆ And if our lives are to be connected to God, we turn away from Jesus to our own peril.

- God has made the world subject to Jesus.

  - ◆ God never did this with the angels, so, again, Jesus is superior to them.

  - ◆ But this only happened because Jesus first fully identified with the world.

- Jesus willingly came into the world to fully experience its pain.

- And this is to our benefit for three reasons:

  - ◆ To fully identify with us as sisters and brothers.

  - ◆ To make atonement for our sins (which cause the pain of this world).

  - ◆ To bring us with him fully into the house of God.

- So Jesus is greater than (over) the angels, but Jesus is also greater than (over) Moses.

- Therefore, be careful that you don't disconnect from Jesus (who is God):

  - ◆ Remember how those in our past who disconnected from God came under punishment.

  - ◆ The same can happen to you if you do not stay true and committed to Jesus.

- Let God's people in the earlier redemptive sequence be your instructors:

  - ◆ Like us, they were saved and led to their "(sabbath) rest" in the promised land.

- But they failed to stay connected to God by way of the word of the prophet (Moses) and died before reading "rest."

  ◆ Now God has promised us a coming "rest" (i.e., "heaven" when we die).

    - But we will receive it only if we remain connected to God by way of the word of the prophet (Jesus) and live faithfully through these trials.

- And, again, the only one who can keep you connected to God is Jesus:

  ◆ He is our true high priest, who will take us boldly to God's merciful throne through his actions on our behalf on the Day of Atonement. He is fully human, so he completely understands the struggles of our lives and sympathizes deeply, to the point of anguished cries.

- In fact, he is as fully committed to fulfilling the mandate and responsibilities of his priestly order as are others.

  ◆ They in their "Aaronic/Levitical priestly order."

  ◆ He in his "Melchizedek priestly order."

- I wish you were getting this. You should be mature enough to teach others, but it seems you have lost your passion for Jesus and are trying only to protect yourselves.

  ◆ Though I write strong words, I am confident that you will continue in our faith in Jesus.

  ◆ After all, God has made absolute promises of care toward us that are our hope.

  ◆ And Jesus is the only anchor we have today to ensure that we will receive what was promise.

- After all, Jesus is a priest after the order of Melchizedek.

  ◆ The Levitical order priests could not fully satisfy needs, since its sacrifices needed repeating.

  ◆ That is why someone from Melchizedek's order was needed.

    - Someone who was a descendant of David (of the tribe of Judah), perfect and never dying.

Message: Larger than Life

The name "Melchizedek" has always intrigued me. I wonder what a "Melchizedek" would look like—rather imposing, I'm sure. The name rolls around for a while before it comes out. You begin with soft sounds and warm touches, and then you sort of sneeze the rest of it out. In my mind, Melchizedek would have to be rather tall; a short Melchizedek just wouldn't be Melchizedek. Maybe "Melchy" or "Chizy," but not the whole thing.

A Melchizedek would have to be fairly old, too. A handle like that could crush a baby. Can you imagine youngsters playing ball and the coach calling for Melchizedek to get in the game? He'd be laughed off the field.

No, there's something old and tall and wise and authoritative about a person who fits the name Melchizedek.

Uncommon

You can't have too many people in your community by the name of Melchizedek either. It loses its punch if you see it on every thirty-seventh mailbox. Melchizedeks are few and far between. They have to be or they can't be Melchizedeks. Not that you don't want one around; a good Melchizedek in the family line sort of spruces it up. You can point to that name back in the pages of the family Bible and it gives importance to your bloodline: "See. I come from a good family."

But it's not one of those names that you want to pass down from generation to generation, either. You can understand it when someone wants to call a baby Franklin, Jr. or Theodore Geisbert IV. But you have to handle a name like Melchizedek with care. One Melchizedek is enough; you wouldn't want to try to clone him or force someone else to walk in his shoes.

No Wimp

There's something royal in the name, of course. A Melchizedek deserves to rule. Maybe that's not putting it strongly enough: a Melchizedek *needs* to rule. Authority goes with the name. You can't be a Melchizedek and be a wimp at the same time. In fact, you might find a Melchizedek in kingly legends, like the quest for the Holy Grail. A Melchizedek shouldn't just sit there on his throne and grow benignly old; he should have a mission, a purpose, a cause to champion, a crusade to march in. If a Melchizedek sits around too long, you start calling him "the old man" or "the head honcho," or something demeaning like that. But when you see him on his steed, something in you stirs magnificently. His face is slightly weather-beaten and his hair is brushed by the wind. You know he's a man of purpose. You know there's depth to him.

Where Legends Live

So what's this all about? Am I dancing around in ignorance, trying to make something out of a name that's only mentioned twice in the Old Testament and in a single New Testament passage? Is this an exercise in theological silliness?

Not really. Melchizedek is a strange figure, scattered lightly across the Scriptures. Of himself, he doesn't really amount to much, I suppose. But his very insignificance, coupled with the single act of faith to which he's tied in the life of Abraham, has given him the stature of prince among legends.

And that's really the point of the writer of Hebrews. With whom can you compare a divinely appointed mediator who stands taller than the priests of ancient Israel and more competent even than a king like the great David? Certainly David did not fit the mold of the other monarchs around him. In fact, when David resembled them most, he was least like his truest self. David was the stuff that becomes a legend. And before David became one himself, you could only talk about him and his sons in the hushed terms of larger-than-life figures. Like Melchizedek.

The Bible doesn't allow us to read too much theology into Melchizedek. But when it comes to thinking about David, our thoughts naturally turn to those few who stand slightly above the natural order of things. Melchizedek comes to mind.

That is probably why David's later, greater Son ran into the same family history, generations further along. Someone probably bumped into him one day and started thinking, "That man's got a Melchizedek in the family tree, I'm sure." The rest, as the writer of Hebrews shows, is history. Good history. The true history of salvation.

Chapter 12

Splitting the *Day of the Lord*

Text: Hebrews 8:1–13

Now the main point in what we are saying is this: we have such a high priest, one who is seated at the right hand of the throne of the Majesty in the heavens, a minister in the sanctuary and the true tent that the Lord, and not any mortal, has set up. For every high priest is appointed to offer gifts and sacrifices; hence it is necessary for this priest also to have something to offer. Now if he were on earth, he would not be a priest at all, since there are priests who offer gifts according to the law. They offer worship in a sanctuary that is a sketch and shadow of the heavenly one; for Moses, when he was about to erect the tent, was warned, "See that you make everything according to the pattern that was shown you on the mountain." But Jesus has now obtained a more excellent ministry, and to that degree he is the mediator of a better covenant, which has been enacted through better promises. For if that first covenant had been faultless, there would have been no need to look for a second one.

God finds fault with them when he says:

"The days are surely coming, says the Lord,
when I will establish a new covenant with the house of Israel
and with the house of Judah;
not like the covenant that I made with their ancestors,
on the day when I took them by the hand to lead them out of the land
of Egypt;

for they did not continue in my covenant,

and so I had no concern for them, says the Lord.

This is the covenant that I will make with the house of Israel

after those days, says the Lord:

I will put my laws in their minds,

and write them on their hearts,

and I will be their God,

and they shall be my people.

And they shall not teach one another

or say to each other, 'Know the Lord,'

for they shall all know me,

from the least of them to the greatest.

For I will be merciful toward their iniquities,

and I will remember their sins no more."

In speaking of "a new covenant," he has made the first one obsolete. And what is obsolete and growing old will soon disappear.

Backstory: A Two-Phased Divine Mission

JEREMIAH LIVED ALMOST A century after Isaiah. By his time, Assyria had long ago destroyed Judah's northern brother neighbor Israel. Judah was itself only a tiny community now, limping along with diminishing resources, and constantly tossed around by the bigger nations of its world.

But things were changing rapidly on the international scene. Assyria was being beaten down, beginning in 612 BC, by its eastern bully province, the rising power of Babylon. After wrestling the capital city of Nineveh to the ground, and snapping the backbone of Assyrian forces at Carchemish, Babylon immediately took over Palestine, the newer name for the old region of Canaan.

Judah was experiencing a rapid turnover of kings, many of whom were puppets of Babylon. For decades already, the country had been paying yearly tribute or security bribes to Babylon. Since 606 BC, Judah had been forced to turn over some of its promising young men for propaganda retraining exile in the capital of the superpower, in anticipation that they would return to rule the nation as regents of Babylon.

For reasons like these, Egypt began to loom large in many minds as the only possible ally strong enough to withstand Babylon's domination of the region. Even though Israel's identity had been forged through a divine exit strategy from oppressive Egyptian mastery several centuries before, now a good number of voices were publicly suggesting that the remaining citizens of Jerusalem get out of town before a final Babylonian occupation, and find refuge in the safer haven of Egypt.

A Moral Man in an Immoral Society

Into these times and circumstances Jeremiah was born. From his earliest thoughts, he was aware of Yahweh's special call on his life. This knowledge only made his prophetic ministry more gloomy, for it gave him no out in a game where the deck was stacked against him. So he brooded through his life, deeply introspective. He fulfilled his role as gadfly to most of the kings who reigned during his adult years, even though it took eminent courage to do so. Although he lived an exemplary personal lifestyle, political officials constantly took offense at his theologically charged political commentaries, and regularly arrested him, treating him very badly. Jeremiah was passionately moral, never allowing compromise as a suitable temporary alternative in the shady waters of international relations, or amid the roiling quicksand of fading religious devotion. He remained pastorally sensitive, especially to the poor and oppressed in Jerusalem, weeping in anguish as families boiled sandals and old leather to find a few nutrients during Babylonian sieges, and especially when he saw mothers willing to cannibalize their dying babies in order to keep their other children alive. Above all, Jeremiah found the grace to be unshakably hopeful. He truly believed, to the very close of his life, that though Babylonian forces would raze Jerusalem and the temple, Yahweh would keep covenant promises, and one day soon restore the fortunes of this wayward partner in the divine missional enterprise.

Jeremiah's name and the often haranguing tone of his prophecies came into the English language as a unique word in the late eighteenth century. A "jeremiad" is a diatribe, rant, or tirade against sin, social ills, or some undesired social group. While the term unfortunately stereotypes the good prophet's larger identity and message, it is hard to deny that this portion of the Bible is one of the most caustic and condemning. Jeremiah's times were politically, socially, economically, and religiously challenging, and the general character of life in Jerusalem was in great disharmony with the covenant lifestyle espoused in the Torah.

Toward the end of his ministry, Jeremiah was aided by his good friend Baruch, whose very name meant "blessing." It was Baruch who made sure Jeremiah got at least a little food, even when the prophet was thrown to the slimy bottom of a dry cistern as punishment for his opposition to the current government and its practices. And Baruch salvaged Jeremiah's writings when kings were systematically burning them as treasonous. Baruch patiently wrote and rewrote the messages of Yahweh that were delivered through the mouth of Jeremiah.

Prophetic Proclamations

Jeremiah's prophecies are not collected in a chronological order. When tracked against the reigns and events of various kings, the following challenges, indictments and promises can be chronicled:

- King Josiah (640–609): The indictments of chapters 3–6 and the support for reforms as spelled out on chapters 30–31.

- King Johoahaz (609–608): The brief lament found in chapter 20:10–12.

- King Jehoiakim (608–597): In 607–606 the Babylonians made their first official incursion into Jerusalem, confirming Jehoiakim as king only if he would declare his small country a vassal territory of Babylon. The invaders were allowed to retrain some of the maturing sons among the noble families (including Daniel and his friends) in Babylon, so that they could return one day as proper Babylonian regents. Jeremiah gave his famous "Potter's House" sermon at this time and later wrote about the battle of wills taking place that would ultimately result in Judah's captivity by Babylon for seventy years.

- King Jehoiakin (597): After Jehoiakim grew reckless with false bravado and thought he could declare independence from Babylon, Nebuchadnezzar sent his troops again and replaced him with his son Jehoiakin. The eighteen-year-old lasted less than a year before the Babylonians took him away to exile (along with Ezekiel and others) and installed his uncle Zedekiah as the final ruler of Judah. Jeremiah's messages were warnings for the people to prepare themselves for deportation, the only outcome they could expect after so many years of flaunting Yahweh's ways.

- King Zedekiah (597–586): The last king of Judah seems to have been spineless, placating all in sight, and making secret deals with everyone. In the end, he tried secretly to flee Jerusalem in order to save his own skin. During these dark times Jeremiah wrote a letter to the people of Judah who had already been deported to Babylon, urging them to settle in. Although Yahweh would surely restore the nation in the future, said Jeremiah, the current generation had to suffer punishment for its sinfulness. At the same time, during the final siege of Jerusalem, when the entire economy and real estate market had collapsed, Jeremiah bought a field deemed worthless as a token of good faith that Yahweh would call the people back from exile to prosperity. But when Zedekiah got overly confident about his valued position as Babylon's local appointee, Jeremiah warned him that the judgment of Yahweh was irreversible and days of destruction were just around the corner.

- Governor Gedaliah (586): The Babylonians were willing to take Jeremiah to join the other exiles in deportation, or to leave him with the small and impoverished remnant left to scrounge in the rubble of Jerusalem. Jeremiah chose the latter, soon witnessing the assassination of Governor Gedaliah, who was left in charge, and the complete collapse of whatever social organization might have been left.

- Remnant Leader Johanan (586–585): Another person loosely connected with the royal family took over after Gedaliah's assassination and then feared Babylonian reprisals because of the anarchy in Jerusalem. Johanan decided to take the remaining people down to Egypt to find safety. Jeremiah refused to go along, reminding the remnant that Judah was their homeland and that Yahweh had promised peace following the deportation of the rest to Babylon. Johanan and his thugs played bully politics, however, and bound Jeremiah, taking him along with them to Egypt against his will.

The theme of the Sinai covenant is very prominent in Jeremiah's prophecies. Most striking is his recognition that it governs both Israel's success and its demise, and that one day soon Yahweh will have to find a way to renew that covenant in a manner which will keep the restored nation more faithful to its identity and true to its mission. This is why the writer of Hebrews quotes Jeremiah 31:31–34 at length; from his perspective, the time of the renewed covenant has arrived. Jesus is the high priest of this new expression of God's ages-old redemptive plan.

Splitting the "Day of the Lord"

The prophets began to emerge on Israel's scene shortly after its settlement in Canaan. At first they functioned as lingering echoes of Moses' booming voice, now fading in the historic distance. Although they continued in this role, seeking ways to translate the theology and social lifestyle of the Sinai covenant into new and changing circumstances for Israel, the prophets also became a third national leadership team, standing somewhere between the cultic role of the priests and the political venue of the kings. There is little evidence that they considered themselves as providing new revelations for Israel. Rather, they were interpreters of the Sinai covenant, subservient to Moses and the original suzerain-vassal documents. Their authority, while rooted in contemporary visions, was derived from the ancient standards, and never ran ahead of Exodu, Leviticus, or Deuteronomy.

What eventually coalesced from their common declarations, however, was the rallying point of the "Day of the Lord." Increasingly the prophets heard Yahweh declaiming that things were getting so bad, both within Israel and among the nations of her world, that only a direct divine intrusion could set things right again. This impending divine visitation became known as the great and terrible "Day of the Lord."

While God's visible actions in this imminent momentous occasion would probably span a lengthy period of time, the outcomes would be so decisive that it could be termed a single event. Three major things would happen when Yahweh arrived on that "day":

- There would be a catastrophic judgment meted upon all the nations of earth, including Israel/Judah. It would fall as a divine judicial assessment that none were living appropriately to the lifestyle of the Sinai covenant, or changing their behaviors toward that direction because of the missional influence of God's people.

- In spite of the conflagration, a remnant of Israel would be spared. This small group would be evidence that not all of the people had forgotten their God and, similarly, that God would never forget the divinely created community.

- After the cleansing of judgment and the restoration of the remnant, a new and vibrant messianic age would be ushered in. This would be a time in which all the implications of the Sinai covenant would be lived out with fresh and natural devotion by the renewed people of Yahweh. Furthermore, throughout the world, every nation would actively seek to conform its moral behaviors to that same pattern of life. The creation itself would be reinvigorated with its Edenic glories, and the Creator and all creatures would find themselves enjoying the harmony and unlimited bounty intended by God at the beginning of time.

The "Day of the Lord," thus, was to be no less than re-creation itself. It might take a direct intervention of God into human history to bring about, but when it happened, everything would be set right. This is the message of

Jeremiah in chapter 31:31–34 that the author of Hebrews rides into the story of Jesus.

The Creator remains on a mission to recover the lost citizens of the kingdom of heaven, as well as renew the painfully twisted elements of nature. In order to make this restoration happen, the family of Abraham was enlisted as a witnessing partner. Unfortunately, the nation of Israel proved to be unequal to the task, and the divine redemptive enterprise limped toward an inglorious demise, even while the prophets were seeing and stating grander visions of the coming age. In the end, a muted but stirring prophetic voice charmed the hearts of all who waited in longing for the imminent "Day of the Lord."

What everyone in the covenant community anticipated actually was about to happen, but in a way that none had expected. Yahweh finally did show up, but appeared as a weak child rather than in the guise of a mighty warrior. Moreover, the "Day of the Lord" itself was split in two so that the beginnings of the messianic age blessings arrived in whispers, long before the warning trumpets of judgment would be sounded.

Where Have We Come So Far?

- God has spoken in times past.

    - This is our source of direction and confidence.

    - We know who we are because of the prophets.

- God has recently spoken a stronger, better, and clearer message through Jesus.

    - So when we, who live by the prophetic message, hear Jesus, we had better listen.

- Jesus is superior to the angels.

    - The great divine message that formed us came through Moses, but the message itself was delivered to him by angels (Deut 33:2; Acts 7:53).

    - Yet Jesus is superior to angels, and therefore delivers a more important prophetic message than that through the great prophet Moses.

- So stick with Jesus, even though you are tempted to turn away from him.

    - There is no higher authority or source of connection with God.

- ◆ And if our lives are to be connected to God, we turn away from Jesus to our own peril.
- God has made the world subject to Jesus.
  - ◆ God never did this with the angels, so, again, Jesus is superior to them.
  - ◆ But this only happened because Jesus first fully identified with the world.
- Jesus willingly came into the world to fully experience its pain.
- And this is to our benefit for three reasons:
  - ◆ To fully identify with us as sisters and brothers.
  - ◆ To make atonement for our sins (which cause the pain of this world).
  - ◆ To bring us with him fully into the house of God.
- So Jesus is greater than (over) the angels, but Jesus is also greater than (over) Moses.
- Therefore, be careful that you don't disconnect from Jesus (who is God):
  - ◆ Remember how those in our past who disconnected from God came under punishment.
  - ◆ The same can happen to you if you do not stay true and committed to Jesus.
- Let God's people in the earlier redemptive sequence be your instructors:
  - ◆ Like us, they were saved and led to their "(sabbath) rest" in the promised land.
    - ▪ But they failed to stay connected to God by way of the word of the prophet (Moses) and died before reading "rest."
  - ◆ Now God has promised us a coming "rest" (i.e., "heaven" when we die).
    - ▪ But we will receive it only if we remain connected to God by way of the word of the prophet (Jesus) and live faithfully through these trials.
- And, again, the only one who can keep you connected to God is Jesus:

- He is our true high priest, who will take us boldly to God's merciful throne through his actions on our behalf on the Day of Atonement. He is fully human, so he completely understands the struggles of our lives and sympathizes deeply, to the point of anguished cries

- In fact, he is as fully committed to fulfilling the mandate and responsibilities of his priestly order as are others.
  - They in their "Aaronic/Levitical priestly order."
  - He in his "Melchizedek priestly order."

- I wish you were getting this. You should be mature enough to teach others, but it seems you have lost your passion for Jesus and are trying only to protect yourselves.
  - Though I write strong words, I am confident that you will continue in our faith in Jesus.
  - After all, God has made absolute promises of care toward us that are our hope.
  - And Jesus is the only anchor we have today to ensure that we will receive what was promise.

- After all, Jesus is a priest after the order of Melchizedek.
  - The Levitical order priests could not fully satisfy needs, since its sacrifices needed repeating.
  - That is why someone from Melchizedek's order was needed.
    - Someone who was a descendant of David (of the tribe of Judah), perfect and never dying.

- This brings us back to the main thing we have been saying: Jesus is the best high priest ever.
  - He is God (seated at the right hand of the majesty in heaven).
  - He is owner of the house of God.
  - He is high priest of the house of God.
    - The true house of God, with dimensions given by God on the mountain.
    - The visible house of God, here below (under the care of the Levitical priests), important as it is, is only a shadow of the real thing.
  - He is faultless.

- He is the mediator of the new covenant (remember Jer 31:31–34?).

- This is very important: God found fault with the old covenant.

  - God is causing the old covenant age to come to an end.

  - Jesus is the only source of hope in the new covenant age.

Message: Plan B (Which Is Really Plan A)

There is something wonderfully paradoxical about the Christian church. Its origin as a unique social phenomenon clearly dates from the Pentecost events described in Acts 2. Yet, at the same time, Jesus' disciples, who were at the center of the church from its very beginning, would say that this "new" community of faith was simply part of a centuries-old, already existing people of God, stretching back all the way to Abraham and his family. In God's initial encounter with Abram, recorded in Genesis 12, it is clear that the relationship between God and Abram was missional in character. The Creator wished to "bless" all nations of the earth, but would enact that blessing through Abram and his descendants. This became the source of Israel's unique identity: bound to Yahweh through the Sinai covenant and positioned on the great highway between the nations in the territory known as Canaan. For the mission to work, people would have to flow to and through this piece of property, and Israel would have to be the visible face of God and God's intentions.

Yet after thirteen centuries of tenuous existence in the "promised land," the larger world of human spread and discover was expanding and "Canaan" could no longer be considered the center of all civilizations. Along with that, the witness of Israel to the nations had become muted through historical circumstances and internal challenges. So the Creator became a creature in the person of Jesus. He taught and expressed the divine mission, and then initiated the "new" Christian church from among the "old" people of Israel. What had once been geographically based now became a mobile, international community of witness within every culture. The missional engagement which began centuries earlier through Abram's little family as a centripetal force, pulling all nations into Israel's witnessing orbit, was now flung out as a centrifugal spray, invading and influencing every territory on earth.

Steps in a Big Plan

But how are these two developments connected? The whole message of the author of Hebrews is based, as becomes apparent in chapter 8, on the continuing relationship between the old and the new. This association is rooted in a number of theological axioms:

- First, it is built upon the confession that there is a God who created this world, and uniquely fashioned the human race with attributes that reflected its Maker.

- Second, through human willfulness, the world lost its pristine vitality and is now caught up in a civil war against its Creator.

- Third, intruding directly into human affairs for the sake of reclaiming and restoring the world, the Creator began a mission of redemption and renewal through the family of Abraham, the nation of Israel.

- Fourth, Israel's identity as a missional community was shaped by the suzerain-vassal covenant established at Mount Sinai.

- Fifth, in order to be most effective in its witness to other nations, Israel was positioned at the crossroads of global societies, and thus received, as its "promised land," the territory known as Canaan.

- Sixth, the effectiveness of this divine missional strategy through Israel was most evident in the eleventh century BC, during the reigns of David and Solomon, when the kingdom grew mightily in size and influence among the peoples of the ancient near east and beyond.

- Seventh, this missional witness eroded away, almost to oblivion, through a combination of internal failures and external political threats, until most of the nation of Israel was wiped out by the Assyrians and only a remnant of the tribe of Judah (along with religious leaders from among the Levites and a portion of the small tribe of Benjamin) retained its unique identity as the people of Yahweh.

- Eighth, because of the seeming inadequacy of this initial method of witness, as the human race expanded rapidly to places beyond ready contact with Israel in Canaan, the Creator revised the divine missional strategy and interrupted human history in a very visible manner, once again, through the person of Jesus.

- Ninth, Jesus embodied the divine essence, taught the divine will, and went through death and resurrection to establish a new understanding of eschatological hope, which he then passed along to his followers as the message to be communicated to the nations.

- Tenth, Jesus' teachings about this arriving messianic age were rooted in what the prophets of Israel had called the "Day of the Lord": a time when divine judgment for sins would fall on all nations (including Israel); a time when a remnant from Israel would be spared to become the restored seed community of a new global divine initiative; and a time when the world would be transformed as God had intended for it to be, so that people could again live out their intended purposes and destinies.

- Eleventh, instead of applying all aspects of this "Day of the Lord" in a single cataclysmic event, Jesus split it in two, bringing the beginnings of eternal blessings while withholding the full impact of divine judgment for a time.

- Twelfth, the Christian church became God's new agent for global missional recovery and restoration for the human race, superseding the territorially-bound witness of Israel, with a portable and expanding testimony influencing all nations and cultures.

- Thirteenth, since the "Day of the Lord" has begun but is not yet finished, Jesus will return again to bring its culmination.

- Fourteenth, the church of Jesus exists in this time between Jesus' comings as the great divine missional witness.

Each of these themes is implied or explicit in the first eight chapters of Hebrews. God, sin, and the divine mission are all part of the fabric of the narrative, while Israel's role in the divine mission, along with the changing strategies, is declared openly. Jesus is at the center of all these things, bringing a unique redemptive intrusion into the current story of the human race. It is, as the writer of Hebrews notes, a brand new era.

In the "former age," God spoke through prophets, ministering divine care through angels and Moses, using a temporary house called the tabernacle, with its Levitical priesthood, whose officiants were imperfect and offered sacrifices that had to be repeated. In contrast, now that this "new age" has come, God speaks through the Son, ministering divine care through Jesus (who is better than the angels and Moses), as he shapes the true house of God with its Melchizedek priesthood, whose officiant is perfect and has offered a single sacrifice that does not need to be repeated. The divine mission remains the same, but the strategy by which God reaches to all people has shifted. The "old" is good; the "new" is better.

A Divine Decision

Using the idea of newness found in Jeremiah's prophecy, the writer of Hebrews makes a very striking point. It is not we but God who finds fault with the earlier expression of the covenant. Because of this, God is causing the old covenant age to come to an end. And, if that is the case, then Jesus is the only source of hope in this new covenant world.

Once again we are learning something about the mindset of those to whom this document is being written. They are deeply religious. They are strongly attached to the forms of Israel's religious expressions. They understand that God is working out a centuries-long mission of recovery toward fallen humanity. They know how powerful this was articulated through Israel's covenant ceremonies.

But what they are not sure of is whether Jesus fits into this picture. Maybe the old forms are sufficient. Maybe the old ways are all we need.

No, says the author of Hebrews. The times are changing, by divine initiative. And God has spoken clearly: Jesus is the only mediator for our age. The new covenant times have arrived.

They do not negate the faith or practices of the old covenant manifestations, but Jesus has superseded these things so that, in this new covenant age, the old forms no longer work. Do not stick with the old when the new has replaced it. Jesus is the only way of salvation today. Trust him. Trust in him.

Chapter 13

Atonement Day Revisited

Text: Hebrews 9:1–28

Now even the first covenant had regulations for worship and an earthly sanctuary. For a tent was constructed, the first one, in which were the lampstand, the table, and the bread of the Presence; this is called the Holy Place. Behind the second curtain was a tent called the Holy of Holies. In it stood the golden altar of incense and the ark of the covenant overlaid on all sides with gold, in which there were a golden urn holding the manna, and Aaron's rod that budded, and the tablets of the covenant; above it were the cherubim of glory overshadowing the mercy seat. Of these things we cannot speak now in detail.

Such preparations having been made, the priests go continually into the first tent to carry out their ritual duties; but only the high priest goes into the second, and he but once a year, and not without taking the blood that he offers for himself and for the sins committed unintentionally by the people. By this the Holy Spirit indicates that the way into the sanctuary has not yet been disclosed as long as the first tent is still standing. This is a symbol of the present time, during which gifts and sacrifices are offered that cannot perfect the conscience of the worshiper, but deal only with food and drink and various baptisms, regulations for the body imposed until the time comes to set things right.

But when Christ came as a high priest of the good things that have come, then through the greater and perfect tent (not made with hands, that is, not of this creation), he entered once for all into the Holy Place, not with the blood of goats and calves, but with his own blood, thus obtaining eternal redemption. For if the blood of goats and bulls, with the sprinkling of the ashes of a heifer, sanctifies those who have been defiled so that their flesh is purified, how much more will the blood of Christ, who through the eternal Spirit offered himself without blemish to God, purify our conscience from dead works to worship the living God!

For this reason he is the mediator of a new covenant, so that those who are called may receive the promised eternal inheritance, because a death has occurred that redeems them from the transgressions under the first covenant. Where a will is involved, the death of the one who made it must be established. For a will takes effect only at death, since it is not in force as long as the one who made it is alive. Hence not even the first covenant was inaugurated without blood. For when every commandment had been told to all the people by Moses in accordance with the law, he took the blood of calves and goats, with water and scarlet wool and hyssop, and sprinkled both the scroll itself and all the people, saying, "This is the blood of the covenant that God has ordained for you." And in the same way he sprinkled with the blood both the tent and all the vessels used in worship. Indeed, under the law almost everything is purified with blood, and without the shedding of blood there is no forgiveness of sins.

Thus it was necessary for the sketches of the heavenly things to be purified with these rites, but the heavenly things themselves need better sacrifices than these. For Christ did not enter a sanctuary made by human hands, a mere copy of the true one, but he entered into heaven itself, now to appear in the presence of God on our behalf. Nor was it to offer himself again and again, as the high priest enters the Holy Place year after year with blood that is not his own; for then he would have had to suffer again and again since the foundation of the world. But as it is, he has appeared once for all at the end of the age to remove sin by the sacrifice of himself. And just as it is appointed for mortals to die once, and after that the judgment, so Christ, having been offered once to bear the sins of many, will appear a second time, not to deal with sin, but to save those who are eagerly waiting for him.

Backstory: The Initial Day of Atonement

ALL THE IMAGES PAINTED in Hebrews 9 are intended to recall the annual Israelite national cleansing ceremony called the Day of Atonement. This ritual was established by God at Mount Sinai, just after the suzerain-vassal covenant of Exodus 20–24 officially transferred the "ownership" of Israel from the Pharaoh of Egypt (who had been defeated by Yahweh in the battle of the ten plagues and annihilated in the waters of the Red Sea) to Yahweh, the Creator of all and Lord of the nations.

When God moved into the Israelite camp to live and journey with the people, everything changed. There was a sense of nervous tension and excitement. How should the people act, now that this powerful deity actually resided at the heart of the community? The atmosphere was charged with energy and anticipation.

A New Book of Culture

And the lifestyle of the people did change, just as would be the case whenever a ruler of power visited or established a new royal home. The book of Leviticus functioned as a sort of new operator's manual for the changing expressions of culture and behaviors when God moved in with God's people.

Although readers might quickly get bogged down in the seemingly endless list of commands and regulations found in Leviticus, if one steps back to view the book as a whole, there are clear groupings of materials. The collection might be outlined like this:

- Instructions regarding offerings (1–7)
- Instructions for the priests in their ritual activities (8–10)
- Instructions regarding general hygiene in the community (11–15)
- Instructions about the Day of Atonement (16)
- General instructions about clean and unclean living (17–25)
- Curses and blessings (26)
- Appendix: Instructions concerning dedications (27)

While these instructions are understandable for the most part and provide a general outlook on life in the Israelite camp, they remain somewhat arbitrary until viewed in light of what appears to be the primary rationale undergirding the entire social ethos. In Leviticus 19:1–2 Moses received this command: "The Lord said to Moses, 'Speak to the entire assembly of Israel and say to them: "Be holy, because I, the Lord your God, am holy."" Holiness was a lifestyle intrinsic to the Creator's character. So, naturally, when Yahweh moved into the camp of Israel as its suzerain, some behavior modification among the vassals was necessary. In essence, the commands and regulations of Leviticus explored and explained the unique culture of Israel's modified society, now that she was under new authority and her champion had chosen to identify closely with this people.

In this light, the various sections of Leviticus take on new and vibrant meaning. Rather than merely cataloguing certain rituals or practices (because these are the way things have always been done and are now simply being codified), there was a new and pervasive dynamism, along the lines of a town getting ready for its recently elected mayor, the inauguration of a new president in a superpower nation, or the affirmation of a new constitution and governing body after a great revolution. The lack of any significant historical narrative or context-setting materials at the outset of Leviticus indicates that these instructions are elaborations upon the big covenant declarations of Exodus 20–24, along with the raising of the tabernacle at the center of the community. Now the day-to-day operations are explained and nuanced. In fact, the detailed notes about offerings in chapters 1–7 form a perfect bridge between finishing the tabernacle and getting on with life. The five types of sacrifices commanded and explained may be seen as vehicles for communicating inward "cleansing" or "holiness," both to Yahweh and also to others in the newly reshaped community. These offerings were visible prayers and may, in fact, picture the idea of the Israelites engaged in the dynamics of mealtime rituals with God. Notice that these offerings were to take place in the courtyard of the tabernacle at the same time as the typical meals, in the rhythm of Israelite custom, were eaten.

Levites to the Center

The ceremonial purification of the priests, in their special role as caretakers of the house of Yahweh and the rites practiced in it, were explored next. Since the clan of Moses and Aaron had been particularly vigilant for Yahweh's honor in the recent horrible golden calf incident, these Levites became symbolic in their functionary cleansing rituals for the washing of the entire nation. By vicarious extension, the people together, through the Levites, practiced hospitality at this tent at the center of the camp. This was particularly seen through the negative lesson given by the events surrounding the death of Aaron's sons, Nadab and Abihu; these two young men apparently wrote their own rules for how the rituals were supposed to take place, and through their folly the entire nation was warned to take note.

The Levites thus took center stage within the community. They cared for the house of Yahweh on behalf of the Israelites. And since the family of priests was contained within their numbers, these officials were to process the approach of the community as a whole toward Yahweh through their administration of the sacrifices of Leviticus 1–7, just as they were also to oversee the details of the "cleansing/holiness" practices throughout the camp. For these reasons, the entire collection of regulations, in its later Greek translation, was fittingly titled "Leviticus," or the activities pertaining to the Levites in the administration of Yahweh's holiness among his people.

This is how the concerns about mold, mildew, foods, blood flow, sores, and diseases in chapters 11–15 ought to be viewed. These instructions were more than simply good sanitation practices for forty years of camping. Instead, they reflected the fully-orbed shalom that was part of the Creator's understanding of how things were to operate in this realm that was originally divinely designed and now was recovering its natural identity. When Yahweh moved into the neighborhood, the place ought not to look, feel, or smell like a dump.

The Big Event

All of this was made explicit in chapter 16, with the yearly prescription of the Day of Atonement. This highly ritualized annual event was to be a national time of quick, thorough, and pervasive symbolic cleansing which encompassed the on-going and regular concerns for holiness/cleansing that had already been mentioned. First, the priests went through a ceremonial purification which involved both washings and the offering of a bull. Then two male goats were selected, with one becoming the sin offering for the people and the other transformed into the scapegoat, which carried any residual pollution outside of the camp, expelling it as alien and ungodly. Next, the high priest alone entered the most holy place, filled the room with a cloud of incense, and sprinkled blood from both offerings on the throne of Yahweh. Finally, the high priest re-emerged from his intimate conversations with Yahweh, bathed again, washing away even the splattering of sin or pollution that might have come back upon him in the business of the day. Through this lengthy ritual, the nation was cleansed, and the "holiness" of Leviticus 19:1–2 reigned.

As the writer of Hebrews reminds his readers about the symbols of the Day of Atonement and then re-visions them in this new age, under the new ministry of the greatest high priest, Jesus, he makes a few comments that also reimage for them the rebellions and fallings away told in the book that follows Leviticus. The "golden urn holding the manna, and Aaron's rod that budded" (Heb 9:4) were permanent reminders of two among the many uprisings and clashes which threatened both Yahweh's rule and the structures of this reconfigured community. The former had to do with divine provisions for food which were violated by a Sabbath-breaker, and the latter pointed to insurrections which challenged divine leadership appointments. Both of these stories are found, originally, in the book of Numbers.

Aaron's Budding Staff and Other Symbols Pointing to Jesus

While Leviticus describes the mood, climate, and atmosphere in the community where Yahweh had taken up residence, Numbers functioned more like the spats of newlyweds and the marriage counseling necessary to revitalize the relationship. First came lists of family trees and social responsibilities, which prepared the nation for travels toward their promised land destination. Then occurred a series of specific tests of covenant loyalty, many of which deeply troubled both the community and its divine partner. After Moses' leadership was challenged by his siblings and then, a short while later, by other members of his tribe, the biggest showdown occurred. Both Moses and Aaron were attacked by the entire community of Israel and threatened with death. Yahweh intervened and, in a tempered display of restrained anger, affirmed Aaron's role as high priest after only a small number of rebels had succumbed to a divine plague. It was the intercession of Moses and Aaron, on behalf of their rebellious friends, that ended judgment before it ran its full course. Instead, Yahweh requested that the leader of each tribe bring his staff to the tabernacle in what would become an official selection ceremony. The staffs, with each man's name carved deeply into the wood, were set up in the holy place of the tabernacle and left there overnight. The next morning, when Moses went in to retrieve them, eleven were unchanged, remaining merely sticks of wood. But Aaron's staff had become a living, portable tree, even though it was without roots or nourishment. It had produced branches and leaves and blossoms, even almonds. The election was over. Aaron was confidently reaffirmed as the only high priest of the people, clearly chosen by God. This is the story referenced by the author of Hebrews in 9:4.

Once again, the author of Hebrews has expressed his profound knowledge of Scripture. He ticks off references to stories, sometimes nearly obscure, and ceremonies that dot the pages of the Torah. He has memorized the Psalms and much of the covenant literature, and brings quotes and allusions into his teaching as if they were the language of everyday communication. For him, the Scriptures truly are the words of life.

What becomes apparent in reading Hebrews is that the original readers were as familiar with these things as was the writer. They, too, lived and breathed and drank in the Hebrew Scriptures as the very essence of meaning itself. It is precisely this devotion that provides the author of Hebrews with his interpretations that become, repeatedly, a call—not to abandon these things but to receive them as signs and pointers to Jesus. If they trusted in the revelation of God through the ceremonies of the past as outlined in Scripture, they should more fully trust Jesus now. All that happened before, all that was written in the covenant documents and the holiness codes, now finds its fulfillment in Jesus.

Where Have We Come So Far?

- God has spoken in times past.
  - This is our source of direction and confidence.
  - We know who we are because of the prophets.
- God has recently spoken a stronger, better, and clearer message through Jesus.
  - So when we, who live by the prophetic message, hear Jesus, we had better listen.
- Jesus is superior to the angels.
  - The great divine message that formed us came through Moses, but the message itself was delivered to him by angels (Deut 33:2; Acts 7:53).
  - Yet Jesus is superior to angels, and therefore delivers a more important prophetic message than that through the great prophet Moses.
- So, stick with Jesus, even though you are tempted to turn away from him.
  - There is no higher authority or source of connection with God.
  - And if our lives are to be connected to God, we turn away from Jesus to our own peril.
- God has made the world subject to Jesus.

- ✦ God never did this with the angels, so, again, Jesus is superior to them.

- ✦ But this only happened because Jesus first fully identified with the world.

- Jesus willingly came into the world to fully experience its pain.

- And this is to our benefit for three reasons:

  - ✦ To fully identify with us as sisters and brothers.

  - ✦ To make atonement for our sins (which cause the pain of this world).

  - ✦ To bring us with him fully into the house of God.

- So Jesus is greater than (over) the angels, but Jesus is also greater than (over) Moses.

- Therefore, be careful that you don't disconnect from Jesus (who is God):

  - ✦ Remember how those in our past who disconnected from God came under punishment.

  - ✦ The same can happen to you if you do not stay true and committed to Jesus.

- Let God's people in the earlier redemptive sequence be your instructors:

  - ✦ Like us, they were saved and led to their "(sabbath) rest" in the promised land.

    - ▪ But they failed to stay connected to God by way of the word of the prophet (Moses) and died before reading "rest."

  - ✦ Now God has promised us a coming "rest" (i.e., "heaven" when we die).

    - ▪ But we will receive it only if we remain connected to God by way of the word of the prophet (Jesus) and live faithfully through these trials.

- And, again, the only one who can keep you connected to God is Jesus:

  - ✦ He is our true high priest, who will take us boldly to God's merciful throne through his actions on our behalf on the Day of Atonement. He is fully human, so he completely understands the struggles of our lives and sympathizes deeply, to the point of anguished cries.

- In fact, he is as fully committed to fulfilling the mandate and responsibilities of his priestly order as are others.
  - They in their "Aaronic/Levitical priestly order."
  - He in his "Melchizedek priestly order."
- I wish you were getting this. You should be mature enough to teach others, but it seems you have lost your passion for Jesus and are trying only to protect yourselves.
  - Though I write strong words, I am confident that you will continue in our faith in Jesus.
  - After all, God has made absolute promises of care toward us that are our hope.
  - And Jesus is the only anchor we have today to ensure that we will receive what was promise.
- After all, Jesus is a priest after the order of Melchizedek.
  - The Levitical order priests could not fully satisfy needs, since its sacrifices needed repeating.
  - That is why someone from Melchizedek's order was needed.
    - Someone who was a descendant of David (of the tribe of Judah), perfect and never dying.
- This brings us back to the main thing we have been saying: Jesus is the best high priest ever.
  - He is God (seated at the right hand of the majesty in heaven).
  - He is owner of the house of God.
  - He is high priest of the house of God.
    - The true house of God, with dimensions given by God on the mountain.
    - The visible house of God, here below (under the care of the Levitical priests), important as it is, is only a shadow of the real thing.
  - He is faultless.
  - He is the mediator of the new covenant (remember Jer 31:31–34?).
- This is very important: God found fault with the old covenant.
  - God is causing the old covenant age to come to an end.

- Jesus is the only source of hope in the new covenant age.
- These changes are symbolized by the "houses" of the two covenant ages:
  - The tabernacle with God hidden and symbolic actions repeated.
  - The heavenly dwelling with Jesus bringing us directly to the throne.
- Both "houses" required blood sacrifice for God's people to approach God.
  - But in the earthly tabernacle, repeated animal sacrifices by Levitical priests were needed.
  - While in the heavenly dwelling, Jesus offered himself once for all.
- Thus, Jesus is the best mediator and the only source of our eternal security.
  - The tabernacle and Levitical priesthood were only types of this ultimate expression of God's love.

Message: Why Did Jesus Die?

When Canadian missionaries Don and Carol Richardson entered the world of the Sawi people in Irian Jaya in 1962, they were aware that culture shock awaited them. But the full impact of the tensions they faced didn't become apparent until one challenging day.

The Sawi lived in dwellings constructed high in the trees, partly to escape the ever-damp rain forest jungle floor, partly to catch cooling breezes that were otherwise blocked by dense growth, and partly to avoid mosquitoes as much as possible. Don committed himself to language acquisition and soon had learned enough of the Sawi language to carry on elementary conversations. He often spent time at the evening communal gathering of men, practicing his rudimentary Sawi skills by articulating Bible stories.

Storytellers

The Sawi were great tellers of tales. The best among them could weave word pictures for hours, captivating and entrancing everyone within earshot. Don was a novice working under the limitations of a foreign language. Some listened politely as he tried to express himself, but most ignored him and carried on other conversations and activities.

Then came the night that turned out to be horrifyingly different. At first, the gathering of men was as restless as usual while Don spoke. The narrative he had chosen, of Jesus' final days with his disciples before the crucifixion, did not seem to grab them. But Don pressed on, and began the story of Judas, one of Jesus' closest associates, plotting to have his friend killed. Suddenly Don felt a measureless energy connecting everyone in the room. No one moved. No one made a noise. All were listening.

Startled and pleased, Don carried on. The drama heightened with a dark night, Jesus' worried conversations, the arrival of soldiers, and the kiss of betrayal. The room shivered with anticipation at each move. And when the details of Judas's awful murderous act danced before them, Don felt a keen sense of involvement in every eye.

Super-Sawi

Then came the uneasy crawling of his skin. What was it about the story that drew the Sawi? Why did this story of treachery draw such enthusiasm? He was about to find out.

When the last words were spoken, one man whistled in delight. Others chuckled in glee and some touched their fingertips to their chests in awe. In their animated responses, it quickly became apparent that to them, *Judas* was a great man. He was the hero of the story. Judas might even be called a super-Sawi. He had played the greatest trick a Sawi man could ever hope to pull off—the "fattening of a friend for the slaughter."

Don was horrified. What was this Sawi ritual that seemed to make Judas the person to emulate in the crucifixion story? It was rooted in the cannibalistic heritage of the Sawi.

Over generations, the Sawi found no excitement that could match that of eating the flesh of someone who first had been groomed as a friend. It was the ultimate expression of power, of control, of vindication. To eat the flesh of a friend was the ultimate trip since it took all of the vital energy of someone who was respected (and thus made a friend), and infused this vitality into one's own self. To "fatten a friend for the slaughter" made the betrayer a truly big man. In fact, his story would be told again and again, around nighttime fires, as a lesson to future generations.

So, for the Sawi, Judas was the hero of the gospel. Jesus was a great man, a wonderful friend. But Judas was an outstanding man who managed, through subterfuge, to incorporate all of Jesus' goodness into Judas' own larger personhood first by befriending him, and then, even more significantly, by betraying him to his death.

Trembling at the Mystery

Don and Carol Richardson could not sleep that night. After all, they had been welcomed into the village as guests. They had been "befriended." Now they wondered whether they were to become the next victims of such a value system. Which among those who had treated them kindly would soon plunge the knife after they had been sufficiently "fattened for the slaughter"?

The Richardsons decided, with deep fears and much prayer, to remain among the Sawi. Don scavenged his few theological books for different ways to express the Christian understanding of the atonement. How could he proclaim the gospel message, centered as it was on Jesus' death, in a meaningful manner for Sawi who were enamored with Judas?

There are three major families of atonement theory, he recalled. Each began with Jesus on the cross. But each moved in a different direction as it unpacked the meaning of what took place on that grim and gruesome Friday afternoon.

Earliest among Christian reflections on the meaning of Jesus' death was the "ransom" theory. The gospel message was, from the first, really "good news." After all, no one had ever before experienced a dead man getting up out of his grave. That, coupled with the miracles that Jesus had done, both before and after his resurrection, made a huge impact on his closest contacts and friends. They were scared and amazed, terrified and overjoyed, all at the same time. Jesus could do anything.

And what Jesus did was good. He was not a tyrant, using power as a weapon. He was a friend, a healer, a provider. He blessed bread and it multiplied until everyone was fed. He spoke words of kindness and encouragement and demons left the house. He touched sores and painful rashes and health glowed in the eyes of those previously troubled by diseases. He was God's agent of grace. In fact, many believed he was, himself, actually God.

More than that, although Jesus had disappeared from them, the message from his closest disciples was that he would return soon. During this brief interlude, Jesus' friends and followers were commissioned to tell everyone they could about the great things Jesus had done. Early followers of Jesus soon earned the name "Christians," since they could not stop talking about Jesus, the Christ. They were like little Jesuses walking around. Whether people appreciated them or despised them, these were certainly "Christians."

Of course, beyond all the tales of Jesus' miracles and the huge story of his resurrection, there was the *big event* that needed explanation. Yes, Jesus was powerful. Yes, he was God or godlike. Yes, he did many good things that changed peoples' lives. But why was he killed in the first place? And how could such a one who wielded enormous divine resources that sent away demons and overturned diseases and defied death in others himself succumb to death? What was going on?

Face Toward the Devil

The initial response of Christians to such questions is that Jesus willingly traded his life for that of others. After all, he had talked about both his coming and his death in that manner: "For the Son of Man came not to be served but to serve, and to give his life a ransom for many." During the age of persecution, early Christian theologians portrayed Jesus' cross as the point of transaction between himself and the devil. This line of argument was rooted in Genesis 3 where the devil, in the form of a serpent, tempted the first human parents into seeking meaning apart from their Creator. Through the unfortunate choices of Eve and Adam, all their offspring would begin life dominated by Satan and compromised by evil. From birth, Lucifer owned our souls and snagged us on his deadly lures as we swam the oceans of time and existence. Powerless to save ourselves, Jesus provided, by way of his own death, the ransom that bought us back from the devil.

Justin Martyr (100–165) articulated this already early in the second century. "[Christ]" he said, "was in these last days, according to the time appointed by the Father, united to His own workmanship, inasmuch as He became a man liable to suffering . . . He commenced afresh the long line of human beings, and furnished us, in a brief, comprehensive manner, with salvation; so that what we had lost in Adam—namely, to be according to the image and likeness of God—that we might recover in Christ Jesus." Soon after, in his commentary on Matthew 16:8, Origen (184–254) wrote: "To whom did [Christ] give his life a ransom for many? Assuredly not to God; could it then be to the evil one? For he was holding us fast until the ransom should be given him, even the life of Jesus; [Satan] being deceived with the idea that he could have dominion over it, and not seeing that he could not bear the torture in retaining it." He draws out this image again later in his commentary, and Gregory of Nyssa (c. 335–394) and Augustine (c. 354–430) pick it up in turn.

The idea of Jesus' death as a ransom is intriguing. It makes the gruesome reality of crucifixion even more powerful. Yes, Jesus could have avoided the cross, but he chose to offer himself in exchange for the whole of humanity who, by their willful disobedience or through the dastardly trickery or the devil, had come to be owned by evil. Only someone who has power greater than Satan, but who chooses to wield that might in the guise of helplessness, could subvert the tyranny of wickedness by feinting defeat in a single battle in order to win the cosmic war.

C. S. Lewis twice carried the ransom theory of the atonement in our modern world. First, he named his space hero "Dr. Ransom" in the trilogy that wrestled over the past, present, and future of earth and its neighboring planets. Ransom is a scientist (knowledgeable, source of hope and healing) who gets abducted by aliens (evil incarnated), visits Mars (to see how one species resisted temptation), and travels to Venus as the Creator is planting a new civilization that might replay humankind's fall into sin.

Later, the act of a ransoming Messiah was central to Lewis' Narnia Chronicle, *The Lion, the Witch and the Wardrobe*. Aslan, the Jesus-like lion ruler of Narnia, is reclaiming his kingdom that has been under a long spell of wintery frigidity brought on by the White Witch. According to ancient prophecies, Aslan can only redeem his Narnia world through the assistance of two sons of Adam and two daughters of Eve. The Pevensie children from London, living temporarily in the country home of Professor Digory Kirke to escape the Second World War bombing blitz, stumble into Narnia just in time. But all is not well. Peter, Susan, and Lucy are right for redemptive leadership and will go on to rule as king and queens. But brother Edmund sneaked into Narnia on his own and fell prey to the Witch's influences. She "owns" him, and because this "son of Adam" has now become an agent of evil, Aslan cannot win the war for Narnia. The only way that Edmund can be released from her clutches is if Aslan himself will become the ransom. Of course, this defeats all of Narnia's hopes, since the "savior" of this world is now killed by the evil ruler who has usurped the throne.

Whimpering in darkness as the demons and ogres strip the mane and life from Aslan on the Stone Table, with magical writing from the beginning of time that dictates these outcomes, Lucy and Susan believe all is lost. But at dawn they are wakened by a loud *crack*. Peering from their hiding place, they see the Stone Table shattered, and the evil creatures scattered. Then Aslan bounces in, larger than ever. When they ask him what has happened, he tells of a magic that is found before time itself. In this magic, Aslan was able to offer himself as ransom to the White Witch, without her realizing that she would never be able to keep or destroy him.

Face toward the Father

The ransom perspective regarding the work of Jesus was strong in the church's first centuries. It has been maintained through to the present in popular form by Lewis' creative Narnia imaginings and also by astute theologians such as Gustav Aulen, who asserted Jesus' triumph over evil as *Christus Viktor*. Aulen unfolded the history of atonement theories in three stages. The second group of atonement explanations, initiated by Anselm (1033–1109), imagined Jesus' death more as an intentional dialogue with his Father. On Monday of what has come to be known as passion week, Jesus told a story that summarized all of Israelite history, including Jesus' own coming into the world, as a teaching parable. A great landowner established a vineyard guarded by walls and complete with a winepress and a fortified tower. Before leaving on an extended journey, the master of the estate rented it out to tenants. After harvest, the landlord sent servants to collect his mandated share of the proceeds. The tenants, however, beat some and killed others, despising the one who had given them their very livelihood.

Finally, the master sent his own son, believing that the troublesome renters would respect this flesh of his own flesh. But the rebels saw things differently. "This is the heir," they said to one another. "Come, let's kill him and take his inheritance." And this they do.

Jesus' story ends with the landowner bringing judgment on those horrible tenants. Of course, all who heard the story knew that they were implicated in the fiendish plot, for they were the tenants of God's great world. Even more, they had received ambassadors from God throughout their history—the prophets sent to call them back to obedience and loyalty to their good master. In each Gospel's rendition of this parable, the last lines talk about the religious leaders of the day going out to foment a plot against Jesus, desiring to kill him. The rest of passion week will mark their progress until Jesus is on the cross.

Of course, Jesus' own disciples recalled this parable for its profound theological richness as the centuries unfolded. God had been righteous and good in preparing this world for humankind. God had even nurtured a special relationship with the nation of Israel, giving them unique lead-tenant status at the heart of his creation. To them God had sent prophets, reminding the people of their character and obligations. Yet virtually every "servant of Yahweh" had been despised or brutally treated. Some had even been killed in response to their righteous messages.

And now, the Son had come. But he was rejected and tortured as well, until he hung on the cross in shame. Yet in his steadfast commitment to the ways and the will of his Father, Jesus restored dignity and honor in heaven and transformed life on earth. In Anselm's pivotal work, *Cur Deus Homo*, Anselm carries on a dialogue with his student Boso about these things. Anselm argues that humanity has offended God, but that humankind is incapable of living faithfully or restoring honor. In fact, even if we were able to overcome our innate tendencies toward evil, continuing to defame God, any righteous acts would only be reasonable and expected and would not cleanse the tarnishment debt that had been growing for centuries. Only Jesus, beginning with a perfect righteousness, could also stand in for us as we faced our Creator. Taking it upon himself to offer his own life on our behalf, Jesus' crucifixion provides absolute redemption, since Jesus is a human without sin (thus not needing to negotiate on his own behalf for his own transgressions) and also divine (thus acting in infinite ways toward ultimate and transcendent fulfillment of outcomes).

Aquinas (1225–1274) elaborates on the satisfaction atonement theory in his *Summa Theologica*. He writes, "Consequently Christ by His Passion merited salvation, not only for Himself, but likewise for all His members." Later, both Martin Luther (1483–1546) and John Calvin (1509–1564) expounded further on this view of Jesus' crucifixion, although separating it from the sacramentalism of the medieval church. Calvin put it this way: "This is our acquittal: the guilt that held us liable for punishment has been transferred to the head of the Son of God (Is. 53:12). We must, above all, remember this substitution, lest we tremble and remain anxious throughout life—as if God's righteous vengeance, which the Son of God has taken upon himself, still hung over us.

This perspective on the meaning and effects of Jesus' death emerges most directly from biblical passages like Hebrews 9. The write of Hebrews, using the Day of Atonement as his canvas, paints a picture of Jesus performing the duties of high priest in order to make the people right with their sovereign. There is sin. There is sacrifice. There is expiation and atonement. Redemption is accomplished when Jesus officiates at the place of death, since "without the shedding of blood there is no forgiveness" (Hebrew 9:22).

Face toward Humanity

A third family of atonement theories focuses the attention of Jesus on humanity, rather than on the devil or the Father. Most frequently this is called the "moral example or influence" view of the atonement. While it has been around since the beginning of the church, this perspective gained a lot of traction in our modern world. Since it points to the cruelty of Jesus' death and the fact that he did not deserve what happened to him, the moral influence atonement theory asserts Jesus' crucifixion as a scandal that is intended to shock us back from our immoral stupor, re-engaging us with a higher morality.

Most articulate and influential for this perspective was Immanuel Kant, the German philosopher who set the stage for much of our current metaphysical thinking. Reacting to David Hume's skepticism about God and the transcendent beliefs of Christianity, Kant sought to ground religious perspectives in the rationality of common human thinking. Kant remained a theist all his life but rewrote the manner in which God is apprehended by us or influences our lives. The consistency of our many human perceptions about the world in which we live convinced Kant that God has provided innate categories of thinking, organizing, and moralizing within the common human mind. These shape our experiences of life, as well as our ethical practices, in similar ways, regardless of our cultural backgrounds or contexts.

Jesus was important for Kant but not in a manner similar to either the "ransom" or "satisfaction" portraits for understanding why Jesus came among us or died a cruel death. Instead, for Kant, Jesus was the greatest expression of human self-awareness and compliance with the intrinsic moral codes stamped into our rational processes. Jesus thus serves humanity as the pinnacle example of moral rectitude and the role model of best ethical choices.

Kant expressed this most profoundly in the third book of his, *Religion Within the Limits of Reason Alone* (1793). Jesus of Nazareth is, for Kant, the prime archetype symbolizing what can take place when we as evilly-inclined humans reach instead for the virtues which God has embedded into our most authentic rational thinking. Kant never explores Jesus' origins, or connects Jesus with divinity. Instead, the fullness of the best of our humanity oozes from Jesus' every pore, and we become better through our imitation of him.

Friedrich Schleiermacher adapted Kant's Enlightenment philosophical perspectives and used them to shape what would come to be known as liberal protestant theology. Schleiermacher broke from the orthodox German pietism of his family heritage in a stunning declaration to the youthful intelligentsia of his times by publishing *On Religion: Speeches to Its Cultured Despisers* (1799). Rejecting miracles and the historic Christian views of Jesus as divine, Schleiermacher instead described religion as an innate human longing for mystery and the transcendent. Jesus most clearly articulated these things and demonstrated them in his personal commitments to others, including his great example of love in volunteering to go to death if it would spare his friends and allow them to escape and live on.

In 1832, after having formulated his mature Enlightenment theology for publication as *The Christian Faith*, Schleiermacher taught a course on "The Life of Jesus." Although these assertions were never published as a finished literary work by Schleiermacher, they have been reassembled from his own lecture outlines, supplemented by quotes and elaborations found in classroom notes taken by his students. Schleiermacher believed Christianity was the best expression of human religious questing and that the Jesus at the center of Christianity was humanity's greatest ethical teacher, its finest example of authentic moral living.

Schleiermacher's "example theory" of Jesus' life and death was multiplied throughout the nineteenth and twentieth centuries in what has become known as the initial "quest for the historical Jesus." Ernest Renan (1823–1892) and David Strauss (1808–1874) broadly popularized this perspective in their influential biographies of Jesus, each titled *Life of Jesus* (1835; 1863). Both asserted that Jesus was a heroic man who separated his deep moral authority from the Judaism into which he had been born and established Christianity as the best expression of truly moral rational religion. Culminating this "quest" was Albert Schweitzer (1875–1965), who wrote a history of this Enlightenment take on Jesus and the religion he founded. Invariably Jesus was portrayed as a uniquely insightful human who provided his followers with a meaningful moral matrix defined by a rational understanding of the best that life can become when properly conceived and executed by ethically astute people and societies.

Back to the Gospel

While each of these families of atonement theory is rooted in some aspect of Jesus' life and teachings, and each holds merit for deepening our appreciation of Jesus' world-changing ministry and death, there are clearly a number of contradictory points made by various extended reflections on these themes. The writer of Hebrews would keep us focused on the "satisfaction" aspect of Jesus' death. Building his argument upon his readers' shared understanding of the actions and significance of the annual Israelite "Day of Atonement," the author declares Jesus to be a unique high priest, offering himself as the substitute sacrifice that will renew God's relationship with God's people.

And how did Don Richardson fare in his attempt to bring this message regarding Jesus to the Sawi people who were enamored with strongman Judas who had, in Sawi fashion, "fattened the pig (Jesus) for the slaughter"? As Don and Carol continued their lives with these people in the rain forests of

Papua, New Guinea, climate conditions precipitated stresses that eventually caused a new insight.

In an unusually dry rainy season, river flows diminished and vegetation suffered from drought. Sawi men ranged further and longer to find adequate game and fish and local sources of fruits and vegetables became scarce. Rarely an afternoon would pass without deepening concerns expressed in the tree house where the men huddled to mend nets, create hunting weapons, and pass along gossip and wisdom. Now the talk was turning ugly, particularly after several Sawi were wounded in skirmishes with neighboring tribes who fought them over territorial claims for hunting grounds and fishing rights in a world of receding resources. After these clashes brought death to more than a few of both Sawi and their enemies, Don heard murmurings of the possible need for a "peace child."

A "peace child"? Don asked what this meant. With troubled voices, the older men revealed another stream of Sawi tradition. Sometimes in the distant past, they said, when tensions ran high between clans and tribes, and when warfare threatened to destroy their villages and families, a wise chief would grab the youngest newborn male from its mother's loving embrace and run with the child, chased by horrified maternal cries, across the distance between the Sawi and their enemies. Emerging suddenly into the settlement of their foes, the chief would thrust this baby into the arms of a young woman there. While adrenaline flared and testosterone ignited menacing passions, a sudden stillness would calm them all. This was a "peace child," and everyone was aware of what was taking place. A single life of a Sawi boy had been entrusted to the care of the other tribe. In this action, their communities were knit toward a common purpose: one of us live with them; we have become brothers and sisters and family and partners; to kill them is to take our own life; to fight with them is to destroy ourselves.

In an instant, all rules in the game of war were changed. What had been combat against foreigners to gain and use turf and resources now was transformed into a growing family that needed all interests to provide safety and nourishment for every individual who was part of this newly amalgamated collective. The "peace child" knit disparate elements of humanity together into a larger whole where mutual care superseded violent competition.

Don was intrigued—a "peace child" who reconciled embattled enemies.

He had one important follow-up question. What would happen, he asked, if someone harmed the "peace child"?

Fierce emotions erupted immediately. Harm the "peace child"? Impossible. No one would ever do that. It was unthinkable.

"Let me tell you a story," said Don. He told of a time in the distant past when the tribe of humanity was at war with the tribe of heaven. He told how antagonism mounted and words became weapons and alienation threatened to destroy this world. But just when things looked most critical, the chief of heaven's tribe took his only son and thrust him into the hands of a young human woman. She became his mother, and the "peace child" reconciled earth to heaven.

As murmurs of approval hummed in every Sawi throat, Don went on. One day, he told them, a brash young man connected with the "peace child." This fellow decided to draw the "peace child" into his personal quest for power and played the manly Sawi game of "fattening the pig for the slaughter." After three years of building trust and friendship, the cunning young fellow was able to betray and kill his buddy.

The Sawi were horrified. When did this happen? Who was this terrible young man? How could anyone violate the foundational principle of reconciliation that was essential to the "peace child" rite?

In simple terms, Don Richardson told the Sawi men about Jesus (the "peace child") and Judas (the betrayer). With cries of anguish, the Sawi wondered what could be done, and how this plight might be remedied.

That was the day that the Sawi became Christians.

Chapter 14

A Tale of Two Covenants

Text: Hebrews 10:1–18

Since the law has only a shadow of the good things to come and not the true form of these realities, it can never, by the same sacrifices that are continually offered year after year, make perfect those who approach. Otherwise, would they not have ceased being offered, since the worshipers, cleansed once for all, would no longer have any consciousness of sin? But in these sacrifices there is a reminder of sin year after year. For it is impossible for the blood of bulls and goats to take away sins. Consequently, when Christ came into the world, he said,

"Sacrifices and offerings you have not desired, but a body you have prepared for me; in burnt offerings and sin offerings you have taken no pleasure. Then I said, 'See, God, I have come to do your will, O God' (in the scroll of the book it is written of me)."

When he said above, "You have neither desired nor taken pleasure in sacrifices and offerings and burnt offerings and sin offerings" (these are offered according to the law), then he added, "See, I have come to do your will." He abolishes the first in order to establish the second. And it is by God's will that we have been sanctified through the offering of the body of Jesus Christ once for all.

And every priest stands day after day at his service, offering again and again the same sacrifices that can never take away sins. But when Christ had offered for all time a single sacrifice for sins, "he sat down at the right hand of God," and since then has been waiting "until his enemies would be made a footstool for his feet." For by a single offering he has perfected for all time those who are sanctified. And the Holy Spirit also testifies to us, for after saying,

"This is the covenant that I will make with them after those days, says the Lord: I will put my laws in their hearts, and I will write them on their minds,"

he also adds,

"I will remember their sins and their lawless deeds no more."

Where there is forgiveness of these, there is no longer any offering for sin.

Backstory: Shadow and Substance

THE WRITER OF HEBREWS continues his analysis of the Day of Atonement and its relation to Jesus. This is clear from his reference to "the blood of bulls and goats" in verse 3. The Day of Atonement was built around the sacrifice of these two kinds of animals and there was no other event or celebration in Israel's ceremonial life which shared the same featured sacrificial combination.

At the start of the Day of Atonement, a bull would be offered in the cleansing ritual for the high priest. Since the high priest represented the nation of Israel as a whole, the largest possible single animal sacrifice was made, standing in for this largest expression of the national population. Later in the day, two goats were selected for further cleansing rituals. One was sacrificed as a sin offering while the other became the "scapegoat," channeling the sins of the people symbolically out into the wilderness where it was turned loose.

The author is summarizing and reiterating the point he made just prior to this: the very fact that the Day of Atonement had to be repeated yearly in the cycle of Israel's national cleansing before God indicated that it was only modestly powerful to cleanse. But Jesus, who is a different kind of high priest (after the order of Melchizedek), provided a single once-for-all-time sacrifice that needed no repetition.

Old and New

This immediately leads the writer to a new topic—the relationship between the old and new expressions of God's saving, cleansing activity among God's people. In what has come to be known as typology, the author uses two words to describe the two sides of a single redemptive coin. The former is called Σκιὰν, while the latter is identified as εἰκόνα τῶν πραγμάτων. One might pair these as "shadow and substance." It is impossible to have a shadow if the substantial thing is not present. At the same time, in the world of planet Earth, during the daylight, when we are able to see things because of the light provided by the sun, no reality exists without casting a shadow. Shadow and substance co-exist in a symbiotic manner. One cannot be had without the other. Where one is present, its companion is also evident.

But that does not make the substantial thing and its shadow identical or equivalent. The person and her shadow may have the same outline form but one could never mistake the one for the other. Also, there is an unequal relationship of dependency between the two, shadow and substance. The thing of substance creates the shadow, not the other way around. While both are inextricably tied to each other, the substance carries the weight of their common identity. It is not the shadow that dictates terms to the substantive thing but the substantive thing which forces the shadow to take shape and meaning.

So it is, according to the author of Hebrews, in the relationship between the Day of Atonement (along with all that was part of the "Law" and the ceremonial system of Israel) and Jesus. Although the former occurred prior to Jesus' recent appearance in human history, it is actually symbiotically dependent upon Jesus for both its existence and its meaning. Jesus is the means by which God brings salvation to this world, while the sacrifices and ceremonies of the Day of Atonement and its kin were only typologically prefiguring this culminating reality.

Thus, in the former age, God spoke through prophets and God's care was ministered through angels, Moses, and the temporary house of God (the tabernacle), with its Levitical priesthood whose priests were imperfect, and offered sacrifices that had to be repeated. Meanwhile, in this new age, God speaks through Jesus while God's care is ministered through the Son (who is better than the angels or Moses), by way of the true house of God (the arena of heaven and earth), under the care of the one who is ordained to the Melchizedek priesthood, offering a perfect sacrifice that does not need to be repeated.

Typology

This typology lends itself toward a kind of dualism—the former and the latter, the imperfect and the perfect, the repeated and the once-for-all, the shadow and the substance. But it is not the same kind of dualism as one encounters in the cosmology of Plato, where all materiality is but temporary copies and imitations of the true forms and eternal ideals that populate the realm of transcendent spirituality. Nor is it like Buddhist dualistic cosmology where the material world is temporary, noisy and engaging, and ultimately destructive to essential identity through its forced isolation of spirit from the oneness of all being, while the spiritual world is eternal, quiet and elusive, and ultimately destructive to essential identity through annihilation of the uniqueness of personhood.

Instead, the typological dualism expressed in Hebrews functions within time rather than expressing substantive cosmology defining the whole of reality. This typological dualism found its earlier expression in the first covenant period, sometimes known as the age of the prophets, where, through the auspices of the tabernacle and its Levitical priesthood, there was an endless cycle of repeated sacrifices, pointing toward the need for a more complete address of the problem of human sinfulness. Now, in this latter expression of the same work of God characterized as the second covenant period, known also as the age of the Son, Jesus provides a once-for-all sacrificial ministry that moves us through the heavenly sanctuary into the very presence of God.

This typological dualism is at the heart of Christian theology. Both expressions are God's means for bringing salvation. Both are built upon blood sacrifice. But the former is temporary (a shadow), although essentially connected to the latter just as a shadow is essentially connected to the thing that causes it, having the same shape, character, and movements. Meanwhile, the latter is everlasting (the perfection that needs no repetition). It is the source of being, even for the shadow reality, but its substantive nature supersedes its shadow reflection.

Hence there is one mission of the Creator (bring back into fellowship the human race that has been alienated) which becomes accomplished through two missional strategies:

- First, through Israel as a temporary teaching measure.
- Now, through Jesus as a permanent connection between God and us.

This is essential to the message of Hebrews, and through it, our Christian understanding of the relationship between the Old Testament and the New Testament.

One Christian Bible, but Expressed in Two Testaments

To define a theology of the New Testament is a modest enterprise and a reasonably uncontroversial task. After all, the textual data is limited and the nuances of interpretation are rather narrow in scope. Although among New Testament theologians there are differences of emphasis or arguments about the significance of certain terms and ideas, they rarely find themselves in fundamentally different camps from one another.

Developing a theology of the Old Testament (or Hebrew Bible) is a much more daunting task. Not only is the literature of this collection considerably more expansive, but it varies extensively among multiple genres, topics, and provenance. Added to these challenges are questions of dating, inherent worldview, and the extent of influence from other ancient Near Eastern cultures. Old Testament theologians can square off from very different ideological points of view.

Most intimidating of all, however, is any attempt at a biblical theology that encompasses both Testaments, seeking to remain faithful to the origins and directions of each, while pursuing the historical, cultural, and religious bonds that have brought them together as the Christian Bible. Fundamental to this challenge is the question of the relationship between the two collections. Choices made here are inherently theological, philosophical, and confessional. Five major options are most often posited:

- *The Old Testament is essential Christian Scripture, with the New Testament serving primarily as its explanatory footnote.* Because Jesus and the first Christians were Jewish, and the preaching of the apostles was based upon the Hebrew Bible, there is a sense in which the Old Testament is sufficient when considering what revelation God might have given. The New Testament documents, in this view, do not alter or add to the theology of the Old Testament. Instead, they provide notes about the life and teachings of Jesus and collect together the interpretive nuances about him that were put forward by the church's first preachers.

- *The Old Testament is prophecy and the New Testament describes its fulfillment.* This is a significantly New Testament-centered approach. It views the Hebrew Bible and its context as an incomplete religious world in which its leaders invariably pointed to meanings and future happenings that could not be apprehended immediately by their contemporaries. God's designs, accordingly, were focused on Jesus, and for that reason Israel's history and religion were inherently still evolving, forming at best a prelude or prologue to the real event.

- *The Old Testament is historical background, while the New Testament is essential Scripture.* In this overtly church-centered analysis, all Christian theology is derived from the New Testament. It, alone, is the complete "Word of God." The Old Testament is, of course, beneficial and convenient, for it gives historical context to the life of Jesus and helps explain some of the terms and ideas bandied about in New Testament writings which are shaped by certain ancient cultures. Clearly, however, the New Testament is the guidebook for the church, and for that reason it can be published separately from the Hebrew Bible and studied independently of that other collection which belongs to a different religion.

- *The Old Testament is primarily an expression of Law, while the New Testament is truly gospel, "good news."* This approach believes that the God of the Judeo-Christian tradition acted in fundamentally different ways when nurturing the lives of these sibling faith communities. The "Law" of Old Testament covenant theology was a somewhat misguided attempt that viewed God as standing like nanny or teacher over a spiritually immature people until an appropriate time when they would hunger for freedom as believers come of age. The New Testament breathes with grace and spiritual maturity that was not possible during Old Testament times. Jesus is the one who explained the new religious outlook and took care of the penal code associated with the Old Testament "Law" so that New Testament believers would not have to worry about it.

- *The Old Testament begins God's covenant mission to reclaim the wayward peoples of earth through a centripetal geographic strategy, and the New Testament reaffirms this core design while retooling its missional thrust centrifugally outward to the far reaches of human settlement and expansion.* In this perspective, there is a single unifying motif that binds the two Testaments together: the mission of God. This mission is largely channeled through Israel in Old Testament times, with a result that the nation needed to be located at a significant crossroad of international interaction so that all peoples might eventually have an opportunity to connect with Israel's God. Furthermore, because the missional activities of God were expressed through a specific cultural context, many of the scriptural teachings were designed in and around and through Israelite culture and history. The New Testament does not alter this divine missional drive, but it renegotiates the parameters so that it becomes more portable and transferable. The critical event that initiated the Old Testament era of the mission was the exodus of Israel from Egypt and the formation of its identity through the Sinai covenant. The critical event that initiated the New Testament era of the mission was the incarnation of the divine identity into human form (Jesus) so that the transition could be made quickly and its redemptive transaction secured once and for all.

An Intriguing Supportive Argument

This fifth perspective seems most consonant with the message of Hebrews, particularly when the writer supports his arguments with a lengthy quote from Psalm 40. Psalm 40 is a song of deliverance attributed to David. It reflects on a very traumatic, life-threatening event for which God brought about a miraculous escape and restoration. Afterward, even while the menacing taunts of enemies continued, David proclaimed the might of Yahweh to the gathering of God's people. Although he likely brought a sacrifice to express his thankfulness, he also declares that life devotion and service are the real expression of appreciation.

It is the unique expression given by David in Psalm 40:6–8 that captures the attention of the writer of Hebrews and provides us with another glimpse of his brilliance and depth of scriptural understanding. For one thing, he appears to have vast portions of the Hebrew Bible memorized and available in his thinking with incredibly rapid links of association. Most likely this document is being dictated in about an hour's time and the author is not poring over texts and manuscripts, weaving the exact intricacies of a theological treatise. All of these Scriptures occur to him as he dictates, connected instantaneously by theme and image and implied meaning.

This becomes more apparent, secondly, when the textual variations on Psalm 40:6–8 are noted, with their vast difference in meaning and momentum. While the Masoretic Text and the Septuagint are closely aligned throughout most Old Testament passages, it is not so in the received texts available for Psalm 40. The New Revised Standard Version translation of these verses relies on the Masoretic Text and expresses verses 6–8 in English in this manner:

> Sacrifice and offering you do not desire, but you have given me an open ear. Burnt offering and sin offering you have not required. Then I said, "Here I am; in the scroll of the book it is written of me. I delight to do your will, O my God; your law is within my heart."

The Septuagint, however, seems to be drawn from another textual tradition, and gives rise to a uniquely different English translation:

> You did not want sacrifice and offering, but a body you restored to me. You did not ask for whole burnt offering, and an offering concerning sin. Then I said, "Behold, I have arrived. In the scroll of the book it has been written concerning me. I delight to do your will, O my God; your law is within my heart."

There is clearly a major difference between an "open ear" (as in the Masoretic Text) and a "restored body" (as in the Septuagint). While the former has more substantial text and tradition support and the latter may, in fact, be based upon some copyist's error rather than a clear reflection of David's original song, the writer of Hebrews deliberately chose the minor and more obscure rendering of Psalm 40:6–8 to support his point. Why?

It seems to be part of a larger arc of mental development tying all the author's ideas together in a truly brilliant manner. First, in verse 5, the writer indicates that Jesus is the voice of Scripture. This is important, for the whole of Hebrews is based on hearing God speak. In the past, connected to the historic Israelite/Jewish tradition, God spoke through the prophets. Now, however, God is speaking through his Son. But if the voice of Jesus is the voice of God because Jesus is God, then the voice of the prophets is actually the voice of Jesus. Therefore, these people who listen closely to the voice of God through the prophets should continue to listen to the voice of God through Jesus because it is one and the same voice.

Second, since it is Jesus who spoke through David when the great king penned Psalm 40, what emerged is actually a self-declaration of Jesu,s even though it also echoed David's own experiences at the time (think typology). So, David was celebrating divine deliverance from the threats on his life by pledging deeper devotion to God, who had saved him. In David's mind, one of the most profound expressions of service and devotion happened when a Hebrew slave chose to remain subject to a good master, even though the bondsman was entitled to go free. This relationship was commemorated publicly with an ear-piercing ceremony. This seems to be the background of David's somewhat cryptic expression in Psalm 40:6—that God has given him "an open ear." The term in Hebrew is ברית, which means "you bore" or "you pierce." This is precisely what took place in the ancient Israelite ceremony binding a faithful slave to a good master. David visualizes himself in that relationship with Yahweh, his good master who has once again recently saved him.

So What Is God (Jesus) Saying?

But now back to the idea that Jesus is the great voice of God speaking through the testimonies of Israelite Scriptures. The Septuagint version of Psalm 40:6 declares that a "body" has been prepared or restored. The Hebrew word for "prepared" or "establish" or "restore" is כנית, which is based on the same root that gives rise to ברית, the term for "bore" or "pierce." This allows the author of Hebrews to take the Septuagint variation of Psalm 40:6 and directly apply it to Jesus. While David was placing himself in relationship with Yahweh symbolically as a slave who might pledge himself to a good master that saved him time and again (therefore getting his ear pierced and remaining indentured to the master for a lifetime), Jesus, who is the true prophet of God speaking through David, declares, by another reading of this text, that in his devotion to the Father he has become the true sacrifice (having his body prepared for both crucifixion and resurrection), nullifying the need for animal sacrifice.

In a matter of a few lines, deeply understood and christologically interpreted, the author of Hebrews has pulled together powerful ideas from the Old Testament and asserted their on-going message in a New Testament age. In order to confirm this, he reiterates his reading through the explanation he provides in Hebrew 10:8–10—

> When he said above, "You have neither desired nor taken pleasure in sacrifices and offerings and burnt offerings and sin offerings" (these are offered according to the law), then he added, "See, I have come to do your will." He abolishes the first in order to establish the second. And it is by God's will that we have been sanctified through the offering of the body of Jesus Christ once for all.

Then, to seal the deal, he reiterates the voice of David in Psalm 110 as functioning essentially as the mouthpiece of Jesus and brings all things together by evoking the memory of Yahweh's call to Israel through Moses in Leviticus 19:1–2. The Israelites are to be holy because their God, coming to live among them in the tabernacle, is holy. Now, because Jesus is the true high priest over the house of God, he makes God's people holy through his unique sacrifice, the offering of his own body.

Culminating these marvelous maneuvers of the mind and heart, the writer of Hebrews quickly nods, once again, to Jeremiah 31:31–34, a passage he exegeted more fully a short while earlier in what we call Hebrews 8. He merges the two expressions of the divine covenant, gives a testimony that both manifestations of the covenant are intended to provide forgiveness from sins through blood sacrifice, and reiterates that Jesus' sacrifice is the one that completes all things, never needing repetition like was true of the animal sacrifices in Israel's past experiences.

Summing up, the writer of Hebrews brings everything together in Jesus:

- Verse 8—Since God declares that sacrifices are not desired, Jesus puts an end to them.

- Verse 8—Since sacrifices are related to the "Law" (old covenant), Jesus abolishes them as he brings in the new covenant age.

- Verse 9—Since Jesus says in Psalm 40:8 (see verse 5) that "I have come to do your will," and God wishes to put an end to the old covenant, Jesus is the transition from the old to the new.

- Verse 10—"it is by God's will that we have been sanctified through the offering of the body of Jesus Christ once for all."

- Verses 11–12—While the priests of the old covenant had to repeat their sacrifices over and over, Jesus offers himself as a once-for-all sacrifice.

- Verses 12–14—This brings us back to Psalm 110, which affirms that Jesus has accomplished his work ("sat down"), is God ("at the right hand of God"), rules over all as God ("since then has been waiting 'until his enemies would be made a footstool for his feet'"), and draws us into the end-times waiting with him ("those who are being sanctified").

- Verses 15–18—This brings us back to Jeremiah 31:31–34, affirming the beginning of the new covenant age where God forgets sins because our sins are once-for-all forgiven by way of Jesus' once-for-all sacrifice, ending the need for repeated sacrifices.

Can the message get any clearer? Jesus has ushered in the new covenant age. All who trust him cling to his benefits, knowing that he is coming soon to finish the work begun.

Where Have We Come So Far?

- God has spoken in times past.

- ◆ This is our source of direction and confidence.
- ◆ We know who we are because of the prophets.
- God has recently spoken a stronger, better, and clearer message through Jesus.
  - ◆ So when we, who live by the prophetic message, hear Jesus, we had better listen.
- Jesus is superior to the angels.
  - ◆ The great divine message that formed us came through Moses, but the message itself was delivered to him by angels (Deut 33:2; Acts 7:53).
  - ◆ Yet Jesus is superior to angels, and therefore delivers a more important prophetic message than that through the great prophet Moses.
- So, stick with Jesus, even though you are tempted to turn away from him.
  - ◆ There is no higher authority or source of connection with God.
  - ◆ And if our lives are to be connected to God, we turn away from Jesus to our own peril.
- God has made the world subject to Jesus.
  - ◆ God never did this with the angels, so, again, Jesus is superior to them.
  - ◆ But this only happened because Jesus first fully identified with the world.
- Jesus willingly came into the world to fully experience its pain.
- And this is to our benefit for three reasons:
  - ◆ To fully identify with us as sisters and brothers.
  - ◆ To make atonement for our sins (which cause the pain of this world).
  - ◆ To bring us with him fully into the house of God.
- So Jesus is greater than (over) the angels, but Jesus is also greater than (over) Moses.
- Therefore, be careful that you don't disconnect from Jesus (who is God):

- Remember how those in our past who disconnected from God came under punishment.
- The same can happen to you if you do not stay true and committed to Jesus.

• Let God's people in the earlier redemptive sequence be your instructors:

- Like us, they were saved and led to their "(sabbath) rest" in the promised land.
  - But they failed to stay connected to God by way of the word of the prophet (Moses) and died before reading "rest."
- Now God has promised us a coming "rest" (i.e., "heaven" when we die).
  - But we will receive it only if we remain connected to God by way of the word of the prophet (Jesus) and live faithfully through these trials.

• And, again, the only one who can keep you connected to God is Jesus:

- He is our true high priest, who will take us boldly to God's merciful throne through his actions on our behalf on the Day of Atonement. He is fully human, so he completely understands the struggles of our lives and sympathizes deeply, to the point of anguished cries.

• In fact, he is as fully committed to fulfilling the mandate and responsibilities of his priestly order as are others.

- They in their "Aaronic/Levitical priestly order."
- He in his "Melchizedek priestly order."

• I wish you were getting this. You should be mature enough to teach others, but it seems you have lost your passion for Jesus and are trying only to protect yourselves.

- Though I write strong words, I am confident that you will continue in our faith in Jesus.
- After all, God has made absolute promises of care toward us that are our hope.
- And Jesus is the only anchor we have today to ensure that we will receive what was promise.

• After all, Jesus is a priest after the order of Melchizedek.

- The Levitical order priests could not fully satisfy needs, since its sacrifices needed repeating.
- That is why someone from Melchizedek's order was needed.
  - Someone who was a descendant of David (of the tribe of Judah), perfect and never dying.
- This brings us back to the main thing we have been saying: Jesus is the best high priest ever.
  - He is God (seated at the right hand of the majesty in heaven).
  - He is owner of the house of God.
  - He is high priest of the house of God.
    - The true house of God, with dimensions given by God on the mountain.
    - The visible house of God, here below (under the care of the Levitical priests), important as it is, is only a shadow of the real thing.
  - He is faultless.
  - He is the mediator of the new covenant (remember Jer 31:31–34?).
- This is very important: God found fault with the old covenant.
  - God is causing the old covenant age to come to an end.
  - Jesus is the only source of hope in the new covenant age.
- These changes are symbolized by the "houses" of the two covenant ages:
  - The tabernacle with God hidden and symbolic actions repeated.
  - The heavenly dwelling with Jesus bringing us directly to the throne.
- Both "houses" required blood sacrifice for God's people to approach God.
  - But in the earthly tabernacle, repeated animal sacrifices by Levitical priests were needed.
  - While in the heavenly dwelling, Jesus offered himself once for all.
- Thus, Jesus is the best mediator and the only source of our eternal security.

- ♦ The tabernacle and Levitical priesthood were only types of this ultimate expression of God's love.

- But keep in mind that there is a symbiotic relationship between the first and second expressions of God's covenant:

  - ♦ The first is the shadow—the meaningful but repetitious type.

  - ♦ While the second is the substance—the perfection of all things through Jesus.

- Jesus has accomplished everything that is necessary and now rules over all, in an age where the new covenant is written on hearts and forgiveness is complete.

Message: One Bible, Two Testaments

As parents of three wonderful daughters, my wife and I can sympathize with the couple who sent their child off to college, only to find out a few months later that she was dating another student and that the two of them were already talking about marriage. The troubled parents urged their daughter to bring her boyfriend home so that they could meet him. When the college twosome arrived and hurried and worried greetings were made at the door, Mom shunted her daughter off to the kitchen while Dad guided the boy firmly into the family room for a little heart-to-heart.

"So," Dad said at last, trying to find out more about this young man, "what are your plans for your future?"

"I'm not sure, sir," the boyfriend replied, "but I know that your daughter and I were destined to be together and that God will provide."

"Well, what about finances? How do you intend to pay the bills if you should get married?"

"To tell you the truth, sir, we haven't given that much thought yet. But we are deeply in love and we are confident that God will provide."

This was not giving the father much confidence, so he pressed on. "Do you have any ideas about careers, where you will live, and whether you will both finish college?"

"We're planning to take it one day at a time, sir," came the reply, "and we're sure that God will provide."

Later that night Mom and Dad were finally alone together, and she said to him, "Well, what do you think?"

"I have mixed feelings," he told her. "On the one hand, the fellow seems to be a deluded, shiftless, irresponsible fool who hasn't even begun to understand how life works. Yet on the other hand, I get the sense that he thinks I am God."

The Human Quest

There is much of that family's conundrum in the way we all live out our existences here. Partly, we breeze through our days and experiences, believing that we can make it on our own no matter what. At the same time, we wrestle with resources and responsibilities, knowing that there are some moral values and cosmic principles which affirm certain directions and activities in life, while denying and negating or punishing others. Caught somewhere in between is our mixed hope and dread that a higher power out there will fill in the gaps and accommodate our weaknesses and make things right when we mess up. We truck along, blissfully in love with others or ourselves or our careers or our daily duties, trusting that "God will provide," whatever we assume "God" to be or mean.

From a historian's viewpoint, it is obvious that the human race is incurably religious and cannot seem to free itself from god-talk, or the language of mystery and transcendence. At the same time, no religion has been able to argue clearly, from within the system of human experience, that a particular deity is inescapably present or that any peculiar worldview is undeniably true, coherent, or all-encompassing. Thus, for several religious systems divine revelation is a necessary corollary, even though what is needed by humanity and what is offered from above are both hotly debated.

Is revelation a form of clarity and insight that rightly discovers the true nature of things, which we are unable to investigate without transcendent help? Or is revelation the accumulating experiences of those who have sought meaning, helping us to stand on the shoulders of others until we can see further? Or is revelation an injection of supernatural knowledge into our limited reasonings, from outside the system, by the one who created the system? Or is revelation an intrusion of divine activity into the human arena, leaving clues and fossils and symbols which must then be interpreted and applied?

The religion of the Bible assumes that all of our experiential reality had a beginning, a big bang explosion that fashioned everything we encounter out of previous nothingness. It also declares that this rigging of substance out of matter and energy was the act of a benevolent and all-powerful Creator. And, the Bible declares this deity desires an on-going relationship with the worlds that have been brought into being. More particularly, according to both Old and New Testaments, this God nurtures a special longing to engage the human race as a partner in the journey of life. Humankind is, so we are informed, God's unique and crowning species within the grand complexity of molecules and moons, of fish and fowl, of galaxies and granite, of emotions and electrons.

But in its understanding of this on-going friendly arm-wrestling between Creator and creature, biblical religion is deeply rooted in human history. The Bible does not merely talk about values and ideas or morals on which to construct easier lives. Nor is it a set of centering exercises which will keep the imminent more fully tuned to the transcendent. Instead, the story put forward in biblical literature is that the creatures of earth have lost their ability to apprehend or understand their Creator, and that the deity must necessarily take not only the first but also many recurring steps, in an effort to reconnect with them. So, revelation is a concept involving both action and content. God must somehow interrupt the normal course of human affairs in a way that will catch our attention. And when we have stopped to notice or ponder or even recoil in fright, there must be some information which we can use in a way that allows and encourages us to rethink the meaning of all things.

Reading the Bible Again for the First Time

This is clearly at the heart of Hebrews and the author's intent as he keeps writing about (Old Testament) Scripture, the sacrifices and ceremonies of the past, and the coming of Jesus. God is clearly the source and authority of life, according to all biblical literature, including this treatise. And God has interrupted human history in two major ways: first through the events of the exodus and Sinai covenant that created Israel as a missional nation, and then second in the unusual and unrepeatable incarnation of deity into the person of Jesus Christ. All of the literature of the Bible is gathered around these two redemptive events and their implications. For this reason, the Pentateuch and the Gospels are the critical elements shaping the biblical religion. They are not codes of law or wise ethical teachings from a distinguished school of thought; they are the documents articulating an unusual intrusion of divine will into the human arena for the threefold purpose of actively transforming lives by redemptive transactions, teaching the Creator's original worldview and establishing a missional community which will live out and disseminate those perspectives.

Appended to these central documents are the on-going declarations of guidance provided by divinely authorized and spiritually attuned spokespersons, who called others to remember the redemptive events and their significance, and challenged them to live as if these things matter. In the Old Testament expression of biblical religion, these persons are identified as "prophets"—those who speak on behalf of God; in the New Testament, they are called "apostles"—those who are sent by God.

Finally, accreted to these collections are a few other writings that became recognized by the faith community for their depth of spiritual insight or for their helpful clarification of recurring issues. Whether by divine determination or political maneuvering or the whims of history (or even, perhaps, some combination of all of these), the resulting literary product came to its current shape and is known as the Bible. It cannot be fully understood apart from its assumptions about divine revelation. Yet at the same time, it does not presume to be merely a trans-historical injection of supernatural mysteries into the human arena for the use of those who alone are inducted into secret societies where the mind of God is supposedly explored.

Focused on Jesus

If the Bible is to have any on-going religious value, its two historical nodes of divine redemptive activity have to be taken seriously, as the writer of Hebrews constantly asserts. Stripped of the exodus/Sinai covenant, or of the redemptive divinity of Jesus, the Bible makes little sense. Suddenly its moral codes are no better than others that have been formed and articulated at various points throughout history; its pilgrimage images are little different from other quests for significance and the sacred, and its personalities become only another bunch of interesting heroes and drifters who give moral lessons through their flawed frolicking.

But if there is a God, and if that God wished to reclaim, by creatorial right, a relationship with those brought into being as an extension of the divine fellowship and heavenly energy, the Bible makes a good deal of sense. It is a collection of covenant documents which trace the divine redemptive mission through two stages: its early history in locating a transformed community at the crossroads of human society in order to be seen and desired, and its later expression through an expanding and transforming presence in every culture, that tells the story of God along with the other tales of life. These two manifestations of divine redemptive activity are inextricably intertwined. Yet the latter supersedes the former, according to Hebrews (and the rest of the New Testament along with it). For just as a thing and its shadow cannot be separated, God's intents and dealing with the world through ancient Israel and through Jesus are irreducibly linked. Yet also, just as the shadow is produced by the thing that substantively norms its size, shape, and motion, and not the other way around, it is only through God's second great redemptive act that the first one is more fully understood. The Old Testament may not give us a clear picture of Jesus, but when Jesus comes, what happened in the Old Testament is suddenly more fully understood. The shadow testifies to the substance, while the substance give reason for the shadow.

Like the rest of literature, the Bible can be ignored or misread or improperly used. But like the best of literature, when allowed to speak from its own frame of reference, and respected as a collection of documents that are inherently seeking to enhance human life rather than deviously attempting to exploit it, the Bible is truly, in a very powerful and exciting way, the Word of God.

Chapter 15

Let's Keep Going

The Text: Hebrew 10:19–25

Therefore, my friends, since we have confidence to enter the
sanctuary by the blood of Jesus, by the new and living way that
he opened for us through the curtain (that is, through his flesh),
and since we have a great priest over the house of God, let us
approach with a true heart in full assurance of faith, with our
hearts sprinkled clean from an evil conscience and our bodies
washed with pure water. Let us hold fast to the confession of
our hope without wavering, for he who has promised is faithful. And let us consider how to provoke one another to love and
good deeds, not neglecting to meet together, as is the habit of
some, but encouraging one another, and all the more as you see
the Day approaching.

The Backstory: Faithful in Urgent Times

HEBREWS IS UNQUESTIONABLY BUILT upon the foundation of Old Testament
linear thought. It tells of the progression in God's activities with human history, pointing to specific events like the revelations at Sinai, the construction
of the tabernacle, and the ministry of the prophets. This unfolding redemptive work of God has recently reached its apex, according to Hebrews, in the
coming of Jesus (Hebrews 1:1–4). Everything—past, present, and future—
becomes meaningful only as it intersects with Jesus Christ. Jesus' entrance

into human time has changed even our understanding of time and we are now living in the new messianic era.

Although there are many smaller sections and parenthetical notes, the thrust of Hebrews as a whole is on explaining the unique identity and role of Jesus, and drawing out the implications this has for all who know him:

- Jesus is the superior way to God (Hebrews 1–6):

    - Angels delivered the Torah, but Jesus is himself the living Word (chapters 1–2).

    - Moses received the Torah, but Jesus is a new and living symbol (chapters 3–4) of God among us.

    - Aaron and the priests sacrificed daily and yearly, but Jesus sacrificed himself once for all (chapters 5–6).

- Therefore Jesus is like Melchizedek, uniquely filling a mediatorial role (Heb 7–10).

- So keep following him in spite of challenges and tribulations (Heb 10–13).

Since Jesus has entered our history as the definitive revelation of God's eternal plans and designs, he has fulfilled the intent of the sacrificial system and thus made it obsolete. This message, along with the enthusiasm of the divine Spirit, energizes the community of faith that now spreads its witness in this messianic age as the Christian church.

Steeped as he is in Jewish culture and covenantal outlook, the author reduces all of life to the symbolic representations of the tabernacle. When God took up residence on earth, the furnishings of the tabernacle were designed to provide means by which sinful human beings could approach a holy deity. In the tabernacle courtyard, on the altar of burnt offering, a sacrificial transaction took place, atoning for inner sin and alienation from God. The Bronze Sea standing nearby, although used only by the priests and Levites, symbolized the external cleansing necessary when making contact with Yahweh. In the holy place, the first room of the tabernacle proper, were the visible representations of fellowship—a table always prepared for mealtime hospitality, a lamp giving light for Yahweh and his guests, and the altar of incense which, with its sweet smells, overcame the stench of animal sacrifices outside and created a pleasant atmosphere for relaxed conversation. Finally, intimacy with God could be had by passing through the curtain and stepping into the throne room itself, the most holy place. Here, the ark of the covenant, with its mercy seat throne, was the actual place where Yahweh appeared to his people. Because this spiritual journey was too large a leap for most sinfully compromised humans to make, access was granted and taken only once a year in the person and representative acts of the high priest. Israel, as a people, met Yahweh in the tabernacle (the "house of God") through these symbolic representations.

What Jesus has recently done, according to Hebrews, is short-circuited these feeble and repetitious efforts at renewing human relations with God. He did this by fulfilling all the deep-down meanings of these practices in the grand once-and-for-all activity of his death and resurrection. Now the old meanings, good and proper as they were, are connected to new symbols: the cross becomes the altar of burnt offering; Baptism is the cleansing washing that replaces the waters of the Bronze Sea; the Lord's Supper is the on-going experience of the hospitality table; the Holy Spirit is the illuminating presence previously offered by the lamp; prayers (both ours and Jesus') form the new incense that sweetens the atmosphere when we seek God; and the most holy place, with its Mercy Seat atop the ark of the covenant, is nothing less than God's grand throne room in heaven itself. Indeed, if the microcosm worldview of the tabernacle is expanded and inverted, we can sketch out the meaning of Jesus and the true religion of our lives as a journey from outside the camp into the holy presence of God.

It is obvious from the writer's argument that he and those he is addressing are deeply steeped in the worldview, culture, practices and religious rites of Judaism. Not only so, but theirs is a conservative, orthodox, historical understanding of the religion of Israel. The Old Testament is the revelation of God, and Israel holds a special place in transmitting the divine outlook and purposes with the human race. Israel's identity was shaped around its religious ceremonies which themselves emanated from the tabernacle, its furnishings, and its symbolism. From his review and comparison, interjecting the recent revelation of God in Jesus, the author makes a bold statement. We are, he indicates, all on a religious pilgrimage. We are all seeking God, who alone provides mercy in this troubling world. In this quest we rely on external symbols to make the spiritual connections, but not all external symbols are equal in their efficacy. Only Jesus can get us where we want and need to go. Therefore, in these pressing times of looming persecution, don't neglect your connection with Jesus.

Although the author shares these perspectives with his audience, there appears to be one significant difference between him and them: the writer of Hebrews fully believes Jesus has ushered in a culminating change that transcends and makes obsolete these previous expressions of religious identity, while his readers, due to cultural pressures around them, are not as certain about that. This treatise is being written precisely to convince a community, which is on the verge of slipping away from Jesus back into a pre-Jesus Jewish ritualistic context, that such a move would be both unwise and inappropriate.

Where Have We Come So Far?

- God has spoken in times past.
  - ◆ This is our source of direction and confidence.
  - ◆ We know who we are because of the prophets.
- God has recently spoken a stronger, better, and clearer message through Jesus.
  - ◆ So when we, who live by the prophetic message, hear Jesus, we had better listen.
- Jesus is superior to the angels.
  - ◆ The great divine message that formed us came through Moses, but the message itself was delivered to him by angels (Deut 33:2; Acts 7:53).
  - ◆ Yet Jesus is superior to angels, and therefore delivers a more important prophetic message than that through the great prophet Moses.
- So, stick with Jesus, even though you are tempted to turn away from him.
  - ◆ There is no higher authority or source of connection with God.
  - ◆ And if our lives are to be connected to God, we turn away from Jesus to our own peril.
- God has made the world subject to Jesus.
  - ◆ God never did this with the angels, so, again, Jesus is superior to them.
  - ◆ But this only happened because Jesus first fully identified with the world.
- Jesus willingly came into the world to fully experience its pain.
- And this is to our benefit for three reasons:
  - ◆ To fully identify with us as sisters and brothers.
  - ◆ To make atonement for our sins (which cause the pain of this world).

- ◆ To bring us with him fully into the house of God.
- So Jesus is greater than (over) the angels, but Jesus is also greater than (over) Moses.
- Therefore, be careful that you don't disconnect from Jesus (who is God):
    - ◆ Remember how those in our past who disconnected from God came under punishment.
    - ◆ The same can happen to you if you do not stay true and committed to Jesus.
- Let God's people in the earlier redemptive sequence be your instructors:
    - ◆ Like us, they were saved and led to their "(sabbath) rest" in the promised land.
        - ▪ But they failed to stay connected to God by way of the word of the prophet (Moses) and died before reading "rest."
    - ◆ Now God has promised us a coming "rest" (i.e., "heaven" when we die).
        - ▪ But we will receive it only if we remain connected to God by way of the word of the prophet (Jesus) and live faithfully through these trials.
- And, again, the only one who can keep you connected to God is Jesus:
    - ◆ He is our true high priest, who will take us boldly to God's merciful throne through his actions on our behalf on the Day of Atonement. He is fully human, so he completely understands the struggles of our lives and sympathizes deeply, to the point of anguished cries.
- In fact, he is as fully committed to fulfilling the mandate and responsibilities of his priestly order as are others.
    - ◆ They in their "Aaronic/Levitical priestly order."
    - ◆ He in his "Melchizedek priestly order."
- I wish you were getting this. You should be mature enough to teach others, but it seems you have lost your passion for Jesus and are trying only to protect yourselves.
    - ◆ Though I write strong words, I am confident that you will continue in our faith in Jesus.

- After all, God has made absolute promises of care toward us that are our hope.
- And Jesus is the only anchor we have today to ensure that we will receive what was promise.

- After all, Jesus is a priest after the order of Melchizedek.
  - The Levitical order priests could not fully satisfy needs, since its sacrifices needed repeating.
  - That is why someone from Melchizedek's order was needed.
    - Someone who was a descendant of David (of the tribe of Judah), perfect and never dying.
- This brings us back to the main thing we have been saying: Jesus is the best high priest ever.
  - He is God (seated at the right hand of the majesty in heaven).
  - He is owner of the house of God.
  - He is high priest of the house of God.
    - The true house of God, with dimensions given by God on the mountain.
    - The visible house of God, here below (under the care of the Levitical priests), important as it is, is only a shadow of the real thing.
  - He is faultless.
  - He is the mediator of the new covenant (remember Jer 31:31–34?).
- This is very important: God found fault with the old covenant.
  - God is causing the old covenant age to come to an end.
  - Jesus is the only source of hope in the new covenant age.
- These changes are symbolized by the "houses" of the two covenant ages:
  - The tabernacle with God hidden and symbolic actions repeated.
  - The heavenly dwelling with Jesus bringing us directly to the throne.
- Both "houses" required blood sacrifice for God's people to approach God.

- • But in the earthly tabernacle, repeated animal sacrifices by Levitical priests were needed.

- • While in the heavenly dwelling, Jesus offered himself once for all.

- Thus, Jesus is the best mediator and the only source of our eternal security.

    - • The tabernacle and Levitical priesthood were only types of this ultimate expression of God's love.

- But keep in mind that there is a symbiotic relationship between the first and second expressions of God's covenant:

    - • The first is the shadow—the meaningful but repetitious type.

    - • While the second is the substance—the perfection of all things through Jesus.

- Jesus has accomplished everything that is necessary and now rules over all, in an age where the new covenant is written on hearts and forgiveness is complete.

- So, let's go! Grab each other, keep your focus, and let's let Jesus take us right to God's throne of grace.

Message: Carry On

Anne Sexton wrote a volume of poetry describing her religious journey as *The Awful Rowing Toward God.*[1] Faith is difficult, she said in her poems, not so much because God wants it to be that way but because other elements including our own hearts conspire against us on the journey.

In her concluding poem, "The Rowing Endeth," Anne pictured herself docking her spiritual boat at the island of God's home. There she sat down to play poker with God, attempting to win access to God's wealth. In the heat of the game she knew she held a winning hand, laying down a straight royal flush. Even God couldn't beat that.

But God only smiled and spread down a hand of *five* aces. The joke was on Anne and they laughed together in great gusto, echoing grace to the corners of heaven.

It was a strange parable that Anne Sexton penned, yet one rich with biblical meaning, connected deeply to the situation addressed by Hebrews. Like these early Christians, we are forever playing games with God, trying

1. Sexton, *Awful Rowing.*

to win heavenly chips and bankroll divine mercy. Still, sly and wily as we might be, God always manages to pull out a trump card we never expected. Sometimes it even seems like God isn't playing by the rules (our rules, of course). Yet when God shows his hand and takes the game, it is only to share the winnings with us in lavish ways we didn't deserve.

Anne's picture is a delightful portrait of grace. The same is true of Hebrews' encouragement to us in these verses. Grace, as many have written, is very difficult to define. Frederick Buechner said that most tears are grace, as is the smell of rain and having somebody love you. Lewis Smedes said that grace is amazing because it works against our common sense. Inside we know that we are too weak, too harassed, and too human to change for the better, and life shouts that we are caught in a rut of fate or futility; yet God somehow gives us a tomorrow better than we could have chosen for ourselves, were we to have the strength to make it happen. That's grace.

A friend of mine knows it too well. One day she took me out to lunch and spilled another tale of woe. Life has been very unkind to her. Few of us could survive with the hand she has been dealt. Even when she tries to play with the cards she has, the numbers on them keep changing, and she must start all over learning the game.

Three things, however, have made it possible for her to keep going: friends who cared enough to look past her quirks and craziness, medications that kept her from winding up a bag-lady on the streets, and grace. At every corner in her life, just as the traffic was threatening her from both directions, God met her. God took her hand. God played a trump card and she had safe passage to the next corner.

Call it chance, if you will. Call it luck. Maybe it was all in the cards.

But then, with Anne Sexton, the writer of Hebrews calls for us to believe in the one who dealt them. And, with these struggling people of wavering faith, in the one who holds five aces when needed.

Chapter 16

The Grace of Reproof

Text: Hebrews 10:26–39

For if we willfully persist in sin after having received the knowledge of the truth, there no longer remains a sacrifice for sins, but a fearful prospect of judgment, and a fury of fire that will consume the adversaries. Anyone who has violated the law of Moses dies without mercy "on the testimony of two or three witnesses."[1] How much worse punishment do you think will be deserved by those who have spurned the Son of God, profaned the blood of the covenant by which they were sanctified, and outraged the Spirit of grace? For we know the one who said, "Vengeance is mine, I will repay."[2] And again, "The Lord will judge his people."[3] It is a fearful thing to fall into the hands of the living God.

But recall those earlier days when, after you had been enlightened, you endured a hard struggle with sufferings, sometimes being publicly exposed to abuse and persecution, and sometimes being partners with those so treated. For you had compassion for those who were in prison, and you cheerfully accepted the plundering of your possessions, knowing that you yourselves possessed something better and more lasting. Do not, therefore, abandon that confidence of yours; it brings a great reward. For you need endurance, so that when you have

---

1. Deut 19:15.
2. Deut 32:35.
3. Ps 135:14.

done the will of God, you may receive what was promised. For yet

"in a very little while, the one who is coming will come and will not delay;but my righteous one will live by faith.[4] My soul takes no pleasure in anyone who shrinks back."[5]

But we are not among those who shrink back and so are lost, but among those who have faith and so are saved.

Backstory: Learning from Forebears

WHILE THERE IS A deep and strong theological teaching at the heart of Hebrews, the purpose of the document as a whole is a call to stay true to Jesus during a very challenging time in which these readers were tempted to slink back into the protective shelter of ceremonial Judaism because Christians were being persecuted while Jews were not. We learn a bit more about the background and context of these readers in Hebrews 10:32–34. But first comes a strident admonition, the first of three parts in this next "Altar Call."[6]

The initial phase is another stern warning,[7] pulling together the stories, ideas, and themes that had previously appeared in the two earlier "Altar Calls." Near the beginning of this treatise, in Hebrew 3:7–19, the readers were reminded of their Israelite ancestors who died in the wilderness on the way to the promised land, never setting foot in Canaan. Even though the tribes had together experienced the miraculous deliverance of God from Egypt, and trembled before Yahweh in their covenant encounter at Mount Sinai, they lost this trust before receiving the fullness of what God had in store for them. The result was a forty-year wilderness campout which eventually accomplished the deaths of the entire generation of faithless followers. Then later, in Hebrews 5:11–6:3, the author chides his addressees for being dull and for failing to mature. The comparison is to that of children who are difficult students or who do not grow up, and therefore always need repetitive teachings. Appended to that admonition is a reminder of the "falling

---

4. Hab 2:3–4.

5. This part of the quote from Hab 2:3–4 is clearly derived from the Septuagint version, although there are some unusual terms recorded, both from obscure variations of the textual traditions and also, seemingly, influences from Ps 85:8; Ezek 3:20; 18:24; and/or Zeph 1:6.

6. Note the earlier ones in Heb 3:7–19 and 5:11–6:3.

7. Heb 10:26–31.

away" of the ancient Israelites,[8] which provides the theme for this section of the current "Altar Call."

Remembering Shared Experiences

Part two gets personal. In Hebrews 10:32–34 we learn a lot about those to whom Hebrews was written, through a staccato series of recollections:

- The process of coming to faith in Jesus for them began with an "enlightenment" (32).[9]
- Early on, after becoming Christians, they "struggled" and "suffered" (33).
- They were publicly abused and persecuted, along with family and friends (33).
- Some were imprisoned (34).
- Many had their property confiscated (34).
- Through all of this they had been cheerful, strong, and had endured (34).

These descriptors help us understand both the original readers of Hebrews and also something of their times and circumstances. Most illumining is, in fact, the reference to their "enlightenment" in verse 32. This was an expression used by Paul, the master architect of early Christian theology, to indicate the coming-to-faith of gentiles. In Ephesians 4:17–24 Paul uses the idea of darkness and darkened minds to describe gentiles apart from salvation in Jesus.[10] It is clear, from the context, that Paul is deliberately applying this metaphor to gentiles and not to Jews. In Ephesians 2:11 he addresses these

---

8. Heb 6:4–8

9. Heb 10:32. The Greek word used is φωτισθέντες, which means "having been illumined or enlightened." This is the only occurrence of the word in the Bible. It seems to have the same meaning as the φωτισθέντας used in Hebrews 6:4 (which is the only use of that word in the Bible).

10. "Now this I affirm and insist on in the Lord: you must no longer live as the Gentiles live, in the futility of their minds. They are darkened in their understanding, alienated from the life of God because of their ignorance and hardness of heart. They have lost all sensitivity and have abandoned themselves to licentiousness, greedy to practice every kind of impurity. That is not the way you learned Christ! For surely you have heard about him and were taught in him, as truth is in Jesus. You were taught to put away your former way of life, your old self, corrupt and deluded by its lusts, and to be renewed in the spirit of your minds, and to clothe yourselves with the new self, created according to the likeness of God in true righteousness and holiness."

readers as "you Gentiles by birth," repeating this nomenclature in verses 12, 13 and 19. Immediately following comes Paul's strong testimony that he has been called to witness to gentiles.[11] So, when Paul uses darkness and coming to light as the process of gentiles being drawn into faith, he is employing the same metaphorical move as the writer of Hebrews does in 6:4 and 10:32.

This is very significant. The gentile Christian Paul addresses in Ephesians were likely brought into Christianity without first becoming participants in the Jewish ceremonial community. They came from the "darkness" of alienation from their Creator into the light of understanding through the teachings, ministry, and redemptive death and resurrection of Jesus.

A Unique Religious Journey and Community

These Christians addressed by the author of Hebrews, however, knew a different path. The whole focus of the letter is on their hesitancy to stay with Jesus and their tendency to slip into the ritualized religion of Jewish ceremonialism. Yet these early Christians seem to be Jews by affiliation while also, apparently, gentiles by birth and background. This would likely mean that they were first proselytes to Judaism before coming to appreciate Jesus as the Jewish Messiah. The term προσήλυτος is used is used in the Septuagint as a Greek translation of the Hebrew term for those who were "strangers" (אֶת־הַגֵּרִים) in Israel, yet nevertheless participated in the life and culture of God's people.[12] The Sinai covenant gave specific regulations regarding admission into Israelite identity and status those who were not born from Abraham's bloodlines.[13]

During the reign of Solomon, 153,600 of these "strangers" were actually numbered, in a national census, as a meaningful subgroup of Israel.[14] Later, the prophets speak of a time coming in the future when these "strangers" would eventually share fully in all the privileges of Israel.[15] So deeply was this anticipated expansive nature of the witness and people of

11. Eph 3:1–13.

12. See 1 Chr 22:2, and compare with Exod 12:48; 20:10; and 22:21, along with Isa 56:3; Neh 10:28; and Esth 8:17.

13. Exod 12:19; 12:48; 20:10; 23:12; Deut 5:14; 16:11; 16:14, among others. The Kenites, Gibeonites, Cherethites, and Pelethites were all admitted to the privileges of Israelites through these ritual processes. This is why a number of non-Israelites are identified among the military leadership of the nation, over time (e.g., Doeg the Edomite, Uriah the Hittite, Araunah the Jebusite, Zelek the Ammonite, Ithmah and Ebedmelech the Ethiopians).

14. 2 Chr 2:17.

15. Isa 2:2; 11:10; 56:3–6; Ezek 47:22; Mic 4:1.

God engrained in the faith community that by New Testament times, "proselytes" are mentioned regularly as part of the Jewish communities that then experienced conversions to Christianity.[16]

Jewish rabbis distinguished "proselytes" within two types. Based on the explanations regarding cessation of work on the Sabbath in the Fourth Commandment,[17] one form of "alien" was the "stranger of the gate." These "proselytes" within Israel (and later, Judaism) were not required to be circumcised nor to comply with the Mosaic ceremonial law. If they desired to remain among God's people as permanent members of the larger community, however, they were required to abide by what were termed the "Seven Precepts of Noah."[18] These were commands forbidding idolatry, blasphemy, bloodshed, uncleaness, the eating of blood, and theft, and the instruction to obey Jewish authorities. Added to these laws, later, were requirements to abstain from work on the Sabbath and to refrain from eating leavened bread during the time of the Passover.

On the other hand, "proselytes of righteousness" were perceived to be full, devout participants within Jewish communities of faith.[19] These gentiles were completely bound to all the doctrines and practices of the Jewish social and ceremonial systems and, because of this, were allowed to become members of the synagogue in full communion. In other words, the "proselytes of righteousness" had, in fact, fully become Jews in lifestyle, beliefs, identity, and practices, even though they were born outside of the Jewish faith and biological threadings.

The term "proselyte" appears in the New Testament four times,[20] always describing this latter type of gentile proselyte to Judaism. Although born outside of Jewish genealogies, these gentiles in ethnic origin had crossed the threshold to become Jews in identity and practices. They are also referred to as "devout men," or men "fearing God" or "worshipping God."

16. Luke 7:5; Acts 10:2; 10:7; 13:42–43; 13:50; 17:4; 18:7.

17. "Remember the sabbath day, and keep it holy. Six days you shall labor and do all your work. But the seventh day is a sabbath to the Lord your God; you shall not do any work—you, your son or your daughter, your male or female slave, your livestock, or the alien resident in your towns. For in six days the Lord made heaven and earth, the sea, and all that is in them, but rested the seventh day; therefore the Lord blessed the sabbath day and consecrated it" (Exod 20:8–11).

18. According to rabbinical teachings that took shape in medieval Europe, since Noah lived prior to the declarations of the Sinai covenant but was considered a leader of God's people within God's redemptive history, he had received a set of social norms that governed all people who wished to affiliate with the family of faith. See Hilkhot M'lakhim 9:1 and Bavli, Sanhedrin 59a, among other references in the Talmud.

19. Note the reference to such people in Acts 13:43.

20. Matt 23:15; Acts 2:10; 6:5; 13:43.

The initial recipients of Hebrews appear to have emerged from this gentile-cum-Jew-cum-Christian branch of the early church. At one point, from the "darkness" of non-Jewish and non-Christian alienation from God, they had become "enlightened" and moved, originally, into a pious and practicing Jewish community with a major Roman population center, becoming "proselytes of righteousness." They gained a strong attachment to Jewish rituals and theology, identifying completely with Israelite history and cultic ceremonial practices.

At some point, however, as the news about Jesus raced through the Jewish communities, these "proselytes" took a next step and were converted to Christianity.

This was doubly challenging, because Jews who did not receive Jesus as their Messiah initiated a new alienation from the very community that originally welcomed, taught, and affirmed them. At the same time, the Roman government was becoming aware of this rapidly growing religious group, and a number of emperors began pogroms against it. This apparently was when, not that long ago, they "struggled" and "suffered,"[21] were publicly abused and persecuted, along with family and friends,[22] some were imprisoned,[23] and many had their property confiscated.[24]

Although during that time of persecution these readers had remained strong, fortified by their faith and its commitments in a cheerful expression of endurance,[25] things were different now. They were losing heart and hope, with some drifting away from the group. Many were becoming disillusioned, perhaps by Jesus' delay in returning to take them in the promised land of culmination, recreation, and perfection. And the strength of mutual care through crisis was unraveling. These people were threatened and many escaped the constant attacks by not mentioning Jesus any longer, easing away from identifiable Christian groups and practices and remelding into the ancient familiarity of ritualized Jewish ceremonies.

A Stern Voice from the Past

At this point, the author of Hebrews moves into part three of his current "Altar Call." He stridently demands that they stay true through the increasing

21. Heb 10:33.
22. Heb 10:33.
23. Heb 10:34.
24. Heb 10:34.
25. Heb 10:34.

challenges,[26] asserting through the bleakness of these oppressive mists, the rewards asserted by God will shortly emerge.

Once again, his incredible mastery of the Scriptures (Hebrew Bible) are astounding. He reaches into one of the mini minor prophets and pulls out a promise given at another moment of crisis to a previous faithful follower who was then questioning his religious commitments. The voice of God which had once righted Habakkuk when he nearly fell from faith now resonates for the readers of Hebrews.

By the time the seventh century BC rolled around, Israel's prophets were rarely welcome in the royal palaces, even though all that was left of the once proud and expansive nation was a tiny mountainous territory now called Judah. During the 600s, although Assyria kept threatening Jerusalem, that bully nation was increasingly occupied in defending itself against its rebellious eastern province of Babylon. During those years, while Jeremiah developed his gloomy diatribes in the heart of the capital city, several among "the Twelve" also made brief statements about coming judgment. Zephaniah (630–610 BC) provided a few paragraphs against Judah and the nations that surrounded it,[27] couching the imminent intervention of Yahweh in the increasingly common term, "the Day of the Lord." In a final, somewhat lengthier chapter, Zephaniah turned his attention toward restoration and renewal, pointing to a future time when the fortunes of Yahweh's people would be made full once again.

Also, for just a brief moment (probably around 615 BC), Nahum renewed the mission of Jonah against Nineveh and the Assyrians. This time, however, there was no outcome of repentance and restoration. Instead, the short-lived turnabout that had followed Jonah's challenge evaporated entirely, and Nahum declared irreversible divine judgment against this fierce kingdom which had wreaked so much havoc on its neighbors in the Fertile Crescent. Yahweh's word through Nahum would come true a few years later when the Assyrians were trounced by the Babylonians, first in the destruction of the capital city of Nineveh (612 BC), then at their secondary administrative center Harran (610 BC), and decisively in the battle of Carchemish (605 BC), where even the allied armies of Egypt proved insufficient to turn the Chaldean tide.

Finally, during this era as well, came the disconcerting dialogue between Habakkuk and Yahweh. Formulated around the year 600 BC, just as Babylon was rapidly overwhelming the whimpering remnants of the old Assyrian regime, Habakkuk asked Yahweh a series of questions which were

---

26. Heb 10:35–39.

27. Zeph 1–2.

answered in ways that almost brought more pain than the situations they were supposed to resolve. If summarized, the conversation would sound something like this:

> Habakkuk: "Why do you ignore the social evils that plague our land (Judah)?" (1:1–4).
>
> Yahweh: "I'm working on it. Very soon now I will bring punishment through my dreaded scourge, the growing Babylonian conquest machine that is rolling through the area" (1:5–11).
>
> Habakkuk: "O God, no! You can't do that! They are even worse than the most evil among us! How can you talk about balancing the scales of justice with such an unfair sentence?" (1:12–2:1).
>
> Yahweh: "I understand your frustration. That's why I'm giving you a message for all to hear. The sins of my people are terrible, and require drastic measures. For this reason, I am bringing the Babylonians against them. But the Babylonians, too, are my people, and will come under my judgment for the wickedness they perform. In the end, all will bow to me, as is appropriate when nations come to know that I am the only true God. So hang in there; after all, the just will live by faith, and I will hold on to him" (2:2–20).

At this point Habakkuk breaks into a song of confidence and trust (chapter 3) that rivals anything found in the Psalms. Habakkuk charts the terrifying movements of Yahweh on earth, bringing death and destruction as the divine judgments swirl. But in the end, Habakkuk raises a marvelous testimony of faith.

The strong divine encouragement Habakkuk noted in 2:3–4 of his short prophecy now becomes the rousing voice of God for Hebrews' struggling readers. Just as God's message would soon emerge in the form of deliverance for Habakkuk and his community,[28] so Jesus will soon return to affirm these weary gentile-Jewish Christians and reward them for steadfast perseverance.[29] Of course, only those who are "righteous"[30] and who hang on till all is resolved[31] will share in the delights of that culmination.

28. Hab 2:3.
29. Heb 11:37.
30. Hab 2:4.
31. Heb 11:38.

Where Have We Come So Far?

- God has spoken in times past.
  - This is our source of direction and confidence.
  - We know who we are because of the prophets.
- God has recently spoken a stronger, better, and clearer message through Jesus.
  - So when we, who live by the prophetic message, hear Jesus, we had better listen.
- Jesus is superior to the angels.
  - The great divine message that formed us came through Moses, but the message itself was delivered to him by angels (Deut 33:2; Acts 7:53).
  - Yet Jesus is superior to angels, and therefore delivers a more important prophetic message than that through the great prophet Moses.
- So, stick with Jesus, even though you are tempted to turn away from him.
  - There is no higher authority or source of connection with God.
  - And if our lives are to be connected to God, we turn away from Jesus to our own peril.
- God has made the world subject to Jesus.
  - God never did this with the angels, so, again, Jesus is superior to them.
  - But this only happened because Jesus first fully identified with the world.
- Jesus willingly came into the world to fully experience its pain.
- And this is to our benefit for three reasons:
  - To fully identify with us as sisters and brothers.
  - To make atonement for our sins (which cause the pain of this world).
  - To bring us with him fully into the house of God.
- So Jesus is greater than (over) the angels, but Jesus is also greater than (over) Moses.

- Therefore, be careful that you don't disconnect from Jesus (who is God):

  - Remember how those in our past who disconnected from God came under punishment.

  - The same can happen to you if you do not stay true and committed to Jesus.

- Let God's people in the earlier redemptive sequence be your instructors:

  - Like us, they were saved and led to their "(sabbath) rest" in the promised land.

    - But they failed to stay connected to God by way of the word of the prophet (Moses) and died before reading "rest."

  - Now God has promised us a coming "rest" (i.e., "heaven" when we die).

    - But we will receive it only if we remain connected to God by way of the word of the prophet (Jesus) and live faithfully through these trials.

- And, again, the only one who can keep you connected to God is Jesus:

  - He is our true high priest, who will take us boldly to God's merciful throne through his actions on our behalf on the Day of Atonement. He is fully human, so he completely understands the struggles of our lives and sympathizes deeply, to the point of anguished cries.

- In fact, he is as fully committed to fulfilling the mandate and responsibilities of his priestly order as are others.

  - They in their "Aaronic/Levitical priestly order."

  - He in his "Melchizedek priestly order."

- I wish you were getting this. You should be mature enough to teach others, but it seems you have lost your passion for Jesus and are trying only to protect yourselves.

  - Though I write strong words, I am confident that you will continue in our faith in Jesus.

  - After all, God has made absolute promises of care toward us that are our hope.

- ✦ And Jesus is the only anchor we have today to ensure that we will receive what was promise.

- After all, Jesus is a priest after the order of Melchizedek.
  - ✦ The Levitical order priests could not fully satisfy needs, since its sacrifices needed repeating.
  - ✦ That is why someone from Melchizedek's order was needed.
    - ▪ Someone who was a descendant of David (of the tribe of Judah), perfect and never dying.

- This brings us back to the main thing we have been saying: Jesus is the best high priest ever.
  - ✦ He is God (seated at the right hand of the majesty in heaven).
  - ✦ He is owner of the house of God.
  - ✦ He is high priest of the house of God.
    - ▪ The true house of God, with dimensions given by God on the mountain.
    - ▪ The visible house of God, here below (under the care of the Levitical priests), important as it is, is only a shadow of the real thing.
  - ✦ He is faultless.
  - ✦ He is the mediator of the new covenant (remember Jer 31:31–34?).

- This is very important: God found fault with the old covenant.
  - ✦ God is causing the old covenant age to come to an end.
  - ✦ Jesus is the only source of hope in the new covenant age.

- These changes are symbolized by the "houses" of the two covenant ages:
  - ✦ The tabernacle with God hidden and symbolic actions repeated.
  - ✦ The heavenly dwelling with Jesus bringing us directly to the throne.

- Both "houses" required blood sacrifice for God's people to approach God.
  - ✦ But in the earthly tabernacle, repeated animal sacrifices by Levitical priests were needed.

- ✦ While in the heavenly dwelling, Jesus offered himself once for all.

- Thus, Jesus is the best mediator and the only source of our eternal security.

  - ✦ The tabernacle and Levitical priesthood were only types of this ultimate expression of God's love.

- But keep in mind that there is a symbiotic relationship between the first and second expressions of God's covenant:

  - ✦ The first is the shadow—the meaningful but repetitious type.

  - ✦ While the second is the substance—the perfection of all things through Jesus.

- Jesus has accomplished everything that is necessary, and now rules over all, in an age where the new covenant is written on hearts and forgiveness is complete.

- So, let's go! Grab each other, keep your focus, and let's let Jesus take us right to God's throne of grace.

- Again, I want to remind you about those in the past who failed to keep faith with God and lost out.

  - ✦ You have come through some tough times in the past. Remember how you stayed strong?

  - ✦ Some of you seem to be dropping out now, as new threats loom. Remember that Jesus can keep us going.

Message: Stick with it

C. Knight Aldrich, a medical doctor and the first chairperson of the Department of Psychiatry at the University of Chicago (1955–1964), was a keen analyst of the motivations for our behaviors. He worked with the social services agencies of Chicago for a time, particularly spending hours with teenagers who had been arrested for shoplifting or other theft. Aldrich interviewed them to find out how they had come to this.[32] He also talked with the parents, attempting to discover how they had handled the problem from the first time they knew about it.

Over the years he kept records of his interviews, noting that they seemed to separate into two types. One group of teens became repeat

32. Aldrich, *Introduction*.

offenders and showed up in the criminal justice system again and again. The other was a collection of those who were with him one time and then stayed straight.

Dr. Aldrich concluded that there were basically two different ways that parents responded to initial shoplifting incidents. Some confronted their children with words like this: "Now we know what you're like. You're a thief. We're going to be watching you now, buddy. Don't think you can get away with this again."

The others usually said something like this: "Tom, that wasn't like you at all. We'll have to go back to the store and clear this thing up, but then it's done with, okay? What you did was wrong. You know that it was wrong. But we're sure you won't do it again."

Aldrich said that the parents who assumed the worst usually got the worst and the parents who assumed the best most often got the best. The writer of Hebrews might well be reading Aldrich's notes as he pens this section of his treatise to friends who are struggling with mounting social pressures.

Eyes of Love

Much that pretends to be Christian religion seems to have a rather negative view of the human spirit. Although the Bible speaks prophetically in judgment against blatant sinfulness, there are also many passages in Scripture that tell of God's delight in his children. More than that, the Fruit of the Spirit, which the apostle Paul says becomes the way of life for someone who is loved by God, is itself "love, joy, peace, patience, kindness, goodness, faithfulness, gentleness and self-control."[33] As God looks with tender eyes at us, so we are encouraged to view others with grace.

That can be a powerful influence in a person's life. Alan Loy McGinnis tells of attending a business conference where awards were being given for outstanding achievements during the past fiscal year.[34] A woman was called to the podium to receive the company's top honor. Clutching her trophy, she beamed out at the crowd of over three thousand people. Yet in that moment of triumph, she had eyes for only one person. She looked directly at her supervisor, a woman named Joan.

The award-winner told of the difficult times that she had gone through only a few years earlier. She had experienced personal problems, and for a

33. Gal 5:22–23.
34. McGinnis, *Bringing Out*.

time, her work had suffered. Some people turned away from her, counting it a liability to be seen with her. Others wrote her off as a loser in the company.

The worst part was that she felt they were right. She had stopped at Joan's desk several times with a letter of resignation in her hand. She knew she was a failure.

But Joan said, "Let's just wait a little bit longer. Give it one more try." And Joan said, "I never would have hired you if I didn't think you could handle it."

The woman's voice broke. Tears streamed down her cheeks as she softly said, "Joan believed in me more than I believed in myself."

From Prosecutor to Prism

Isn't that the message of the gospel? Isn't that the story of the Bible? That God believed in us while we were still sinners, while we were still failures, while we were at the point in our lives that we couldn't seem to make it on our own?

Sometimes we need the straightedge of God's righteousness in order to see how bent we are. But sometimes, as we find in the words of Hebrews' author in this passage, it helps us learn to smile at others like God has at us. Carry on. God's got your back. Remember how you made it through, by God's grace and good help, during the last crisis? You can do it again. And don't forget the divine promises and expectations that sustain you.

Chapter 17

In Good Company

Text: Hebrews 11:1–12:13

Now faith is the assurance of things hoped for, the conviction of things not seen. Indeed, by faith our ancestors received approval. By faith we understand that the worlds were prepared by the word of God, so that what is seen was made from things that are not visible.

By faith Abel offered to God a more acceptable sacrifice than Cain's. Through this he received approval as righteous, God himself giving approval to his gifts; he died, but through his faith he still speaks. By faith Enoch was taken so that he did not experience death; and "he was not found, because God had taken him."[1] For it was attested before he was taken away that "he had pleased God."[2] And without faith it is impossible to please God, for whoever would approach him must believe that he exists and that he rewards those who seek him. By faith Noah, warned by God about events as yet unseen, respected the warning and built an ark to save his household; by this he condemned the world and became an heir to the righteousness that is in accordance with faith.

By faith Abraham obeyed when he was called to set out for a place that he was to receive as an inheritance; and he set out, not knowing where he was going. By faith he stayed for a time in the land he had been promised, as in a foreign land, living

1. Gen 5:24.
2. Gen 5:23–24.

in tents, as did Isaac and Jacob, who were heirs with him of the same promise. For he looked forward to the city that has foundations, whose architect and builder is God. By faith he received power of procreation, even though he was too old—and Sarah herself was barren—because he considered him faithful who had promised. Therefore from one person, and this one as good as dead, descendants were born, "as many as the stars of heaven and as the innumerable grains of sand by the seashore."[3]

All of these died in faith without having received the promises, but from a distance they saw and greeted them. They confessed that they were strangers and foreigners on the earth, for people who speak in this way make it clear that they are seeking a homeland. If they had been thinking of the land that they had left behind, they would have had opportunity to return. But as it is, they desire a better country, that is, a heavenly one. Therefore God is not ashamed to be called their God; indeed, he has prepared a city for them.

By faith Abraham, when put to the test, offered up Isaac. He who had received the promises was ready to offer up his only son, of whom he had been told, "It is through Isaac that descendants shall be named for you."[4] He considered the fact that God is able even to raise someone from the dead—and figuratively speaking, he did receive him back. By faith Isaac invoked blessings for the future on Jacob and Esau. By faith Jacob, when dying, blessed each of the sons of Joseph, "bowing in worship over the top of his staff."[5] By faith Joseph, at the end of his life, made mention of the exodus of the Israelites and gave instructions about his burial.

By faith Moses was hidden by his parents for three months after his birth, because they saw that the child was beautiful; and they were not afraid of the king's edict. By faith Moses, when he was grown up, refused to be called a son of Pharaoh's daughter, choosing rather to share ill-treatment with the people of God than to enjoy the fleeting pleasures of sin. He considered abuse suffered for the Christ to be greater wealth than the treasures of Egypt, for he was looking ahead to the reward. By faith he left Egypt, unafraid of the king's anger; for he persevered as though he saw him who is invisible. By faith he kept the Passover and the sprinkling of blood, so that the destroyer of the firstborn would not touch the firstborn of Israel.

3. Gen 15:5.

4. Gen 17:19.

5. Gen 48:15.

By faith the people passed through the Red Sea as if it were dry land, but when the Egyptians attempted to do so they were drowned. By faith the walls of Jericho fell after they had been encircled for seven days. By faith Rahab the prostitute did not perish with those who were disobedient, because she had received the spies in peace.

And what more should I say? For time would fail me to tell of Gideon, Barak, Samson, Jephthah, of David and Samuel and the prophets—who through faith conquered kingdoms, administered justice, obtained promises, shut the mouths of lions, quenched raging fire, escaped the edge of the sword, won strength out of weakness, became mighty in war, put foreign armies to flight. Women received their dead by resurrection. Others were tortured, refusing to accept release, in order to obtain a better resurrection. Others suffered mocking and flogging, and even chains and imprisonment. They were stoned to death, they were sawn in two, they were killed by the sword; they went about in skins of sheep and goats, destitute, persecuted, tormented—of whom the world was not worthy. They wandered in deserts and mountains, and in caves and holes in the ground.

Yet all these, though they were commended for their faith, did not receive what was promised, since God had provided something better so that they would not, apart from us, be made perfect.

Therefore, since we are surrounded by so great a cloud of witnesses, let us also lay aside every weight and the sin that clings so closely, and let us run with perseverance the race that is set before us, looking to Jesus the pioneer and perfecter of our faith, who for the sake of the joy that was set before him endured the cross, disregarding its shame, and has taken his seat at the right hand of the throne of God.

Consider him who endured such hostility against himself from sinners, so that you may not grow weary or lose heart. In your struggle against sin you have not yet resisted to the point of shedding your blood. And you have forgotten the exhortation that addresses you as children—

"My child, do not regard lightly the discipline of the Lord, or lose heart when you are punished by him; for the Lord disciplines those whom he loves, and chastises every child whom he accepts."[6]

Endure trials for the sake of discipline. God is treating you as children; for what child is there whom a parent does not

6. Prov 3:11–12.

discipline? If you do not have that discipline in which all children share, then you are illegitimate and not his children. Moreover, we had human parents to discipline us, and we respected them. Should we not be even more willing to be subject to the Father of spirits and live? For they disciplined us for a short time as seemed best to them, but he disciplines us for our good, in order that we may share his holiness. Now, discipline always seems painful rather than pleasant at the time, but later it yields the peaceful fruit of righteousness to those who have been trained by it.

Therefore lift your drooping hands and strengthen your weak knees, and make straight paths for your feet,[7] so that what is lame may not be put out of joint, but rather be healed.

Backstory: Faith as Activating Conviction

THE CONCEPT OF FAITH is central in the New Testament, and a core element of Christianity. Largely expressed through a single Greek term (πιστις) and its cognates,[8] Christian faith leans heavily on Old Testament explanations of the relationship of trust between God and humans.

Hebrew Roots: Dependence and Commitment

There are six Hebrew terms that connote dimensions of faith such as belief, trust, or loyalty. Words derived from the root *bth* [בָּטַח] express safety or security. This confidence can be misdirected, as when Yahweh speaks through the prophet Ezekiel, warning those who are living in Jerusalem just before its destruction by the Babylonians that their presumed righteousness will not save them,[9] or when Hosea urges God's people against trusting in

---

7. Prov 4:26.

8. πιστις emerges from the verb πειθω, which means I persuade. As a noun, πιστις occurs 243 times in the New Testament:

πιστει—dative (fifty-eight times)
πιστεως—genitive (ninety-four times)
πιστιν—accusative (fifty-five times)
πιστις—nominative (thirty-six times)

Along with these, other forms of the word appear as verbs or modifiers:
πιστεύσετε—2; πιστεύσω—2; πιστεύσωμεν—3; πιστεύσωσιν—4; πιστεύσομεν—1; πίστευσον—2; πιστεύσουσιν—1; πιστευθῆναι—1; πιστικῆς—2; πίστει—58; πίστιν—55; πίστις—36; πιστά—2; πιστὰς—1; πιστέ—2; πιστὴ—1; πιστὴν—1; πιστῆς—1; πιστῷ—4; πιστῶν—2.

9. Ezek 33:13.

the might of armies[10] and Jeremiah dismisses the safety of wealth.[11] When the term is used regarding dependence on Yahweh, however, it is a call to deep confidence,[12] and the way of living which transcends our limited experiences.[13]

A second Hebrew root, *hsh* [חסה] focuses on a relationship of dependence between two parties. In Judges 9, for instance, when Gideon's despotic son Abimelech cruelly tyrannizes Israel, a prophet named Jotham draws out a parable in which a prickly thornbush[14] is asked to be king over the trees and then demands that the trees "take refuge" under it,[15] to their own demise. Alternatively, when David is pursued by one of his enemies, he begs for Yahweh's protection because, he asserts, "I take refuge in you."[16] In another Psalm,[17] David pleads with all of God's people to have the same confidence in Yahweh, and thus experience divine salvation.

Three Hebrew terms, *qwh* [קוה], *yhl* [יחל], and *hkh* [חכה] share a common sense of persistence and the faithful waiting dimension of hope. In a very familiar passage, Isaiah urges that "those who hope in the Lord will renew their strength."[18] Several times David prays for God to bring salvation to the people because they "hope"[19] in him or "wait"[20] for Yahweh. Lacking hope or failing to move forward with persistent trust in God is identified as breaking faith.[21]

The dominant image of faith in the Old Testament emerges from the Hebrew concept denoted by *mn* [אמן],[22] which gives us the term "amen."[23]

---

10. Hos 10:13.

11. Jer 49:4.

12. See Isa 50:10.

13. As in Prov 3:5–6.

14. Allegorical code for nasty Abimelech.

15. Judg 9:15.

16. Ps 7:1.

17. Ps 17:7.

18. Isa 40:31.

19. E.g., Psa 33:22.

20. E.g., Psa 33:20.

21. Note, for example, 2 Kgs 6–7, where Aram's armies invade Israel, laying siege to its capital city, Samaria. Elisha predicts a miraculous divine deliverance while the king blames God for the plight of the city and its people and says, "Why should I hope in the Lord any longer?" (2 Kgs 6:33).

22. In fact, the Septuagint consistently translates *mn* [אמן] as πιστευει or πιστος, affirming the link between these Hebrew and Greek concepts.

23. Twenty-nine times in the Old Testament (often in doubled expressions: "amen and amen") and another fifty in the New Testament.

It carries with it the concept of stability or firmness which then provides a secure anchor of hope or a place to stand securely even in troubled times. Abraham relied on God's faithfulness[24] and that is why, according to Nehemiah, the homeland divinely promised continued as a possession for Abraham's descendants.[25] It is the central word in Moses' instructions to Israel to stick with Yahweh because "he is the faithful God."[26] Solomon used the term in his prayer requesting that God's promises to David now come true in Solomon's own life.[27] Conversely, when Moses reminded the Israelites as to why the previous generation was unable to enter into Canaan,[28] or when Hosea communicated God's looming judgment, each warned the people using the same term: that God is true and faithful and that these prophecies are sure and certain.[29]

Most clearly, the concept of "faith" in the Old Testament is directly linked to covenant commitments that go both ways between God and God's people. Isaiah, for instance, records a dialogue between Yahweh and King Ahaz, filtered through the prophet himself, regarding trust and fidelity. God challenges Ahaz, "If you do not stand firm in faith, you shall not stand at all,"[30] urging him to ask for a sign confirming God's surety in delivering Judah from the armies of both Aram and Israel.[31] But Ahaz denies his faith in Yahweh, refusing even this proffered divine token,[32] and is thus declared to be faithless.

New Testament Engagements: Wrestling & Hope

When the New Testament rapid-fires the word faith, it means trust in God,[33] affirmation of the uniqueness of Jesus,[34] hope in Jesus' return,[35] and

---

24. Gen 15:6.

25. Neh 9:7–8.

26. Deut 7:9.

27. 1 Kgs 8:26.

28. Deut 9:23.

29. Hos 5:9.

30. Isa 7:9.

31. Isa 7:10.

32. Isa 7:12.

33. E.g., Luke 1:20; 24:25.

34. E.g., Mark 1:11; 1:14–15; 1:21–27; 5:34; 5:36; 9:7; 12:1–12; Matt 3:17; 8:13; 9:2; 17:5; Luke 3:22; 8:12–13; 9:35; 18:42.

35. E.g., 2 Cor 5:5–7; 2 Thess 2:13–17.

participation in the new cosmic order begun in and through Jesus.[36] The Synoptic Gospels speak primarily of faith as affirming the trustworthiness of Scripture or Jesus,[37] while John consistently uses the term for believing "into" Jesus as the object of faith or the means of union with the Savior.[38] Experiencing the presence of Jesus or understanding what Jesus has done and then rejecting it earns a declaration of being without faith.[39]

This is particularly seen in the book of Acts, where faith in Jesus comes alive and transforms people throughout the Roman world as they get caught up in the spreading waves of evangelism. Confronted with the news of Jesus' divine personhood and saving work, hearers are challenged to believe in "the Lord"[40] or in Jesus.[41] In fact, all who accept the gospel message and Christ's lordship are identified as "believing ones,"[42] a term that is synonymous with "Christians." Furthermore, this faith in Jesus is then linked, in the book of Acts to baptism,[43] confession,[44] forgiveness,[45] grace,[46] healing,[47] the enthusing of the Holy Spirit,[48] justification,[49] purification,[50] and sanctification.[51] People who believe in Jesus are sometimes declared to be "full of faith,"[52] while those who reject him turn from faith.[53]

---

36. E.g., Matt 5:19–20; 7:24–27; 12:22–28; Mark 11:23–24; Luke 17:6.

37. Thirty uses of πιϛτις and its variants, most often in οτι clauses that denote trusting in the authority of something or someone.

38. Ninety-eight expressions of πιϛτις and its variants, most often in εις clauses that connote union with Jesus.

39. E.g., Mark 4:40–41; 6:1–6; 6:50–52; 8:31–38; 9:31–37; 10:32–45; 8:34–38.

40. Acts 5:14; 9:42; 11:21; 14:23; 18:8.

41. Acts 3:16; 19:4. See also Acts 4:4; 6:7; 11:21; 13:12; 13:48; 15:5; 15:7; 16:1; 17:34; 18:8; 21:20; 21:25.

42. Acts 4:32; 11:21; 18:27; 19:18; 22:19.

43. Acts 8:12–13; 18:8; 19:2.

44. Acts 19:18.

45. Acts 10:43.

46. Acts 15:11; 18:27.

47. Acts 3:16; 14:9.

48. Acts 19:2.

49. Acts 13:39.

50. Acts 15:9.

51. Acts 26:18.

52. Acts 11:24. It is also possible to "remain true" (Acts 14:22) and be strengthened in faith (Acts 16:5).

53. Acts 13:8.

Paul writes much about faith,[54] particularly in Romans[55] and Gala-tians.[56] Most of his ideas reflect closely those expressed about faith in the book of Acts. Toward the end of his life, however, there were some unique additions to what faith meant. To Titus, when warning his young protégé about the challenges of false teachers within the Christian community, Paul wrote that being "sound in faith" is necessary for propagating right teach-ings.[57] And, in his final communication to Timothy, Paul reviewed his life and ministry, summing it up in a single idea: "I have kept the faith."[58]

While Paul's use of "faith" is primarily as the link between us and Jesus for the purpose of salvation (hence trusting in Jesus or believing in Jesus or union with Jesus), "faith" has a slightly different emphasis in the book of Hebrews. Of its thirty-one occurrences, twenty-four of them happen in chapter 11, along with one more at the opening of chapter 12.[59] This is truly the chapter on and about faith. But faith, here, is about conviction and hav-ing continued confidence in God. It is less focused on the act and process of salvation in its initial stages. Instead, faith carries with it the challenge of endurance or "faithfulness."

More than Theological Affirmation

Because of this focus, the author of Hebrews presents examples of faith that call his readers to action, not merely disposition or assent. They are not in danger of losing connection with God; after all, they remain deeply invested in Scripture as divinely authoritative and in the ceremonial expressions that bind Jews with their Lord. These readers are, however, apparently seem-ing to disconnect from Jesus and, along with that separation, giving up on practices peculiar to the early Christian community. Hebrews' urgent call to faithfulness builds on the readers' faith in God that is not at all in jeopardy, but attempts to attach it more resolutely to Jesus. This, in turn, will have life-style consequences, most of which lead to persecution, loss, and even death.

So faith, writes the author, is ὑπόστασις, "the assurance of things hoped for."[60] This is the same word he used when describing Jesus as the reality of

---

54. Using πιστις or its variant 136 times.

55. Thirty-seven times.

56. Twenty-one times.

57. Titus 2:1.

58. 2 Tim 4:7.

59. The others are in Heb 4:2, 6:12, 10:22, 10:38, 10:39, and 13:7.

60. Heb 11:1.

God made evident to us,[61] and when affirming that we are partners who share fully in what Jesus is and has as divine.[62] This assurance leads to both confidence in God and a commitment to stick with God's plan. The examples of faith from Scripture and Israel's past affirm this. They are presented, by the author, in three waves. First are ancient individuals who stayed the course of trusting in God even when challenged by the entire world around them (11:1–7).[63] Second is the wave that includes an extended treatment of Abraham (and briefly along with him, his family), the father of everything Israelite and Jewish, including faith in God and reliance on God's promises (11:8–22).[64] Abraham is the father of the Israelite/Jewish community. He lived his life on a journey, seeking a better homeland. As we have seen before, all of Israel and the Jews who survive the nation are resident within

61. Heb 1:3.

62. Heb 3:14.

63. Abel (Heb 11:4) believed that the unseen God (talked about by his parents) was truly there and worthy of whole-hearted sacrifice, even though it led to his death (which is similar to the author's expected outcome for these people). Next, in an age where all other stories were of people being selfish and self-centered, Enoch (Heb 11:5–6) "walked with God." Finally, while the rest of the world thought all was peace and prosperity, and all could live as they wished, Noah (Heb 11:7) was confident of both divine judgment and an existence beyond it in which God would bring blessing.

64. Abraham gets the longest treatment among the family of faith. The readers are reminded that he obeyed a call to go to an unknown place, stayed in a land he did not and could not possess, believing that it would belong to his descendants, trusted a divine promise, having a child when it was humanly impossible, and was willing even to sacrifice Isaac (the only means of finding fulfillment to other divine promises). There are two "commentaries" on Abraham's story, each directed specifically toward the recipients of this treatise: Heb 11:13–16—The hope and expectation was not really about receiving a physical territory in fulfillment of the divine promises; rather, the true understanding is that he and his family had a transcendent inheritance that superseded Canaan; Heb 11:19—Included in Abraham's hope is the possibility (essentially experienced) in the resurrection of the dead.

These "commentaries" are directly linked to the plight of the recipients:

1) They have and are about to again lose their properties, but they ought to have faith (confidence) that God has a better homeland, city, property, and inheritance in store for them.

2) They are about to die, but they ought to have faith (confidence) that, like Jesus, they will be raised from the dead into a new life and existence.

3) The rest of the original patriarchal family is quickly brought in: by faith Isaac properly announces the life outcomes of both Esau and Jacob through his parting blessing; by faith Jacob did the same; by faith Joseph foresaw the exodus of Israel, so many centuries later, and trusted (had confidence) that gave him the ability to request his future burial in his true homeland.

The *key theme* in this section is on a kind of spiritual homesickness: living temporarily; seeking something meaningful; not overly attached to either place or possessions; confident of a better homeland; on a journey, a pilgrimage.

the life of Abraham, so Abraham's faith (trust, confidence) is not that of seeking limited, temporal things; it is focused on eternal outcomes which transcend current difficulties or possessions. Thus, the commentary brings the recipients of this letter directly into Abraham's kinship. So, if these good Jewish folks wish to be the best Jews possible, they must follow their father Abraham in seeking what God truly desires and intends to give. And since Jesus is God, this means seeking whatever Jesus is about and can offer. Therefore, wherever these readers are, they are on a journey, a pilgrimage. Whatever they have or experience is temporary and not essential. They need to travel together to find protection and camaraderie. They need to keep their focus on the glow of the distant horizon, where Jesus is. He is the only one who can guide them through these current crises of life, and then bring them home.

Finally, the third wave of witnesses is dominated by Moses, but carries along with him the Israelites that participated in the wilderness wanderings he managed (Hebrew 11:23–40). There are four ideas in this section:

- The faith of Moses protected him through challenges against both his life and his truest identity (11:23–28).

- The faith of Israel protected the nation in miraculously overcoming the challenges to leave Egypt, endure the wilderness, and enter into the promised land (11:29–31).

- The faith of many throughout Israelite history, resulting in heroic deeds and lifestyles, many times without immediate reward but confident of future blessings (11:32–38).

- A note of incompleteness about their journeys and that of the current readers (11:39–40).

Like Abraham, Moses gets a longer treatment than others: his parents saved him in spite of the ruler's threats; he chose ill treatments rather than safety and luxury simply because he fully identified with God's people and not the Pharaoh's family. Verse 26 is quite astounding: "He considered abuse suffered for the Christ to be greater wealth than the treasures of Egypt, for he was looking ahead to the reward."

A Deep Connection to Jesus' Deliberate Suffering

Abuse suffered for the Christ? Where does this come from? These words are actually a paraphrase and commentary on Psalm 89:50–51. There the psalmist prays: "Remember, O Lord, how your servant is taunted; how I bear in my bosom the insults of the peoples, with which your enemies taunt, O Lord, with which they taunted the footsteps of your anointed."

Since the term "the Christ" means "the anointed one," the writer of Hebrews equates these, indicating that the true "anointed one" of God is Jesus. Further, Psalm 89 laments the early demise of a king in David's lineage and calls on God to remember God's covenant promises to David, so that God might restore the fortunes of one who was mistreated. The application to the New Testament readers of Hebrews fits this very well. All of the incidents recorded for Moses involved threats from earthly authorities which Moses rejected in order to follow through on promises from God, even though there was no human certainty that he would see them fulfilled. From Israel's national history, three incidents are selected, two shared by the whole of the nation and one serving as a witness to the nation:

- Crossing the Red Sea—Believing Israel passes through, godless Egyptians perish.

- The taking of Jericho—Seemingly worthless marching around the city is rewarded with the falling walls, which do not protect the seemingly safe people who do not trust in God.

- The saving of Rahab—While all others perish around her, she does not, because she was faithful to those God sent.

This third wave of witnesses is brought to a quick finish by the rapid repetition of names from the times of the Judges and early Kings. The quick list is divided into two parts: initially mentioned are those who had faith and received miraculous outcomes; then the list continues, but now pointing to those who had faith and yet were cruelly treated, even to death. All, nevertheless, were "worthy," precisely because of their faith in a God who promises and fulfills, even if the fulfillment is sometimes delayed, perhaps until after death. This is a direct admonition to the contemporary readers of Hebrews. They, too, are being persecuted. Their faith is tested. Many of them fear capture and torture and even cruel death. Should they not step back from public testimonies about Jesus and spare their skins?

Maybe. But in light of the drama unfolded throughout the history of God's people, those who truly had faith stuck with it even when the outcome was uncertain, God's promises were delayed in their fulfillment, and the world deemed God's people "unworthy." Yet people of faith, says the author, stick with God and God's promises though torture and death be the outcome. What is unworthy in this world will shine with great worth in the heaven of God.

Revving the Psychological Punch

Notice that the pace picks up as this lengthy survey moves along. At the start[65] there is a kind of slow and measured ponderance: consider these things, these people, these events. The length of individual focus keeps shrinking, however, as the focus shifts from the ancients to Abraham to Moses and beyond. At the same time, the pace increases, until the march concludes quick-step, with a whirlwind of faith-filled people, some of whom were "winners" and some of whom were "losers" (in the eyes of the world). All, however, are heroes of faith and those who read this treatise can be numbered among them, most significantly because they have received the fulfillment the others were only looking for with longing and hope. Will we, with them, remain steadfast in faith? How will we pick up the torch? Will we honor them or dishonor them with our own religious expressions?

In the world of the author and his readers, the "witnesses" of the past are still living. They surround us. They call us to faithfulness. They encourage us to action.

Interestingly, the running metaphors are both right and wrong. They are correct in calling all who enter the race to lay aside training weights which were used during practice sessions to strengthen legs, calves and ankles. They are wrong, however, because they jump back to talk of "the sin" that entangles us. For a runner, it is clothing that entangles, like long togas or robes, or even sashes that might wrap or trip. Yet the author of Hebrews takes us back to "sin," which is disbelief and failure to stay close to God.

Moreover, we need to run the race "set before us" (τὸν προκείμενον ἡμῖν ἀγῶνα) like Jesus ran what was "set before him" (τῆς προκειμένης αὐτῷ). There is a sense of necessity in this language, both for Jesus and for us. Jesus certainly believed his course was determined by the Father for a particular outcome. Since Jesus is both the source ("pioneer"/"author"/"originator") and the outcome ("perfecter"/"finisher"/"culmination") of our "faith," we need to see our paths ahead with a similar determined intentionality. This is not fatalism (since the whole treatise speaks regularly about the choices that we make) but rather commitment to the things toward which one is called, and on the road that leads to particular ends of holiness and righteousness.

Most important in this section is the brief ending note: the race set before Jesus, while ending in joy, was itself the way of the cross and shame. And since we are to follow his lead, the journey for us will also likely be a path filled with "hostility." We are to follow Jesus' lead even though it calls for "shedding blood," which we have not yet experienced. Moreover, we

---

65. Heb 11:1.

should consider this movement through suffering as the caring admonition of a loving parent. For this reason, the writer brings in a quote from Proverbs 3:11–12, a direct allusion to Proverbs 4:26, and provides a commentary on their continuing significance for people of faith in this new age of Jesus.

Reworking the Wisdom of the Past

While it may seem at first glance to be a tedious collection of rather dry one-liners, Proverbs is much more than that. It is our doorway into the educational system of the Israelite community. Our word "proverb" is derived from a Latin term which means "for a verb." So these are "words" which take the place of "more words," or concise distillations of wisdom compacted into a few carefully conceived phrases. The wisdom presumed by the proverbs is the worldview of the Sinai covenant, as the prologue[66] indicates. The message of the book derives its direction from Solomon, who was enormously wise because of the special gift of God.[67] Solomon is the father of Proverbs in several ways. First, he created Yahweh's Temple in Jerusalem which gave a permanent home to Israel's covenant marriage partner. Second, the wisdom of Yahweh spoke powerfully through Solomon, so the whole world came to hear his proverbs and pithy sayings.[68] Third, the greatest bulk of this book called "Proverbs" is attributed directly to Solomon.[69] Fourth, Solomon was also known for his wide-ranging and ultimately catastrophic flirtations, courtships, and marriages, which may well be reflected in the pointed moral sermons of the first nine chapters of Proverbs. In truth, both Solomon's early expressions of pithy wisdom (which drew the attention and the attraction of the world[70]) and his disastrous sexual alliances (which caused his downfall[71]), served to shape the collection of Proverbs in its final form.

This is seen in the "Lectures on Wisdom and Folly" that stand at the head of the book and from which the author of Hebrews takes his cue. In the Hebrew language, both "wisdom" and "folly" are feminine nouns. Thus, the use of the repeated literary device, "my son" in Proverbs 1:8–9:18 is intentional. All readers or hearers of these lectures become the "son" who is courted by two women, "Wisdom" and "Folly." By the end of these carefully crafted lectures, in which each woman is given ample opportunity to present

66. Prov 1:1–7.
67. 1 Kgs 3.
68. 1 Kgs 3–4.
69. Prov 1:1, 10:1, 25:1.
70. 1 Kgs 4:29–34, 10:1–13.
71. 1 Kgs 11:1–13.

her case, all of us must choose which woman to wed. The choice is real, and personal, and life-changing. Wisdom brings stability and well-being; Folly offers quick experiences and tragic ends.

Dating often seems to be a trivial pastime and sexuality sometimes merely the arena for power-plays and sporting events. But in Proverbs, the high calling of courtship is held out as the definer of human identity. None of us remains single. All of us are swept up into the drama. Even more, this relational tugging, twisting attraction and repulsion is forever a triangle: whether female or male, in this affair we are the young man pursuing and being pursued by two women, Folly and Wisdom. Each parades her virtues. Each calls for a choice and a commitment. But there the similarities end. For Folly brings us into an endless addiction to one-night stands in which we lose ourselves in the delirium of mere titillation, and ultimately lose all substance and self-respect. Wisdom, however, wants to take things slowly, and seeks as much to get to know us as we her. Wisdom desires a relationship where respect deepens and both parties are enriched.

If, at the close of these lectures, one should choose Folly, the rest of the Proverbs have no meaning. That person should slam shut the book and get on with other destructive behaviors, for she or he cannot understand the language that is used in the house of Wisdom.

If, however, one hears and understands these lectures and responds with an appropriate desire to court and marry Wisdom, the rest of the book of Proverbs becomes the stuff of which her house is made. When one is bound to Wisdom, the Proverbs are the furnishings of her home, the decorations on her walls, the conversation pieces in her rooms, and the lifestyle that organizes her economy. The many, many proverbs are not to be read together as an unbroken narrative but are supposed to be savored and tasted like the multitude of meals taken in the marriage house of Wisdom, and breathed as if they were the life-sustaining rhythms of respiration itself.

In this manner, the wisdom of Solomon becomes the admonition of a parent who wants to bring out the best in those who follow. This is what the author of Hebrews picks up as he uses this firm injunction. He urges, with strong divine demand, that these faith-seeking and faith-filled people run with good form, following the coach's instructions so that they can win, just as Jesus did.

Even though it might well mean punishment, torture and dying. Trouble is ahead and that is why the individual "sport" of running well must become a group task. Each of the Hebrews' readers must prepare and execute well the disciplines of following Jesus. But each, all together, must also form a community of nurture and encouragement, for the race itself, as Jesus modeled, is tough, painful, and debilitating. No lone runner will survive.

Where Have We Come So Far?

- God has spoken in times past.

    - This is our source of direction and confidence.

    - We know who we are because of the prophets.

- God has recently spoken a stronger, better, and clearer message through Jesus.

    - So when we, who live by the prophetic message, hear Jesus, we had better listen.

- Jesus is superior to the angels.

    - The great divine message that formed us came through Moses, but the message itself was delivered to him by angels (Deut 33:2; Acts 7:53).

    - Yet Jesus is superior to angels, and therefore delivers a more important prophetic message than that through the great prophet Moses.

- So, stick with Jesus, even though you are tempted to turn away from him.

    - There is no higher authority or source of connection with God.

    - And if our lives are to be connected to God, we turn away from Jesus to our own peril.

- God has made the world subject to Jesus.

    - God never did this with the angels, so, again, Jesus is superior to them.

    - But this only happened because Jesus first fully identified with the world.

- Jesus willingly came into the world to fully experience its pain.

- And this is to our benefit for three reasons:

    - To fully identify with us as sisters and brothers.

    - To make atonement for our sins (which cause the pain of this world).

    - To bring us with him fully into the house of God.

- So Jesus is greater than (over) the angels, but Jesus is also greater than (over) Moses.

- Therefore, be careful that you don't disconnect from Jesus (who is God):
  - Remember how those in our past who disconnected from God came under punishment.
  - The same can happen to you if you do not stay true and committed to Jesus.
- Let God's people in the earlier redemptive sequence be your instructors:
  - Like us, they were saved and led to their "(sabbath) rest" in the promised land.
    - But they failed to stay connected to God by way of the word of the prophet (Moses) and died before reading "rest."
  - Now God has promised us a coming "rest" (i.e., "heaven" when we die).
    - But we will receive it only if we remain connected to God by way of the word of the prophet (Jesus) and live faithfully through these trials.
- And, again, the only one who can keep you connected to God is Jesus:
  - He is our true high priest, who will take us boldly to God's merciful throne through his actions on our behalf on the Day of Atonement. He is fully human, so he completely understands the struggles of our lives and sympathizes deeply, to the point of anguished cries.
- In fact, he is as fully committed to fulfilling the mandate and responsibilities of his priestly order as are others.
  - They in their "Aaronic/Levitical priestly order."
  - He in his "Melchizedek priestly order."
- I wish you were getting this. You should be mature enough to teach others, but it seems you have lost your passion for Jesus and are trying only to protect yourselves.
  - Though I write strong words, I am confident that you will continue in our faith in Jesus.
  - After all, God has made absolute promises of care toward us that are our hope.

- And Jesus is the only anchor we have today to ensure that we will receive what was promise.

- After all, Jesus is a priest after the order of Melchizedek.
    - The Levitical order priests could not fully satisfy needs, since its sacrifices needed repeating.
    - That is why someone from Melchizedek's order was needed.
        - Someone who was a descendant of David (of the tribe of Judah), perfect and never dying.

- This brings us back to the main thing we have been saying: Jesus is the best high priest ever.
    - He is God (seated at the right hand of the majesty in heaven).
    - He is owner of the house of God.
    - He is high priest of the house of God.
        - The true house of God, with dimensions given by God on the mountain.
        - The visible house of God, here below (under the care of the Levitical priests), important as it is, is only a shadow of the real thing.
    - He is faultless.
    - He is the mediator of the new covenant (remember Jer 31:31–34?).

- This is very important: God found fault with the old covenant.
    - God is causing the old covenant age to come to an end.
    - Jesus is the only source of hope in the new covenant age.

- These changes are symbolized by the "houses" of the two covenant ages:
    - The tabernacle with God hidden and symbolic actions repeated.
    - The heavenly dwelling with Jesus bringing us directly to the throne.

- Both "houses" required blood sacrifice for God's people to approach God.
    - But in the earthly tabernacle, repeated animal sacrifices by Levitical priests were needed.

- ◆ While in the heavenly dwelling, Jesus offered himself once for all.
- Thus, Jesus is the best mediator and the only source of our eternal security.
  - ◆ The tabernacle and Levitical priesthood were only types of this ultimate expression of God's love.
- But keep in mind that there is a symbiotic relationship between the first and second expressions of God's covenant:
  - ◆ The first is the shadow—The meaningful but repetitious type.
  - ◆ While the second is the substance—The perfection of all things through Jesus.
- Jesus has accomplished everything that is necessary and now rules over all, in an age where the new covenant is written on hearts and forgiveness is complete.
- So, let's go! Grab each other, keep your focus, and let's let Jesus take us right to God's throne of grace.
- Again, I want to remind you about those in the past who failed to keep faith with God and lost out.
  - ◆ You have come through some tough times in the past. Remember how you stayed strong?
  - ◆ Some of you seem to be dropping out now, as new threats loom. Remember that Jesus can keep us going.
- Have faith in Jesus.
  - ◆ See the example of those who have gone before?
  - ◆ Besides, don't you believe that God exists and that he rewards those who seek him?
- Remember how our family's first parents all had faith that God would bring a better future than they experienced at the time.
- Remember how Moses, our greatest hero, chose the difficult path of faith and faithfulness rather than ease and worldly success.
- And don't forget the many among our ancestors who won big for God, or lost greatly in a world that was not worthy of them, seeking by faith what we have recently received in Jesus.
- Most importantly, keep your eyes on Jesus.

- He ran the race before you did (and a bloody run it was), confident of the joy at the end.

- Know that the pain of your own race is part of the loving discipline of a Father who is bringing out the best in you.

- So keep running, and encourage each other on the track.

Message: Maranatha Marathon

King Darius was upset with the Greeks. Through battlefield conquests, he had come to "own" Asia Minor (now roughly the same territory as the nation of Turkey). Since, however, this region had largely been settled by the Greeks generations before, and continued to trade more easily westward in cultural kinship than to his Far East foreign palace cities, the people of "his" territory still viewed themselves as Greeks rather than loyal Persians. Darius was enraged. These folks were meddlesome and perplexing.

So, Darius did what tyrants often do: he amassed the largest military force ever conceived and marched it west. Brutally putting down rebellions in Asia Minor, he then headed for the source of his perceived consternations. He crossed the Bosporus and challenged the Greeks to a winner-take-all showdown on their own territory.

The Greeks were far from unified and terrified at this onslaught. Athens and Sparta headed the largest confederations of multiple independent city-states, but the Spartans, even with their fierce training, shied away from this confrontation, explaining that they needed to observe a religious holiday in seclusion. So the Athenians and a few allies stood feebly before the menacing Persian monster. All could see that the Greeks were going down and out, probably before a single sparring round was ended.

Replaying a Miracle

But miracles and strange twists of history happen every now and again. The pip punished the power. The squirt swatted the scorpion. The weakling wounded the warrior, until Darius limped back to Persia in disgrace.

And from the battlefield near a small town named Marathon, the wondering whisper cascaded: νενικήκαμεν![72] Stunned at their own success, the Athenian forces dispatched a runner to bring the good news home to

---

72. *nenikēkamen*, "we have won!"

the worried senate. While the man's name has been lost,[73] his heroic run inspired generations. Striding approximately twenty-five miles from the battlefield to Athens,[74] he gasped in exhaustion and shouted his victory cry before falling dead.

When the Olympic Games were revived in 1896, the original Marathon runner inspired a new event. Set at twenty-five miles, the marathon race drew endurance athletes from around the world. But when London claimed the hosting responsibilities in 1908, planners realized that they needed to bring the grueling course to a conclusion at the box of the royal family in the newly constructed White Stadium. The marathon suddenly lengthened to 26.2 miles, and has settled there ever since.

Most marathon runners do not die at the finish line. Nevertheless, a marathon race is extremely demanding, requiring both adequate preparation and punishing endurance. Starting is fairly easy. A runner simply puts forward a foot and is rapidly carried along by the jostling crowd. The first half-mile, or even the full initial mile, are passed in an instant, vapored away by nervous excitement.

Beyond Endurance

But then the human body is called upon to function beyond its normal boundaries. While muscles cry for rest, the steel will of the runner demands continued momentum. So, the plodding and pacing set in. Mile after mile, footfall after footfall, numbed by repetitious movements that take pain to new levels, the mind kicks into autopilot as the body thuds along crying for release. Mile 4 is a miracle. Mile 9 is a blur. Mile 13 may be half-way, but the racer has long ago given up thoughts of sanity about this crushing torture. Mile 18 sees growing crowds along the route and the rising voice of encouragement. While the body has no more to give, the spirit seems steadied and focused. By mile 21, hope flutters, speculating nervously that maybe there

---

73. Was it Thersipus of Erchius (Plutarch), Eucles (Hereclides), Philippides (Lucian of Samosata, Herodotus), or Pheidippides (Robert Browning)? The sources disagree, but Thersipus is most likely; Philippides was most broadly repeated among the ancients until Robert Browning reconceived of the name as Pheidippides for his modern audience.

74. Mount Penteli stands directly between Marathon and Athens. The shortest route (approximately 21.5 miles) would take a runner around the north side, but required an extremely steep climb to the Pass of Dionysos. Most agree that he probably followed paths around the south side of the mountain, approximately where modern Greece Highway 3 meanders today.

will be an end to this long night of pain, and perhaps, just beyond the next turn, the stadium and its finish line will appear.

The human fences that guard the race concourse thicken, while their shouts of support rise in rapid decibels. Buoyed by the energy of others, each racer finds quicker steps and renewed focus. Up ahead, the "white noise" of indistinct stadium cheering mounts, filling the air with restless anticipation.

Up a hill. Around a corner. Suddenly every other noise is blanked out as each runner charges into the concrete echo chamber channel that connects the world to the coliseum. Thud, thud, thud . . . heartbeats and footfalls blend.

And then a din erupts as the runner emerges from the tunnel's darkness into light and chaos and the thundering urges cascading down the bleacher mountains surrounding the field. Only a lap to go. One time around the track.

My steps spring. My heart sings. My mind feeds on the shouts of encouragement. Dare I glance up at these wonderful people who are investing their time and voices and admirations into me?

So I sneak a peek above. There are my parents, on their feet and yelling. I've never seen them so animated. And all for me. I almost smile through my pain, and my steps get lighter and quicker.

And then I notice it . . . next to my parents are other familiar faces. Uncle George and Aunt Sue. Cousin Cindy. What is she doing here? Friends from college. And friends from high school? And members of the church I used to be a part of?

Wait. And there are Grandpa and Grandma. But they are dead. And others that I recognize from pictures in old photo albums. Something strange is going on here.

As I run, I become more aware of the thousands and the myriads that are cheering me on. Yes, the other runners too, but everyone shouts my name and wishes me well and calls for me to carry on. Some wear out-of-date clothes, looking like they have stepped out of other cultures and times. But all are here for me, all know me by name, all shout their encouragement.

And before I can fully process this strange and transformative scene, I round the last corner and look ahead. There's the finish line. The tapes measure it on both sides. The clock ticks away the seconds. And at the center stands Jesus. Even though I have never met him, face to face, I know it is him. And he smiles at me. And he laughs the most glorious laugh of good will. And he beckons me with his hand as I finish the race and fall into his supportive tenderness.

Eye on the Prize

This is the message of the final big exhortation of Hebrews. You can do it. Others have run this race before you and they are cheering you on. Some climbed mountains, some fell flat; some leapt over tall buildings and others suffered indignations we can't even begin to describe. But all were surrounded, as you have been, by the testimonies and prayers and well-wishes of those who went before.

And, more significantly, Jesus ran this race, this marathon, this cruel, crushing torture. It took all he had, but he gave it his all. And now he is the very one who gives everything to you. In his strength, you can finish the course. In his encouragement, you can keep the faith. In his love, your heart will find resources that your mind and body have lost too long ago.

No one said that it would be easy. It was not easy for Jesus.

But the outcome is clear and good and overwhelming. You are a winner. Maybe not among those who taunt and test you. Maybe not in the demeanor of a mean world. Maybe not even within the context of your family, neighborhood, or work buddies. But where meaning matters, you are a winner. You ran the course of the saints, and they are cheering you on. You ran the race of Jesus, and he will see you through to the end.

Don't give up on him. He has never given up on you.

And make certain that you carry your fellow runners along. If you are tired and discouraged, they are likely to be as well. We all need each other to get to the finish line.

Chapter 18

Mountain Standard Time

Text: Hebrews 12:14–29

Pursue peace with everyone, and the holiness without which no one will see the Lord. See to it that no one fails to obtain the grace of God; that no root of bitterness springs up and causes trouble, and through it many become defiled. See to it that no one becomes like Esau, an immoral and godless person, who sold his birthright for a single meal. You know that later, when he wanted to inherit the blessing, he was rejected, for he found no chance to repent, even though he sought the blessing with tears.

You have not come to something that can be touched, a blazing fire, and darkness, and gloom, and a tempest, and the sound of a trumpet, and a voice whose words made the hearers beg that not another word be spoken to them. (For they could not endure the order that was given, "If even an animal touches the mountain, it shall be stoned to death."[1] Indeed, so terrifying was the sight that Moses said, "I tremble with fear."[2]) But you have come to Mount Zion and to the city of the living God, the heavenly Jerusalem, and to innumerable angels in festal gathering, and to the assembly of the firstborn who are enrolled in heaven, and to God the judge of all, and to the spirits of the righteous made perfect, and to Jesus, the mediator of a new

1. Exod 19:12–13.
2. Deut 9:19.

covenant, and to the sprinkled blood that speaks a better word than the blood of Abel.

See that you do not refuse the one who is speaking; for if they did not escape when they refused the one who warned them on earth, how much less will we escape if we reject the one who warns from heaven! At that time his voice shook the earth; but now he has promised, "Yet once more I will shake not only the earth but also the heaven."[3] This phrase, "Yet once more," indicates the removal of what is shaken—that is, created things—so that what cannot be shaken may remain. Therefore, since we are receiving a kingdom that cannot be shaken, let us give thanks, by which we offer to God an acceptable worship with reverence and awe; for indeed our God is a consuming fire.

Backstory: A Tale of Two Mountains

"REMEMBER, FOLKS," HE SAID quietly. "The central offense of the gospel is Jesus, not you."

The man speaking was a lifelong missionary, born to parents who were serving as gospel witnesses in China and who himself had devoted his career to planting churches in Japan. His words were a reflection on Paul's reflections about the scandal of the cross in 1 Corinthians 1 and Paul's summary declaration of that in Galatians 5:11.

As a man who had moved into and out of several cultures, he was particularly sensitive to the manner in which Christians present both themselves and the gospel. He suggested that much which is presumed "holy" and "religious" is actually more an expression of cultural preconditioning and has little to do with the central elements of the biblical story of salvation. Moreover, he had often observed Christians who were truly obnoxious when they left North America to be missionaries elsewhere. Their offensiveness hid the true central offense of the gospel and prevented others from connecting meaningfully with Jesus. With kind wisdom, he cautioned us to walk carefully as we lived for Jesus in a multi-cultural world.

3. Hag 2:6.

Quiet Counter-Culture

Something of the same warning begins this section of Hebrews. Through hints and reminders, the author of this treatise has revealed aspects of the community to whom it is being sent:

- They are second-generation Christians who learned of the gospel through others.

- They are deeply invested into Jewish rituals and practices, having grown in faith and its expressions through these over most of their lives.

- They know the Jewish Scriptures very, very well and likely have memorized much of the Pentateuch.

- At the same time, they are Greek-speakers and use the Septuagint (Greek translation) of the Scriptures in their worship and devotional practices.

- These people were likely non-Jewish in ethnic origins, but having become disillusioned with the moral laxity and ethical waywardness of Roman society in the transition from the republic to the empire, they had found among Orthodox Jews a home of righteous rigor.

- Within the last decade or so, these people had been persecuted for their faith, with some of them losing their properties, some being thrown into jails, and some of their leaders having been killed.

- After some years of peace, a new persecution was beginning, and it was challenging the community deeply.

- A new twist, however, is that the Roman authorities, who are initiating this pogrom, are now distinguishing between Jews and Christians, providing safety and social affirmations for the former while targeting the latter with increased violence and ostracism.

For this reason, the author urges, "Pursue peace with everyone." If tensions mount in a neighborhood, groups become identified and some are often scapegoated. Since this Christian community is already being pursued by the governing authorities, any rise in social animosity will bring quicker and stronger social antagonism. If at all possible, these folks should try to keep under the radar and not produce any offensive behaviors that call attention to themselves.[4] The bitterness that arises from social inequities and injus-

---

4. Paul makes a similar appeal to Christians living in challenging and unstable conditions in Ephesus in 1 Tim 2.

tices is always a sore point,[5] as is the challenging arena of sexual innuendos and misconduct.[6]

The writer, always thinking in scriptural models and anecdotes, gives an interesting point of reference to support his concerns. He mentions Esau, who did a rash thing on a whim, selling his favored inheritance status as firstborn to his twin brother for a simple bowl of lentil soup[7] and regretted it the rest of his life. The implication is clear: quick actions taken without thought can lead to dire consequences. The readers of Hebrews should think and plan well, particularly with regard to their public behaviors, so that they might not come to unwanted social ill.

But there is also a deeper corollary to this. In spite of the negative press about him, Esau was basically an ordinary person, trying to live right and do things that matter. It is obvious, from later references to him, that Esau would command a great deal of respect in his community. The implication given by the writer of Hebrews, however, is that any good person can make a bad decision now and again, and that while many of these faulty choices hold little lingering consequence, there are some that are critical, and change our futures completely. Just as good man Esau lived well generally, but tossed a huge blessing away in a moment of famished fever, so these Christians, who have maintained a great record of faithfulness and witness, might lose the best that is offered by God if they deny Jesus on a dark day when hands are feeble and knees are limp and hearts are exhausted.

Double Vision

Another moment of inspiration follows, much briefer than the Bolero-like rousing of the Maranatha marathon just prior to these verses. This time an image of two mountains is staged. Each is presented as a metaphor built on top of a geographical place and historical incident. First come allusions to the initial Israelite encounter with God at Mount Sinai in Exodus 19. Recently released from Egyptian bondage, and miraculously sustained through warrior challenges and wilderness deprivations, the people were led by Moses to the spot where he first encountered Yahweh.[8] While Israel's

---

5. Heb 12:15.

6. Heb 12:16. A supposed socially-presumed inappropriate small sexual gesture was reported to have "justified" the horrible killing of Emmett Till in August of 1955. The trial and subsequent acquittal of those charged with his killing became a major point of contention throughout the U.S. Civil Rights Movement.

7. Gen 25:29–34.

8. See Exod 3.

old taskmaster, the Pharaoh of Egypt, was feared due to terrors of the lash and practices of genocide, her new "owner" also produced deep and anxious responses. These, however, were awe-inspiring earth-shakings that made the powers of Egypt seem trite. While heaven opened over the mountain and earth trembled at the footfall of its Creator, the Israelites hid in panic. Who could stand before such a holy presence and live? Even Moses, who had boldly stood in dialogue with Yahweh at this very spot not long before, confessed, "I tremble with fear."

But there is a second mountain in view. This one is also conflated—past with future, existence with hope, imminence with transcendence. Just as Mount Zion, at the upper limit of ancient Jerusalem, buzzed with radiating glory when Solomon completed the grand temple of Yahweh, and all heaven splashed to earth,[9] so, even now, the angels are dancing around the throne at the center of all reality in anticipation of divine glory flooding creation once again. Meeting God at Mount Sinai was good for ancient Israel but terrifying. Meeting God soon, as the Creator brings resolution to all the turmoil on planet Earth, is and will be exhilarating.

Again, there is an underlying nudge connected to this double vision. Mount Sinai stands for the author as a link with the entire Jewish religious ceremonial system. It was at Mount Sinai that the plans for the tabernacle were delivered. It was at Mount Sinai that the Aaronic priesthood was begun. It was at Mount Sinai that the calendar of daily, weekly, monthly, and yearly sacrifices was initiated. In other words, to act and be Israelite/Jewish, Mount Sinai forms the base of identity and operations.

But since Jesus came, according to the author, this Israelite/Jewish identity has been caught up in and subsumed by an even greater identity. Heaven (the dwelling of God and the location of God's real throne, symbolically represented on earth by the ark of the covenant) supersedes earth's temporary wanderings and expressions, including the old sacrificial system. The new Jerusalem where Jesus now resides, after having cleansed the old Jerusalem with his bloody sacrifice, is pushing at the boundaries of time and space and will erupt soon into our experience. And the angels, who for centuries have penetrated the gossamer veil shielding drab earth from heaven's blinding glory to bring a revelation or a message only now and again, will suddenly be citizens and fellow-worshippers in the grand reunification of all reality, both material and spiritual.

So we should not linger with the past and its sacrifices. Instead, we should lean into the future, with its hopes and promises and glory.

9. See 1 Kgs 5–8; 2 Chr 2–7.

The Way Up the Mountain is Bloody

Yet here is another veiled challenge. The way that Jesus went from the expressions of Mount Sinai to the living reality of the new Mount Jerusalem was by shedding his blood. He is "the mediator of the new covenant."[10] There was blood in the old covenant. After all, from the beginning (Abel's blood), this journey of humanity has been one of death. But Jesus lives even though he died. This is why his blood "speaks a better word" than that mouthed by Abel's flowing crimson stain. Still, to participate in Jesus' everlasting life, the transition involves death. Therefore, these readers are being steeled to the greater persecution still in front of them. They can choose Mount Sinai, with its animal blood and sacrifices, and live for a while longer in this restless heartbreak of a world. Or they can choose Mount Jerusalem, with its once-for-all Jesus' blood and sacrifice, and through their own martyr deaths enter into Jesus' on-going life.

The choice remains: temporary life connected with denying Jesus and slipping back into the Jewish sacrificial system or eternal life received through the way of persecution leading to both sure and imminent death, with full access into eternal glory. This is the painfully promising message of Hebrews. Live now, by sneaking back into old covenant forms, but lose your eternal hope. Or die now, by standing with Jesus and reaching into a future promise that only those with faith can see.

A warning follows. Again, the writer of Hebrews is a genius at knowing and using Scripture. Tying together the shaking of Mount Sinai with a rather obscure reference to shaking found in the very tiny prophecy of Haggai, the author grabs both past and future in a continuing vision of Holy God.

A Rousing Voice from the Past

Haggai and Zechariah appeared on the scene at exactly the same time, in the summer of 520 BC. This was an auspicious season for the few folks who had struggled to find themselves after returning to Jerusalem from Babylonian exile over a decade before. The first thing they had done when viewing the rubble of the city was to set up the altar of burnt offering among the toppled stones of the old temple square.[11] Their band was small and neighbors living in the region resented their invasion. Instead of building the temple and city

10. Heb 12:24.

11. See Ezra 3.

as planned and promised by their Persian overlords,[12] the social tensions resulted instead in a stop-work edict that lasted for ten years.[13] Finally, in the summer of 520 BC, King Darius[14] issued a stunning declaration:

> "Now you, Tattenai, governor of the province Beyond the River, Shethar-bozenai, and you, their associates, the envoys in the province Beyond the River, keep away; let the work on this house of God alone; let the governor of the Jews and the elders of the Jews rebuild this house of God on its site. Moreover I make a decree regarding what you shall do for these elders of the Jews for the rebuilding of this house of God: the cost is to be paid to these people, in full and without delay, from the royal revenue, the tribute of the province Beyond the River. Whatever is needed—young bulls, rams, or sheep for burnt offerings to the God of heaven, wheat, salt, wine, or oil, as the priests in Jerusalem require—let that be given to them day by day without fail, so that they may offer pleasing sacrifices to the God of heaven, and pray for the life of the king and his children. Furthermore I decree that if anyone alters this edict, a beam shall be pulled out of the house of the perpetrator, who then shall be impaled on it. The house shall be made a dunghill. May the God who has established his name there overthrow any king or people that shall put forth a hand to alter this, or to destroy this house of God in Jerusalem. I, Darius, make a decree; let it be done with all diligence."[15]

This was a stop-in-your-tracks shaking of heaven and earth. This was a turn-around of epic proportions. This was a massive reversal of fortunes. And it is precisely at the moment when the Persian courier delivered the message to the depressed and seemingly forgotten band of Jews in their ruined and make-shift huts on the windswept heights of Jerusalem that God energized Haggai with an ecstatic proclamation.

Haggai was a cheerleader. He had returned from Babylon to Palestine with the first wave of freed exiles under the leadership of Zerubbabel in 536 BC.[16] Although it took a while for the community to get its bearings, now, suddenly, there was a push to sift among the stones still left at the site of Solomon's Temple and rebuild a house for Yahweh there. When King

---

12. See Ezra 1.

13. 530–520 BC. See Ezra 4–5.

14. Ironically, the instigator of the doomed 490 BC invasion of Greece, which would be stopped decisively at Marathon.

15. Ezra 6:6–12.

16. See Ezra 1.

Darius' announcement was read, Haggai piggy-backed onto it, urging the workers with divine encouragement. No obstacle could stand in the way of this central task, neither disobedient lifestyles,[17] fainthearted leadership,[18] poverty,[19] ritual defilement,[20] or the rattling sabers of bellicose nations.[21] Under Haggai's promptings and Zerubbabel's governing, the temple was rebuilt in the next four years. By 516 BC it stood again, only a mean miniature compared to the glorious structure created generations before by Solomon in his seven-year building project. Nevertheless, with Haggai's oratorical help, Yahweh's house was reborn.

At the heart of God's message through Haggai was this powerful testimony:

> My spirit abides among you; do not fear. For thus says the Lord of hosts: Once again, in a little while, I will shake the heavens and the earth and the sea and the dry land; and I will shake all the nations, so that the treasure of all nations shall come.[22]

The writer of Hebrews understands the times in which he was living, the times of Jesus' coming to earth and recent, temporary return to heaven as these quaking times. Signs, wonders, and miracles were taking place. Nations were in uproar, and all earthly structures were in danger of collapsing.

But heaven itself was unshakeable. And, as the Hebrews treatise has carefully diagrammed to this point, whatever is connected to the heavenly temple, the true throne of God, and the mediator of the new covenant will last. So the shaking continues and these Christians are reeling under it. But if they cling to Jesus and do not deny him, they are attached to permanent promises and rewards.

Just as the smoke and fire atop Mount Sinai caused the mountain and its surroundings to tremble, so the blazing glory of God is already sending shock waves through earth. Rather than running away in fear, however,

17. Hag 1:2–11.
18. Hag 1:12–14.
19. Hag 2:1–9.
20. Hag 2:10–19.
21. Hag 2:20–23.
22. Hag 2:5–7.

those who know the truth should run with Jesus[23] toward the consuming fire. In his shielding, there is safety and steadiness.[24]

Where Have We Come So Far?

- God has spoken in times past.
  - This is our source of direction and confidence.
  - We know who we are because of the prophets.
- God has recently spoken a stronger, better, and clearer message through Jesus.
  - So when we, who live by the prophetic message, hear Jesus, we had better listen.
- Jesus is superior to the angels.
  - The great divine message that formed us came through Moses, but the message itself was delivered to him by angels (Deut 33:2; Acts 7:53).
  - Yet Jesus is superior to angels, and therefore delivers a more important prophetic message than that through the great prophet Moses.
- So, stick with Jesus, even though you are tempted to turn away from him.
  - There is no higher authority or source of connection with God.
  - And if our lives are to be connected to God, we turn away from Jesus to our own peril.
- God has made the world subject to Jesus.
  - God never did this with the angels, so, again, Jesus is superior to them.
  - But this only happened because Jesus first fully identified with the world.
- Jesus willingly came into the world to fully experience its pain.

---

23. Notice that there is no distinction made in Heb 12:25–27 between the voice of "God" and the voice of "Jesus." Since Jesus has been shown again and again in Hebrews to be God, the voice of Jesus is the voice of God, and the voice of God is the voice of Jesus.

24. See also 1 Cor 3:10–17; 1 Thess 4:13—5:11; 2 Thes 1–2; 2 Pet 3.

- And this is to our benefit for three reasons:

  - To fully identify with us as sisters and brothers.

  - To make atonement for our sins (which cause the pain of this world).

  - To bring us with him fully into the house of God.

- So Jesus is greater than (over) the angels, but Jesus is also greater than (over) Moses.

- Therefore, be careful that you don't disconnect from Jesus (who is God):

  - Remember how those in our past who disconnected from God came under punishment.

  - The same can happen to you if you do not stay true and committed to Jesus.

- Let God's people in the earlier redemptive sequence be your instructors:

  - Like us, they were saved and led to their "(sabbath) rest" in the promised land.

    - But they failed to stay connected to God by way of the word of the prophet (Moses) and died before reading "rest."

  - Now God has promised us a coming "rest" (i.e., "heaven" when we die).

    - But we will receive it only if we remain connected to God by way of the word of the prophet (Jesus) and live faithfully through these trials

- And, again, the only one who can keep you connected to God is Jesus:

  - He is our true high priest, who will take us boldly to God's merciful throne through his actions on our behalf on the Day of Atonement. He is fully human, so he completely understands the struggles of our lives and sympathizes deeply, to the point of anguished cries.

- In fact, he is as fully committed to fulfilling the mandate and responsibilities of his priestly order as are others.

  - They in their "Aaronic/Levitical priestly order."

  - He in his "Melchizedek priestly order."

- I wish you were getting this. You should be mature enough to teach others, but it seems you have lost your passion for Jesus and are trying only to protect yourselves.

    - Though I write strong words, I am confident that you will continue in our faith in Jesus.

    - After all, God has made absolute promises of care toward us that are our hope.

    - And Jesus is the only anchor we have today to ensure that we will receive what was promise.

- After all, Jesus is a priest after the order of Melchizedek.

    - The Levitical order priests could not fully satisfy needs, since its sacrifices needed repeating.

    - That is why someone from Melchizedek's order was needed.

        - Someone who was a descendant of David (of the tribe of Judah), perfect and never dying.

- This brings us back to the main thing we have been saying: Jesus is the best high priest ever.

    - He is God (seated at the right hand of the majesty in heaven).

    - He is owner of the house of God.

    - He is high priest of the house of God.

        - The true house of God, with dimensions given by God on the mountain.

        - The visible house of God, here below (under the care of the Levitical priests), important as it is, is only a shadow of the real thing.

    - He is faultless.

    - He is the mediator of the new covenant (remember Jer 31:31–34?).

- This is very important: God found fault with the old covenant.

    - God is causing the old covenant age to come to an end.

    - Jesus is the only source of hope in the new covenant age.

- These changes are symbolized by the "houses" of the two covenant ages:

    - The tabernacle with God hidden and symbolic actions repeated.

- ◆ The heavenly dwelling with Jesus bringing us directly to the throne.
- Both "houses" required blood sacrifice for God's people to approach God.
  - ◆ But in the earthly tabernacle, repeated animal sacrifices by Levitical priests were needed.
  - ◆ While in the heavenly dwelling, Jesus offered himself once for all.
- Thus, Jesus is the best mediator and the only source of our eternal security.
  - ◆ The tabernacle and Levitical priesthood were only types of this ultimate expression of God's love.
- But keep in mind that there is a symbiotic relationship between the first and second expressions of God's covenant:
  - ◆ The first is the shadow—the meaningful but repetitious type.
  - ◆ While the second is the substance—the perfection of all things through Jesus.
- Jesus has accomplished everything that is necessary and now rules over all, in an age where the new covenant is written on hearts and forgiveness is complete.
- So, let's go! Grab each other, keep your focus, and let's let Jesus take us right to God's throne of grace.
- Again, I want to remind you about those in the past who failed to keep faith with God and lost out.
  - ◆ You have come through some tough times in the past. Remember how you stayed strong?
  - ◆ Some of you seem to be dropping out now, as new threats loom. Remember that Jesus can keep us going.
- Have faith in Jesus.
  - ◆ See the example of those who have gone before?
  - ◆ Besides, don't you believe that God exists and that he rewards those who seek him?
- Remember how our family's first parents all had faith that God would bring a better future than they experienced at the time.

- Remember how Moses, our greatest hero, chose the difficult path of faith and faithfulness rather than ease and worldly success.

- And don't forget the many among our ancestors who won big for God, or lost greatly in a world that was not worthy of them, seeking by faith what we have recently received in Jesus.

- Most importantly, keep your eyes on Jesus.

  - He ran the race before you did (and a bloody run it was), confident of the joy at the end.

  - Know that the pain of your own race is part of the loving discipline of a Father who is bringing out the best in you.

  - So keep running, and encourage each other on the track.

- The end is near.

  - So keep confidence, and live kindly; beware of bitterness that can tear you apart in these tense times.

  - Remember the two mountains:

    - Sinai, from which God shook the world in terror as he announced judgment.

    - Zion, from which God will shake the world in awe as he announces the consummation of all things.

Message: Choose Wisely

Harry Emerson Fosdick once reported a strange event.[25] A man bought a Greyhound bus ticket in New York City stamped with Detroit as his destination. He got on the bus, settled down, read for a while, and then slept for most of the rest of the trip. When the bus stopped at other terminals, he would get out, use the restroom, and buy something to eat. Then he got back on the bus again.

When the bus pulled into the terminal of its final destination, the man collected his bag, walked through the terminal and out onto the street. He asked someone which direction he should go to get to Woodward Avenue. Nobody seemed to know. He asked several more people how to get to Woodward Avenue, and each time he was met with blank stares.

Finally he got upset. "Come on," he shouted. "Woodward Avenue is Main Street here. I know Detroit."

---

25. Fosdick, *Riverside Sermons*, 38–45.

That's when they burst into laughter around him. "This isn't Detroit," they said. "This is Kansas City."

He had gotten on the wrong bus.

Good Intentions Are Not Enough

Often it is no big deal to get on the wrong bus or to take the wrong turn. You realize your mistake and then turn around and get back to where you were supposed to be. There are times, though, when taking a wrong turn can be much more serious.

The author of Hebrews says that good intentions are not enough in life. All his readers are deeply religious and want to do the right things before God. But there are choices to be made as to how these profound convictions come to expression.

I think of that sometimes when I am officiating at a marriage ceremony. What exciting times. Everyone smiles. Everybody is dressed up for a celebration. Everything is so beautiful, so radiant, so full of hope and promise.

I stand at the front of the church with the bride and groom, and in their eyes I see the best of intentions—theirs will be the perfect marriage. Theirs will be the strongest home. Theirs will be the deepest vows, the truest commitments, the richest promises, and the surest future.

Yet, within me, there is often this nagging uncertainty. Why, for so many who think they are headed for heaven, does the journey of marriage lead them to hell? I pray for every marriage, "Lord, let them get on the right bus." Good intentions aren't enough.

Hector Berlioz, the great composer, was living in Paris in 1830. He loved a young woman named Camille, and they were engaged to be married.[26]

But then Hector was awarded the Prix de Roma, the Prize of Rome. He could study and compose and perform his music in Italy for a year or two, and all of his financial needs would be covered.

Camille agreed with him that this was an opportunity he needed to take advantage of. Off he went, with a kiss, and a promise that they would soon be married. His intentions never changed.

But life in Rome swallowed him up. And for Camille, life in Paris went on. Other suitors came to call. When Berlioz next heard from her, she was on her way to marry another. Hector, of course, caught the next coach to Paris. Only he got on the wrong one and ended up in Genoa. There he tried again. He booked passage to France once more, but his anxiety must have blinded him because he took the wrong coach again and ended up in Nice.

26. Crabbe, *Hector Berlioz.*

By this time Camille was married, and Hector quit his journey. That's what happens, sometimes, when you catch the wrong bus.

The world is full of good intentions. Nobody wants war. Everybody wants prosperity. There is a hope and a wish and a desire for love in every human heart. But read the morning newspaper or watch the evening news and another picture emerges. The best of intentions is not enough to heal the racial scars that split our communities. The highest ambitions cannot lift the slums out of hell. The purest desires will not, by themselves, chart a course to peace, prosperity, and democracy among the superpower nations.

Having an ideal, catching a vision, or knowing which city you want to go to does not get you there. It is precisely why we all know the proverb, "The road to hell is paved with good intentions." Actions have consequences. Good intentions are not enough. Do you want to go to Detroit? Then get on the right bus. Do you want to make your dreams come true? Then enter the journey of life through the right gate. Do you want to find a good end to the race you are running? Then, according to the writer of Hebrews, head for the right mountain.

Choices Beg for Further Choices

Yet even starting well or making the first good choice is not enough. C.S. Lewis describes our lives so well in *Mere Christianity*.[27] In the chapter on "Christian Behavior," Lewis writes about people who think that Christianity is a kind of one-time bargain with God: you do this for me and I'll do that for you. We bargain our way into heaven based on a one-time negotiation.

Not so, says Lewis. That is not the way of the Bible. We are not people who have managed to bargain our way into heaven. Rather, we are people who make choices. We all start out at a similar point when we enter this world as babies. But then we begin to choose. We choose this way instead of that; we choose these friends instead of those; we pick this career rather than the other.

Little by little, along the way, says Lewis, we begin to turn ourselves toward God or toward something else, something ultimately demonic. Each choice in life is a new gate. Which way will you go? Or, perhaps more accurately, who are you becoming?

God's will is rarely so small that it is merely this choice against that choice. God's will is a way of life, a series of choices, a decision that we keep on making. The two mountains of Hebrews 12 are always in front of us, and it is not just a matter of picking up apples instead of oranges in the produce

27. Lewis, *Mere Christianity*.

department. Rather, it is always a question of values, of motives, of desires. It is a matter of seeing the goal of our lives in our minds and then getting on the right bus over and over and over again.

Lewis says, "Every time you make a choice you are turning the central part of you, the part of you that chooses, into something a little different than it was before." He says that when you look at your life as a whole, with all of those innumerable choices you make from day-to-day, "all your life long you are slowly turning either into a heavenly creature or into a hellish creature."

What We Choose Eventually Chooses Us

Robert Frost summarizes this well in his famous poem "The Road Not Taken." He writes of finding himself in a forest of trees on a glorious autumn afternoon. He was walking down a path, and there was a fork in the way. Which direction should he go? When he made his choice and picked his direction, he said to himself,

> I shall be telling this with a sigh
> Somewhere ages and ages hence:
> Two roads diverged in a wood, and I—
> I took the one less traveled by.
> And that has made all the difference.[28]

That is true for all of us. Years ago, you chose to settle in a particular town and your decision has had lasting effects on how you understand community, neighborhoods, and even race and ethnicity. You chose your course of education. Think of what you could have been if you had gone into engineering instead of medicine. But think also of who you have become because of the decision you made way back then.

You chose your friends, and they have made you into something too. You chose your spouse, you chose your house, you chose your church. And see what you have become because of it all.

Earlier decisions influence later decisions. Because you chose the career you did, you have touched people in a new way. Because you chose your friends well, you have become more friendly, more loving, more trusting. Think of what you would be like today if you had stayed in that crowd you used to run with.

And because you chose your church, you have grown in Christ. You have learned of the grace of God, of the strength of his holiness, of the joy of service, fellowship, and commitment.

28. Frost, "Road Not Taken."

George Mueller's life is a great example of this.[29] Mueller was one of the finest persons who ever walked this earth. He set up orphanages around the world to care for the little ones who had no one else to look after them. He provided for the poor. He preached the love of Jesus, and he lived it every day.

Someone once called Mueller a success. He said, no, he wasn't a success. He was only a servant, a servant of his master who had loved him to life.

Well, said the reporter, how did you manage to do all you've done during the course of your life?

"I don't really know," responded George Mueller. "As I look back on my life, I see that I was constantly brought to a crossroads which demanded a choice of which way I should go." He said that once he had started to follow in the steps of Jesus, all the rest of the decisions that came after seemed easier. He caught the right bus. When he had done that the first time, it became the start of a habit. The second time he knew which bus to take, and by the third and the fourth and the fifth choices, the way was much more clear. Earlier decisions made his later decisions easier.

That kind of spiritual "success" begins when we know where we want to go. What do you want out of life? Where do you hope to be ten or twenty years from now? Why do you hope to be there?

Setting Our Compass by the True North Star

During World War II, the English government knew that Hitler was planning to invade the British Isles. They encouraged the people to prepare as best they could. They bolstered defenses on the Southeast corner. They stationed reserve guards on constant watch. They developed early warning systems and evacuation routes for the people near the coast.

Then they did one more thing. The government passed a law requiring every community to take down all road signs and every other sign that named any town or village. They knew the Germans had maps of England, but if the invaders couldn't locate themselves on those maps, they would be slowed in their progress toward London. Without points of reference, the troops would wander aimlessly.

That is also the way of our lives. If we have no plans or hopes or goals, we find ourselves wandering on any road that beckons. Too often, these lead us to the wrong mountain.

A woman once came running up to Arthur Rubinstein after he finished another spectacular concert. "Oh, Mr. Rubinstein," she said. "I've

29. Mueller, *Autobiography*.

always wanted to play the piano. I'd give anything if I could play like you did this evening."

"No, you wouldn't," he replied. "I know what I've had to give up to be able to play like this, and if that's what you really wanted, you would have done the same."

How true. The great pianist knew his goal. He knew where he wanted to be in life, and then he kept making the necessary choices. He practiced his scales. He put in his hours at the keyboard. He did what he had to do.

Generations ago young William Borden went to Yale University. He was the wealthy son of a powerful family. He could choose to do anything with his life. After he graduated, he chose to become a missionary of the gospel of Jesus Christ. His friends thought he was crazy. "Why throw away your life like that?"[30]

But Borden knew his future. He determined his destiny. He made his choices, and his goals laid hold of him. He set out on a long journey to China, a trip that would take many months. By the time he got to Egypt, some disease ravaged his body. He was placed in a hospital. Soon it became obvious that he would never recover. William Borden would die a foreigner in Egypt. He never reached his goal, and he never went back home.

He could have thought, "What a waste. I should have listened to my family. I should have stayed in America. Why did God do this to me?"

Those, however, were not his dying thoughts. His last conscious act was to write a little note. Seven words that were spoken at his funeral. Seven words that summarized his life, his goals, his choices, and his identity: "No reserve, no retreat, and no regrets."

Can you say that? "No reserve, no retreat, and no regrets."

Does that describe who you are? Can you see your future? Have you determined your destiny? Then continue your journey protected by this old Irish blessing:

> May the road rise to meet you.
> May the wind be always at your back.
> May the sun shine warm on your face,
> and the rain fall softly on your fields;
> And until we meet again,
> may God hold you in the palm of his hand!

---

30. Taylor, *Borden of Yale*.

Chapter 19

Becoming Our Best Selves

Text: Hebrews 13:1–19

Let mutual love continue. Do not neglect to show hospitality to strangers, for by doing that some have entertained angels without knowing it. Remember those who are in prison, as though you were in prison with them; those who are being tortured, as though you yourselves were being tortured. Let marriage be held in honor by all, and let the marriage bed be kept undefiled; for God will judge fornicators and adulterers. Keep your lives free from the love of money, and be content with what you have; for he has said, "I will never leave you or forsake you."[1] So we can say with confidence,

"The Lord is my helper; I will not be afraid. What can anyone do to me?"[2]

Remember your leaders, those who spoke the word of God to you; consider the outcome of their way of life, and imitate their faith. Jesus Christ is the same yesterday and today and forever. Do not be carried away by all kinds of strange teachings; for it is well for the heart to be strengthened by grace, not by regulations about food, which have not benefited those who observe them. We have an altar from which those who officiate in the tent have no right to eat. For the bodies of those animals whose blood is brought into the sanctuary by the high priest as a sacrifice for sin are burned outside the camp. Therefore Jesus

1. Deut 31:6.
2. Ps 118:6–7.

also suffered outside the city gate in order to sanctify the people by his own blood. Let us then go to him outside the camp and bear the abuse he endured. For here we have no lasting city, but we are looking for the city that is to come. Through him, then, let us continually offer a sacrifice of praise to God, that is, the fruit of lips that confess his name. Do not neglect to do good and to share what you have, for such sacrifices are pleasing to God.

Obey your leaders and submit to them, for they are keeping watch over your souls and will give an account. Let them do this with joy and not with sighing—for that would be harmful to you.

Pray for us; we are sure that we have a clear conscience, desiring to act honorably in all things. I urge you all the more to do this, so that I may be restored to you very soon.

Backstory: Outside the Camp

The final multiple ethical exhortations that close this treatise are a common feature of early Christian writings. In the New Testament alone, we find these similar expressions:

- James concludes his brief letter with around a dozen practical encouragements and warnings to live faith in daily behaviors.[3]

- Peter brings his first letter to a culmination with three specific admonitions to live humbly, be on guard against the predations of the devil, and endure well through suffering.[4]

- Jude calls his readers to remember the faithfulness of the apostles and uses their example to call out at least five specific dimensions of spiritual living.[5]

- Paul makes a habit of ending his letters with lists of preferred or commanded moral expressions of Christian faith:

    - To the Galatians, he urged care for one another, submission to scriptural authority, discernment about false teachings, constancy in doing good, and humility.[6]

3. Jas 4–5.
4. 1 Pet 5:5–10.
5. Jude 17–23.
6. Gal 6.

- In his first letter to the Thessalonians, after a final warning against false teachers who deny the second coming of Jesus, he rushes through a rapid-fire staccato list of seventeen instructions about living faithfully as "children of light and children of the day."[7]

- Bringing his poignant and very personal second letter to the Corinthians to a close, Paul quotes a proverb, calls for the church to be involved in spiritual self-examination, and then gives four pointed moral injunctions: "Put things in order, listen to my appeal, agree with one another, live in peace."[8]

- Romans 15:1–12 functions as a similar concluding challenge to godly living, focused particularly on urging the congregation to get along with one another, especially beyond the cultural Jew-gentile separations. Then Paul launches into two new mini-letters (one reaffirming his divine ordination as an ambassador of Jesus to the gentiles and the other outlining his intended travel plans) and a list of greetings before a final, briefer hortatory challenge to be aware of false teachers.[9]

- Ending his letter to the Colossian congregations, Paul urges six very focused social behaviors consonant with the gospel, and then gives six more specifically spiritual discipline instructions[10] before concluding with a number of personal notes about individuals these people know.

- Written at the same time as Paul's letter to the Colossians, his letter called "Ephesians"[11] carries similar ethical injunctions, though less specific and addressed to broader behaviors.[12]

- In his letter to the Philippian congregation, Paul concludes with a mixture of moral urgings and personal references.[13]

- To both Timothy and Titus, in letters that mirror one another in essential content, Paul provides closing instructions that list

7. 1 Thess 5.

8. 2 Cor 13.

9. Rom 15–16.

10. Col 3:18—4:6.

11. Most probably, the letter we call "Ephesians" is actually the letter Paul references in Col 4:16, and was originally a circular letter intended to be read in all of the congregations in the area.

12. Eph 5–6.

13. Phil 4.

good behaviors, call for certain pastoral practices, warn about persons who have opposed either Paul or the gospel enterprise, and urge spiritual disciplines.[14]

- Paul's final letter to Timothy carries reminders of Paul's lifestyle and behaviors, encouraging the same in his protégé, interspersing these instructions with a number of personal issues about people and travels.[15]

Other early Christian writings follow a similar pattern as they end. "The Pastor of Hermas" is sprinkled throughout with moral exhortations, and then culminates these with a final instruction for all to do good.[16] Similar expressions are collected near the end of Ignatius of Rome's first-century *Letter to the Romans*.

Living Faithfully

The list of urged moral behaviors at the close of Hebrews is an interesting miscellany. There are general instructions that apply to all in the practices of daily living, group injunctions that nurture deeper community, and specific behaviors which would come to expression in only some individuals because of their focused nature. In summary:

- Let mutual love continue.
- Do not neglect to show hospitality to strangers, for by doing that some have entertained angels without knowing it.
- Remember those who are in prison as though you were in prison with them; those who are being tortured as though you yourselves were being tortured.
- Let marriage be held in honor by all, and let the marriage bed be kept undefiled; for God will judge fornicators and adulterers.
- Keep your lives free from the love of money, and be content with what you have.
- Remember your leaders, those who spoke the word of God to you; consider the outcome of their way of life, and imitate their faith.
- Do not be carried away by all kinds of strange teachings, for it is well for the heart to be strengthened by grace, not by regulations about food, which have not benefited those who observe them.

---

14. 1 Tim 6; Titus 3.

15. 2 Timothy 3:10–4:22.

16. Hermas, "The Pastor," parable 10.

- Do not neglect to do good and to share what you have, for such sacrifices are pleasing to God.

- Obey your leaders and submit to them, for they are keeping watch over your souls and will give an account. Let them do this with joy and not with sighing—for that would be harmful to you.

- Pray for us.

Interspersed with these exhortations are two final scriptural nods. First, in Hebrews 13:5, the writer applies the promise of God to the Israelites as they were about to enter Canaan[17] to this struggling Christian community: "I will never leave you or forsake you." In doing so, he draws together several strands of biblical interpretation and reinterpretation. For one thing, the continuity between God's first covenant people and God's second covenant people is affirmed. This was a key theme of earlier sections of the treatise, notably chapters 1 and chapters 3–9. Also, the divinity of Jesus is reiterated, since it is by holding onto Jesus that the strength of God's care will be felt.[18] And, along with these things, the writer is picking up the theme of wilderness journeying that was central to chapter 4. Not all the Israelites who received the commands and promises at Mount Sinai made it into the promised land; only those who were truly obedient and kept the faith eventually received what was divinely intended. So with these persecuted Christians: the vow of God remains unchanged, but they must act upon it.

Second, the promise of God through Moses to Israel, now applied to these New Testament strugglers, is further affirmed by way of David's great testimony found in Psalm 118:6–7. Once again, the quote emerges from a time of struggle (David obviously has gone through a serious period of challenges to his life from enemies) and espouses confidence in God's ability to carry faithful followers through.

Splitting the Community

Most significant, however, is a complex allusion to the Day of Atonement[19] in verses 10–13. The writer of Hebrews used this event of spiritual cleansing in the life of ancient Israel at length in chapters 7–10. Now he injects a stunning interpretation and application of one element of the ceremony's activities. According to Leviticus 16, two sacrifices were to be offered on the Day of Atonement. First, a bull was killed and burned. This was the larg-

---

17. Deut 31:6.

18. Note Heb 13:8, which states this explicitly.

19. Originally explained and outlined in Lev 16.

est animal sacrifice in the whole cadre of Israelite offerings commanded by Yahweh. Although it was intended to cleanse the high priest who officiated throughout the rest of the day's activities, the high priest himself carried the symbolic weight of the entire nation within his person. Thus, the largest possible sacrifice was made to atone for the largest expression of Israelite collective identity.

Second, a goat was sacrificed. This was one of two goats selected for the Day of Atonement ceremonies. The other received a transfer of the people's sins by way of the high priest laying hands on its head. That goat was brought out to the wilderness to die as an unclean reject from the community.[20] This goat, however, continued the cleansing process for the nation as a whole.

But there is a procedural note in Leviticus 16:27 that points to the practicalities of these instructions. The portable altar of burt offering used to burn these animals in the courtyard of the tabernacle was not very large,[21] and the time needed to incinerate them completely would exceed the general limits of resources available a day. For that reason, "the bull of the sin offering and the goat of the sin offering, whose blood was brought in to make atonement in the holy place, shall be taken outside the camp; their skin and their flesh and their dung shall be consumed in fire."[22] Using this image, the writer of Hebrews extrapolates theologically:

- Jesus is the new, permanent "Day of Atonement" sacrifice.[23]

- Jesus was not sacrificed on the altar of burnt offering in the tabernacle (temple) court; he was sacrificed on a cross outside the camp (city of Jerusalem).

- So we need to move away from the tabernacle (temple) sacrifices and out of the city to the one who offered the only true and eternal sacrifice for us.

- And, by the way, those who continue to offer sacrifices at the altar of burnt offering in the tabernacle (temple) miss all of this, to their own detriment.

This interesting reflection on the events of the Day of Atonement in ancient Israel, and the fulfillment of its intentions in the death of Jesus, now are

20. This is the origin of the term and concept of "scapegoat."

21. 5 cubits by 5 cubits by 3 cubits, according to Exod 27:1–5. This would be approximately 7 ½ square feet, and 4 ½ feet high, or about the size of two average kitchen tables placed next to one another.

22. Lev 16:27.

23. See Heb 5 and 9.

used to remind this persecuted Christian band that neither Jerusalem or Judaism itself are their true places of residence or citizenship or salvation. They belong, instead, to the eternal city of God that is above and is to come.

Deftly extrapolating and interpolating ceremonial events central to the religious life of Judaism, the author of Hebrews draws one final distinction between the people and rituals of the first covenant expression and the those of God's true community in this new second covenant age. Not only is salvation no longer to be sought within the Jewish ceremonial ritual system, these legitimate heirs of all that God promised and intended must actually separate themselves from on-going expressions of Judaism. Jesus is the way; Judaism is not.

Thus, these gentiles who converted to Judaism because it attracted them to its deep piety and devout connection with the Creator of all, and who had become fervent followers of Messiah Jesus revealed in these recent times, were now to withdraw from the very community that originally nurtured their faith. This continued commitment to Jesus, along with its related rejection of any efficacy to be found in the on-going Jewish ceremonial rites, demanded a new and deep division between peoples who had shared common language, lifestyle, religious practices, scriptural learning, and leadership. They had lived together. They had worked together. They had studied together. They had witnessed together. They had eaten together. They had married one another.

But now they must separate.

Where Have We Come So Far?

- God has spoken in times past.
    - This is our source of direction and confidence.
    - We know who we are because of the prophets.
- God has recently spoken a stronger, better, and clearer message through Jesus.
    - So when we, who live by the prophetic message, hear Jesus, we had better listen.
- Jesus is superior to the angels.
    - The great divine message that formed us came through Moses, but the message itself was delivered to him by angels (Deut 33:2; Acts 7:53).

- ◆ Yet Jesus is superior to angels, and therefore delivers a more important prophetic message than that through the great prophet Moses.
- So, stick with Jesus, even though you are tempted to turn away from him.
    - ◆ There is no higher authority or source of connection with God.
    - ◆ And if our lives are to be connected to God, we turn away from Jesus to our own peril.
- God has made the world subject to Jesus.
    - ◆ God never did this with the angels, so, again, Jesus is superior to them.
    - ◆ But this only happened because Jesus first fully identified with the world.
- Jesus willingly came into the world to fully experience its pain.
- And this is to our benefit for three reasons:
    - ◆ To fully identify with us as sisters and brothers
    - ◆ To make atonement for our sins (which cause the pain of this world).
    - ◆ To bring us with him fully into the house of God.
- So Jesus is greater than (over) the angels, but Jesus is also greater than (over) Moses.
- Therefore, be careful that you don't disconnect from Jesus (who is God):
    - ◆ Remember how those in our past who disconnected from God came under punishment.
    - ◆ The same can happen to you if you do not stay true and committed to Jesus.
- Let God's people in the earlier redemptive sequence be your instructors:
    - ◆ Like us, they were saved and led to their "(sabbath) rest" in the promised land.
        - ▪ But they failed to stay connected to God by way of the word of the Prophet (Moses) and died before reading "rest."

- Now God has promised us a coming "rest" (i.e., "heaven" when we die).

    - But we will receive it only if we remain connected to God by way of the word of the prophet (Jesus) and live faithfully through these trials.

- And, again, the only one who can keep you connected to God is Jesus:

    - He is our true high priest, who will take us boldly to God's merciful throne through his actions on our behalf on the Day of Atonement. He is fully human, so he completely understands the struggles of our lives and sympathizes deeply, to the point of anguished cries.

- In fact, he is as fully committed to fulfilling the mandate and responsibilities of his priestly order as are others.

    - They in their "Aaronic/Levitical priestly order."

    - He in his "Melchizedek priestly order."

- I wish you were getting this. You should be mature enough to teach others, but it seems you have lost your passion for Jesus and are trying only to protect yourselves.

    - Though I write strong words, I am confident that you will continue in our faith in Jesus.

    - After all, God has made absolute promises of care toward us that are our hope.

    - And Jesus is the only anchor we have today to ensure that we will receive what was promise.

- After all, Jesus is a priest after the order of Melchizedek.

    - The Levitical order priests could not fully satisfy needs, since its sacrifices needed repeating.

    - That is why someone from Melchizedek's order was needed.

        - Someone who was a descendant of David (of the tribe of Judah), perfect and never dying.

- This brings us back to the main thing we have been saying: Jesus is the best high priest ever.

    - He is God (seated at the right hand of the majesty in heaven).

    - He is owner of the house of God.

    - He is high priest of the house of God.

- The true house of God, with dimensions given by God on the mountain.
- The visible house of God, here below (under the care of the Levitical priests), important as it is, is only a shadow of the real thing.
  - He is faultless.
  - He is the mediator of the new covenant (remember Jer 31:31–34?).
- This is very important: God found fault with the old covenant.
  - God is causing the old covenant age to come to an end.
  - Jesus is the only source of hope in the new covenant age.
- These changes are symbolized by the "houses" of the two covenant ages:
  - The tabernacle with God hidden and symbolic actions repeated.
  - The heavenly dwelling with Jesus bringing us directly to the throne.
- Both "houses" required blood sacrifice for God's people to approach God.
  - But in the earthly tabernacle, repeated animal sacrifices by Levitical priests were needed.
  - While in the heavenly dwelling, Jesus offered himself once for all.
- Thus, Jesus is the best mediator and the only source of our eternal security
  - The tabernacle and Levitical priesthood were only types of this ultimate expression of God's love.
- But keep in mind that there is a symbiotic relationship between the first and second expressions of God's covenant:
  - The first is the shadow—the meaningful but repetitious type.
  - While the second is the substance—the perfection of all things through Jesus.
- Jesus has accomplished everything that is necessary and now rules over all, in an age where the new covenant is written on hearts and forgiveness is complete.

- So, let's go! Grab each other, keep your focus, and let's let Jesus take us right to God's throne of grace.
- Again, I want to remind you about those in the past who failed to keep faith with God and lost out.
  - You have come through some tough times in the past. Remember how you stayed strong?
  - Some of you seem to be dropping out now, as new threats loom. Remember that Jesus can keep us going.
- Have faith in Jesus.
  - See the example of those who have gone before?
  - Besides, don't you believe that God exists and that he rewards those who seek him?
- Remember how our family's first parents all had faith that God would bring a better future than they experienced at the time.
- Remember how Moses, our greatest hero, chose the difficult path of faith and faithfulness rather than ease and worldly success.
- And don't forget the many among our ancestors who won big for God, or lost greatly in a world that was not worthy of them, seeking by faith what we have recently received in Jesus.
- Most importantly, keep your eyes on Jesus.
  - He ran the race before you did (and a bloody run it was), confident of the joy at the end.
  - Know that the pain of your own race is part of the loving discipline of a Father who is bringing out the best in you.
  - So keep running, and encourage each other on the track.
- The end is near.
  - So keep confidence, and live kindly; beware of bitterness that can tear you apart in these tense times.
  - Remember the two mountains:
    - Sinai, from which God shook the world in terror as he announced judgment.
    - Zion, from which God will shake the world in awe as he announces the consummation of all things.
- Live chaste and ready lives, for God is always with you.

Message: Living Witnesses

Some years ago, a major research firm conducted a survey to determine what people would be willing to do for $10 million.[24] The results were astounding. 3 percent would put their children up for adoption; 7 perecent would kill a stranger; 10 percent would lie in court to set a murderer free; 16 percent would divorce their spouses; 23 percent said they would become prostitutes for a week or longer.

Most astonishing was the category at the top of the list. One-fourth of all surveyed said that they would leave their families for $10 million.

Everyone has a selling price at which he or she will step over a line of conduct and allow someone else to dictate the terms of behavior. It might be $10 million or it might only be one more bottle of wine. It might be a night in the spotlight or a night in bed. In Shusaku Endo's powerful novel *Silence*,[25] the missionary priest Rodriguez steps over the line when torture exceeds what his soul can bear, and he desecrates an image of Jesus. We all have our selling price.

Multiple Identities

Our selling price is linked to our identity, as this passage from Hebrews reminds us. The stronger our sense of who we are, the higher our selling price and the deeper our character. There are, however, several identities that each of us wears.

The first is the identity we receive from others. We get our looks and temperament from our parents. We garner our tastes and styles from our culture. There is even something mystical about us that we receive as a gift from God, unique to our personalities. In Hebrews 13, this is the meaning of the quotations from Deuteronomy and Psalms. We are linked to the community of Israel that stood at Mount Sinai to receive the divine instructions about life. We are tied, inseparably, to David and other psalmists who believed God was true to God's promises.

Poet John Masefield understood that when he reflected on how it was that he started writing and rhyming. One day he picked up a volume of Geoffrey Chaucer's works and was gripped by the art of the lines. Masefield couldn't put the book down. That night, he read until a whole new world opened for him. By the time morning broke, said Masefield, he had finished the entire book, set it down, looked at the dawning day and quietly said, "I too am a poet." And so he was.[26]

24. Patterson and Kim, *The Day America*.
25. Endo, *Silence*.
26. Smith, *John Masefield*.

A second identity we have in life is the one we make. In N. Richard Nash's captivating drama, *The Rainmaker*,[27] the main character is a con artist who calls himself Starbuck. He travels from town to town during the Dirty Thirties scheming to get people to pay him to bring the rains for their parched fields.

Young Lizzie Curry catches his eye and they spar with building passion. But Lizzie is no fool and she challenges him to come clean with her about his true name. It can't really be Starbuck, she knows.

Starbuck admits that he was born a "Smith," but asks, "What kind of name is that for a fellow like me? I needed a name that had the whole sky in it. And the power of a man. Starbuck. Now there's a name—and it's mine."

Lizzie tries to contradict him, telling him he has no right choosing his own name and giving up his family heritage. Yet he will not capitulate quickly. "You're wrong, Lizzie," he says. "The name you choose for yourself is more your own name than the name you were born with."

Starbuck is on to something. Much of what we see in people around has to do with what they have made of themselves. When an English nobleman named Roberts was having his portrait painted the artist asked him if he would like the lines and creases in his face smoothed over.

"Certainly not." he objected. "Make sure you put them all in. I earned every single wrinkle on my face."

He was a man who knew the identity he had made.

There is also a third and deeper human identity. It is the identity that transforms us from what we were to what we are becoming. The poet saw a friend clearly when he wrote:

> And there were three men went down the road
>> As down the road went he:
> The man they saw, the man he was,
>> And the man he wanted to be.

The person we each want to be when we find our truest selves in God is larger than either the identity we have received from others or the one we try to create. This is the thought that the writer of Hebrews hopes to encourage in his close association of faith and ethics, of religion and behaviors. Anything that sullies us by trying to define us on terms less than God's grace limits our best self.

---

27. N. Richard Nash's *The Rainmaker* was first produced at the Cort Theatre in New York City on October 28, 1954; it ran for 125 performances and was quickly translated into over forty languages. By 1956 it had been produced as a film starring Burt Lancaster and Katherine Hepburn.

The Witness of Character

This is why the author of Hebrews focuses on daily behaviors as the expression of meaningful faith. If these theological syllogisms and conclusions are true, they shape how we live and act. Others will know of God only through our lifestyles and moral commitments.

Will Durant, the famous philosopher and historian, was asked for advice by one of his grandchildren. He summarized all his wisdom in "ten commandments."[28] At the heart of them is this advice: "Do not speak while another is speaking. Discuss, do not dispute. Absorb and acknowledge whatever truth you can find in opinions different from your own. Be courteous and considerate to all, especially to those who oppose you."

We would all like to have friends like that. Certainly we expect God to treat us that way.

But "considerateness" is more than just thoughtfulness. It is a profound expression of identity rooted in God's intentions for it. It is also a living testimony that other people are more than brute animals or despised creatures. We and they are important to God. That is why God showers love on us in Jesus. And if we and they are important to God, God's ways of living ought to shape our testimonies about life, lived or spoken.

Stan Wiersma, writing under his pen name "Sietze Buning," explored the religious roots of being considerate in his collection of folk poetry titled *Style and Class*.[29] Much of what we display in life, said Sietze Buning, has to do with "style"—we watch how others dress or act and then we try to imitate those we admire. But "class" is living out of the nobility of your inner character, said Sietze.

He tells this little story to illustrate what he means:

> Queen Wilhelmina was entertaining the
> Frisian Cattle Breeders' Association at dinner.
> The Frisian farmers didn't know what to make of their finger bowls.
> They drank them down.
> The stylish courtiers from the Hague nudged each other,
> and pointed, and laughed at such lack of style.
> Until the queen herself, without a smile, raised her finger bowl and
> drained it, obliging all the courtiers to follow suit, without a smile.[30]

Sietze Buning ends with this note of judgment: "*The courtiers had style, but Queen Wilhelmina had class.*"

28. Durant and Durant, *Lessons of History*.
29. Buning, *Style and Class*.
30. Buning, *Style and Class*, 17.

While that makes for good story telling, Sietze Buning takes it one surprising step further. He links style to the wisdom of the world and class to the wisdom of heaven. The former tries to get us to fit in with the right crowd, looking the right way and eating the right foods, while driving the right vehicles. That's style.

But class—*real* class—happens to us when we realize that we are children of God. If God is King, we are nobility—princesses and princes in the realm of the great ruler.

Children of the King do not need to prove themselves, nor do they need to flaunt their status. If they have learned well at home the true worth of their lives, they can treat others with courtesy and respect. They can be considerate. It is a religious thing, just as the writer of Hebrews instructs.

Taking Our Cue from the Captain

Someone has suggested a powerfully illuminating analogy. When a ship is built, he said, each part has a little voice of its own. As seamen walk the passageways on her maiden voyage they can hear the creaking whispers of separate identities: "I'm a rivet"; "I'm a sheet of steel"; "I'm a propeller"; "I'm a beam." For a while these little voices sing their individual songs, proudly independent and fiercely self-protective.

But then a storm blows in on the high seas—the waves toss, the gales hurl, and the rain beats. If the parts of the ship try to withstand the pummeling independent from one another, each would be lost. On the bridge, however, stands the captain. He issues orders that take all of the little voices and bring them together for a larger purpose. By the time the vessel has weathered, the storm sailors hear a new and deeper song echoing from stem to stern: "I am a ship."

It is the captain's call that creates the deeper identity. So too in our lives, according to this concluding exhortation in Hebrews. Minor stars in a world of glamour try to sing siren songs, pulling bits and pieces of us from the voyage of our lives. Those who hear the captain's call are able to sail true and straight.

Chapter 20

Who Are These People?

Text: Hebrews 13:20-25

Now may the God of peace, who brought back from the dead our Lord Jesus, the great shepherd of the sheep, by the blood of the eternal covenant, make you complete in everything good so that you may do his will, working among us that which is pleasing in his sight, through Jesus Christ, to whom be the glory forever and ever. Amen.

I appeal to you, brothers and sisters, bear with my word of exhortation, for I have written to you briefly. I want you to know that our brother Timothy has been set free; and if he comes in time, he will be with me when I see you. Greet all your leaders and all the saints. Those from Italy send you greetings. Grace be with all of you.

Backstory: Identity Clues

THE INITIAL BLESSING IN the concluding elements of the letter is a very good summary of everything the author has sought to communicate by way of this treatise:

- "The God of peace" recalls the "shalom" or sabbath rest that was an essential focus of the reward promised to those who remained faithful to Jesus, even during perilous times.[1]

1. Heb 4.

273

- The resurrection of Jesus is the undeniable confirmation of Jesus' unique identity and authoritative priesthood, since Jesus is like Melchizedek—in part because neither had a beginning or an end.[2]

- Jesus is the "great shepherd of the sheep" on several levels. First, he is the one and only true Passover Lamb, since all Old Testament ("former covenant") expressions ultimately pointed to him and because his self-sacrifice accomplished all that the repeated Passover Lamb offerings were meant to do but could never fully achieve. Second, Jesus is the great shepherd and we are the sheep, indicating that where he goes, we must follow. This is particularly important during the increased persecution being experienced by this community and the threats of even great pogroms to come. We are the Jesus' faithful followers only if we share in his identity and bloody sacrifice. This means that, just as Jesus died in the execution of his responsibilities, so too we are likely to be executed as we follow him. Jesus spilled his blood, and ours is soon to follow. In a corollary, if we stop following Jesus and revert to merely rigorous righteousness and investments in the ceremonial rites of the former covenant expressions, we have stopped following our shepherd.[3]

- The "blood of the eternal covenant" takes the readers back to Jeremiah 31:31–34 and Hebrews 8, where the heart of Hebrews theology is articulated. Already during the expressions of the former covenant, God made it clear that a fuller and more complete expression of divine love and engagement would soon take place. Jesus fulfills and culminates everything that God intended for Israel, including celebrating the ritual atoning and cleansing sacrifices one last time in a permanent form. The single covenant commitment of God, split into two expressions, is now at its ultimate rendition through the blood of Jesus.

- "Make you complete in everything good so that you may do his will": this phrase has a double meaning. On the one hand, it renews the challenges urged toward faithful commitments to Jesus during these perilous times that the writer previously issued in Hebrews 3:7–19, 5:11–6:3, and 10:26–39. On the other hand, couched within the framework of a testimony of divine blessing, it forms an assurance that God will work things out even though these folks feel tired and weak and powerless. Insofar as they are able, they need to keep true to their testimonies that Jesus is the Messiah and the source of all life and

2. Heb 7.
3. Heb 3, 6, 10–12.

livelihood. But even when they fail and fall, the author of Hebrews is confident of the great power of divine providence that will see them through the sticky times ahead.

- "Working among us that which is pleasing in his sight": while the "pleasing" element of this injunction might seem "pleasant," the reality of God's work in and through these people amounts to likely death. Jesus followed the plan of the Father's working, and it led him to the cross. We are to run the race of life and faith with those who have trusted God before, knowing that many of them were tortured and died precisely because of their faithfulness. And the race marked out for us is crimson because of the blood of both Jesus and Abel.[4]

- "Through Jesus Christ," who is our great high priest and the one who came from the throne of grace (heaven),[5] offered the perfect Day of Atonement sacrifice,[6] rightly rules over the true house of God,[7] and takes us with him to the throne of grace where we receive mercy.[8]

- "To Whom be the glory forever and ever": this final doxology affirms that all praise belonging only to the one Creator God can and should be affirmed and declared to Jesus, since Jesus is himself also truly our eternal God.[9]

The author's genius is again apparent in this short blessing, as is the theological consistency of the message of the book as a whole. We may wonder at the "briefly" character of this treatise, but it is likely that the author was able to preach and teach for hours at a time when personally with this congregation.

Clues about the Recipients

There are a few final personal notes, the first contemporary expressions given by the author: Timothy has recently been released from prison and is on his way to see the author. The author plans to travel with Timothy to visit these people. Greetings are sent, with special regard for the leaders of this

---

4. Heb 11–12.
5. Heb 1.
6. Heb 2, 6, 9.
7. Heb 3.
8. Heb 10.
9. Heb 1, 3, 12.

community and from others who used to live with these recipients in Italy[10] but are now residing, along with the author, at some distance from Italy.

These closing notes raise again two questions: who is the author of this document, and who are its recipients? By the time we reach the end of the treatise, there are quite a few clues about its intended readers:

- They were second generation Christians who had learned of Jesus and the teachings of the Christian faith from others, never having met Jesus personally.[11]

- They had endured challenges to their faith and its expressions some time earlier.[12] These initial persecutions involved public ridicule,[13] the murdering of at least several of their leaders,[14] property confiscated from some of them,[15] and time in prison for a number among their group.[16]

- Implied by the theological content and many scriptural quotations throughout the book is the deep commitment of these people to God, to the Jewish faith and its ritual expressions, and to the authority of Scripture. They knew the Scriptures well and were able to follow lines of teaching that connected various passages to one another easily.

- At the same time, these folks were Greek-speakers, since the scriptural references are consistently taken from the Septuagint (LXX) Greek translation of the Hebrew Bible. Moreover, the reference to their coming to faith through being "enlightened"[17] seems to indicate that these readers originated outside of the ethnic Jewish community and became members originally through proselytism, probably before or around the same time that news about Jesus as Messiah disseminated throughout the Jewish centers of the Roman world.

---

10. The phrase οἱ ἀπὸ τῆς Ἰταλίας ("those from Italy") can mean either "those who live in Italy" or "those who are from Italy but not currently residing in Italy." This ambiguous notation has served to suggest that the author is either in Rome, sending this letter out to readers elsewhere, or has been resident in Rome and is now not there, sending this missive to his friends and acquaintances still living in Rome.

11. Heb 2:1; 2:3; 13:7.

12. Heb 10:32.

13. Heb 10:33.

14. Heb 13:7.

15. Heb 10:34.

16. Heb 10:34; 13:3.

17. Φωτισθέντες, "having been enlightened," in Heb 10:32.

- They lived in Rome. Although the cryptic notation "from Italy" in Hebrews 13:24 can mean either that this group of people had once lived in Italy and now was residing elsewhere, or that the author and his companions had been part of their group in Italy and now lived away from them, the former sense is much more likely. The reference to Timothy's imprisonment and the author's future travel plans do not clarify geographical matters, since Timothy had traveled all over the Mediterranean world with Paul. Even though Timothy had been posted as the lead pastor in Ephesus near the end of Paul's life,[18] it is clear from Paul's second letter to Timothy that Paul had been arrested and was in prison in Rome, expecting Timothy to join him there.[19]

- New persecutions were threatening,[20] causing some to lose heart and give up testimony in Jesus, reverting, instead, into familiar rituals of Jewish faith emerging from its first covenant expressions. Implied by this distinction between the presumed treatment of Jews and Christians is a time when governing officials no longer viewed Christianity as a sect of and contained within the Jewish population.

These last clues to the identity of the original readers of Hebrews lead us to issues of timing. When was this treatise written and sent? Central to finding an answer is the assertion which emerges from Hebrews that Jews would not be persecuted for their faith, but Christians would. This connects with the evolving policies of the Roman government toward both Jews and Christians. Jewish identity and rituals were a fact of life for the Romans. The kingdom they had received from the Greeks included both the Jewish territories of Judea and Galilee in Palestine and also large Jewish communities in every major city of the empire, especially Antioch, Alexandria, and Rome itself.

Clues about the Date of Composition

The intriguing Edict of Claudius expelling all Jews from Rome assists in identifying the earliest time in which Jewish and Christian identities might have been separated from one another. Emperor Claudius ruled from early 41 through late 54. At one point during his reign, according to Suetonius, a biographer of the Roman emperors, Claudius force all Jews to leave Rome because their public arguments about Jesus' possible messiahship had

18. See 1 and 2 Tim.

19. 2 Tim 4:9–13.

20. Heb 10:24–25; 10:35–36; 12:3–13.

disturbed the peace.[21] This event enters the New Testament in Acts 18, where Paul becomes acquainted with Aquila and Pricilla in Corinth. They were Jews from Rome who had been forced from the city by Claudius' edict.[22] This note, along with Luke's further explanation that "Gallio was proconsul of Achaia" while Paul was ministering in Athens,[23] helps focus the date of Claudius' edict further. Gallio was personally in Corinth for approximately the calendar year of 51 AD.[24] This would indicate that Claudius' expulsion of the Jews from Rome took place around 49–50 AD.

Since the cause of Claudius' edict was an uproar in the Jewish community about whether Jesus was the "Christ" (Messiah), Christianity was not yet differentiated from Judaism generally at this time, at least by Roman authorities. Only a decade later, Emperor Nero would clearly distinguish between Judaism and Christianity, affirming the validity of the former while aggressively persecuting the latter. Nero blamed Christians for setting the great fire of Rome in 64 AD[25] and had thousands of them killed, including Peter[26] and Paul.[27]

While local persecutions of Christians continued throughout the first two centuries, only one other major official attack on Christianity happened before the last possible date of the writing of Hebrews.[28] Emperor Domitian (81–96 AD), son Emperor Vespasian (67–79 AD) and brother of Emperor Titus (79–81 AD), ascended to power in a world unsettled by the strange deaths of his predecessors, another great fire in Rome, and the first significant losses to the battle-hardened Roman troops in remembered

21. Suetonius, *Divus Claudius* 25 mentions agitations by the "Jews" which led Claudius (Roman Emperor from AD 41 to 54) to expel them from Rome: "Since the Jews constantly made disturbances at the instigation of Chrestus, he [the Emperor Claudius] expelled them from Rome." See also Cassius Dio, *Roman History* 60.6.6–7; Paulus Orosius, *History* 7.6.15–16.

22. Acts 18:1–2.

23. Acts 18:12.

24. See Westerholm, *Blackwell Companion*, 14; Murphy-O'Connor, "Paul and Gallio."

25. Cassius Dio, *Roman History*, books 62; Suetonius, "Life of Nero" in *Lives of Twelve Caesars*; Tacitus, *Annales* XV.38–44.

26. 1 Clement, 5; Tertullian, *Prescription against Heretics* 106; Tertullian, *Antitode for the Scorpion's Sting* 15; Origen, *Commentarii in Genesim*, III (quoted by Eusebius in *Ecclesiastical History* III, 1); Peter of Alexandria, "Canonical Epistle," Canon 9; Jerome, *De viris illustribus*, chap. 1.

27. Ignatius, *To the Ephesians*, Chapter XII; Eusebius, *Ecclesiastical History*, II.25:8; Tertullian, *Prescription against Heretics*, Chapter XXXVI; Eusebius, *Ecclesiastical History* II.25:5–6.

28. Clement of Rome, who died in 99 AD, quotes from Hebrews in his second letter, 2 Clement.

history. Domitian feared that the empire was losing its strength because it had forgotten its older gods. Particularly challenging was the rapid spread of Christianity, with its stories of a leader killed by Romans but resurrected to speak judgment against them. Domitian responded with the massive assault on Christianity that would, among other consequences, send John in exile to Patmos, where he received the Revelation from Jesus.[29]

If Hebrews is written after a time of mild persecution took place, and during the times when a significantly greater persecution is threatening, the most likely dates for its creation are either between 55–64 AD, after the Edict of Claudius and before Nero, or 70–80 AD, after the great Neronian pogroms and in anticipation of Domitian's tortures. While both periods could work well to set the stage for the themes of Hebrews, two considerations push toward the earlier timeframe. First, confiscation of property, public ridicule and the imprisonment of leaders of the Christian community[30] fit better with the Edict of Claudius than they do with Nero's strong persecutions, especially since the readers are reminded that they have not yet been subjected to threats of death for their faith.[31] Nero certainly went beyond public ridicule and bloodless threats in his attacks on the Christian community.

Second, and more significantly, there is no reference to the Jerusalem temple throughout Hebrews. The writer consistently mentions the tabernacle[32] or "house of God"[33] as the locus of God's presence and the ritual ceremonies of Jewish sacrifices. Even though it is clear that the author of Hebrews is aware of the temple in Jerusalem as the successor of the tabernacle,[34] the tabernacle evokes the original, purer expressions of Israelite/Jewish religious identity and the active interaction between God and God's people that took place.

At the same time, an essential element of the theological movements and arguments of this treatise is that the sacrifices taking place in the temple courts are no longer efficacious or necessary. Since the temple in Jerusalem was destroyed by the Roman armies in 70 AD, if Hebrews had been written afterward, the writer would have had a perfect illustration of God's clear judgment against the temple rituals. Since, it seems, the author did not have the destruction of the temple available to him as a graphic supportive

29. Smallwood, "Domitian's Attitude."

30. Heb 10:33–34.

31. Heb 12:4.

32. Heb 8:2; 8:5; 9:2; 9:3; 9:6; 9:8; 9:11; 9:21; 11:9; 13:10.

33. Heb 3:2; 3:3; 3:4; 3:5; 3:6; 8:8; 8:10; 10:21.

34. See Heb 13:11–13.

illustration of the key themes of his treatise, it appears most likely that this document was written before 70 AD, and thus sometime between the Edict of Claudius and the persecutions of Nero. If the threat of new persecutions was very strong, as the writer seems to indicate, Hebrews was probably written in the early sixties, when memories of the expulsion from Rome under Claudius were still remembered by many, but a clear distinction between the Jewish community and the Christian community was experienced by all, and Nero's public anger with Christians was becoming obvious.

Clues about the Author

One final question remains. Who is the "I" that authored Hebrews? Since the writer does not identify himself by name, this conundrum has been debated throughout the history of the Christian church.

It is clear that Clement of Rome (c. 35–99 AD) knew of Hebrews and quoted it in one of his own letters.[35] Origen (185–254) was the first to reflect on the authorship of Hebrews,[36] tentatively seeming to affirm the

35. "This is the way, dearly beloved, wherein we found our salvation, even Jesus Christ the High priest of our offerings, the Guardian and Helper of our weakness. Through Him let us look steadfastly unto the heights of the heavens; through Him we behold as in a mirror His faultless and most excellent visage; through Him the eyes of our hearts were opened; through Him our foolish and darkened mind springeth up unto the light; through Him the Master willed that we should taste of the immortal knowledge Who being the brightness of His majesty is so much greater than angels, as He hath inherited a more excellent name. For so it is written 'Who maketh His angels spirits and His ministers aflame of fire' but of His Son the Master said thus, 'Thou art My Son, I this day have begotten thee. Ask of Me, and I will give Thee the Gentiles for Thine inheritance, and the ends of the earth for Thy possession.' And again He saith unto Him 'Sit Thou on My right hand, until I make Thine enemies a footstool for Thy feet.' Who then are these enemies? They that are wicked and resist His will." (1 Clement 36:1–6). Although Clement does not identify the author of Hebrews, his quotation indicates at least two things: first, Hebrews was written before the end of the first century (since Clement died in 99 AD) and second, Hebrews was likely kept and read in Rome.

36. Eusebius (c. 260–c. 240), in his *Ecclesiastical History* (6.25.11–14), written around 320–324, quoted Origen in this manner (references to "the apostle" are referring to Paul): "In addition he [Origen] makes the following statements in regard to the Epistle to the Hebrews in his Homilies upon it: That the verbal style of the epistle entitled 'To the Hebrews,' is not rude like the language of the apostle, who acknowledged himself 'rude in speech' {2 Corinthians 11:6), that is, in expression; but that its diction is purer Greek anyone who has the power to discern differences of phraseology will acknowledge. Moreover, that the thoughts of the epistle are admirable, and not inferior to the acknowledged apostolic writings, anyone who carefully examines the apostolic text will admit. Farther on he adds: If I gave my opinion, I should say that the thoughts are those of the apostle, but the diction and phraseology are those of someone who remembered the apostolic teachings, and wrote down at his leisure what had been said by his

widespread view, in his day, that Paul wrote it. Although he left the matter open, in at least eleven references to Hebrews, Origen refers to it as having been authored by Paul.[37]

Why would Origen (and others) think that Paul wrote Hebrews? There are several good reasons:

- The theology: Jesus as the only way of salvation; warnings against dependence on Jewish ceremonial practices.

  - But Paul never refers to Jesus as high priest.

- The blessing (13:20–25): "Grace to you."[38]

  - But this was likely a standard greeting in the early church.[39]

- The connection with Timothy (13:23), who was Paul's pastoral apprentice, assistant, friend, and helper.

  - Still, Hebrews might also have been written after Paul died, when Timothy was living and associating with other leaders in the church.

- The connection with "Italy" (Rome?) (13:24).

- The placing of Hebrews among Paul's letters in early manuscripts.[40]

Yet the Pauline authorship of Hebrews is not convincing. For one thing, Paul always signed his letters. The writer of Hebrews had every opportunity to do so, yet felt this self-disclosure was unnecessary. Second, Paul never refers to Jesus directly as high priest, and this is a major expression about Jesus which lies at the heart of the theology in Hebrews. Third, although Paul was not

---

teacher. Therefore if any church holds that this epistle is by Paul, let it be commended for this. For not without reason have the ancients handed it down as Paul's. But who wrote the epistle, in truth, God knows. The statement of some who have gone before us is that Clement, bishop of the Romans, wrote the epistle, and of others that Luke, the author of the Gospel and the Acts, wrote it. But let this suffice on these matters."

37. Origen, *First Principles* 3.2.4; Origen, *First Principles* 4.1.13; Origen, *First Principles* 4.1.13; Origen, *First Principles* 4.1.24; Origen, *First Principles* 2.7.7; Origen, *First Principles* 2.3.5; Origen, *First Principles* 3.1.10; Origen, *Against Celsus* 7.29; Origen, *Against Celsus* 3.52; Origen, *To Africanus* 9.

38. Very similar to Paul's concluding blessings in Rom 1:7, 16:20; 1 Cor 1:3, 16:23; 2 Cor 1:2, 13:14; Gal 1:3, 6:18; Eph 1:2, 6:24; Phil 1:2, 4:23; Col 1:2, 4:18; 1 Thess 1:1; 5:28; 2 Thess 1:2, 3:18; 1 Tim 1:2, 6:22; 2 Tim 1:2, 4:22; Titus 1:4, 3:15; Phlm 3, 25.

39. See 1 Pet 1:2; 2 Pet 1:2; 2 John 3.

40. See P46 "Chester Beatty Papyri"—c. 175–225 AD—which contains these New Testament writings: Romans 9–16, Hebrews, 1 & 2 Corinthians, Ephesians, Galatians, Philippians, Colossians, and part of 1 Thessalonians. Notice that Hebrews is listed in the middle of Paul's writings.

among Jesus' first disciples,[41] Paul did consider himself directly called and taught by Jesus,[42] which seems to distinguish Paul from the self-perceptions of the author of Hebrews. Fourth, Paul considered himself the apostle to the gentiles,[43] not primarily to the Jews, while Hebrews is clearly written to Jewish Christians, even if these particular folks may have moved from gentile background into the community of faith. Fifth, Paul always uses the Hebrew text of the Old Testament in his references and quotations (translating them into Greek himself), whereas Hebrews consistently uses the Septuagint version of the Old Testament.

For these reasons, by the fourth century, Pauline authorship was generally rejected. Eusebius, in his *Ecclesiastical History* (320–324 AD), strongly questioned Pauline authorship of Hebrews.[44] Jerome, when creating the Vulgate,[45] placed Hebrews after the letters of Paul, thus acknowledging a possible tie to Paul but taking it out of the received works clearly attributed to Paul.

Throughout the centuries, many other writers have been suggested. Since Clement of Rome makes use of Hebrews 13 in 1 Clement 16:1–6 without attributing it to anyone else, some believe he actually wrote the treatise. Luke, the physician and companion of Paul, has been a contender since the fourth century when Eusebius repeated this suggestion that he had garnered from Origen and others. Still, Origen seems to have split his votes between Clement and Luke. Tertullian thought Barnabas was the most likely choice.[46] Martin Luther first suggested Apollos as the author, in a 1522 sermon on Hebrews 1:1–4.[47] While there was no hard evidence, and Apollos' name had never before been tied to Hebrews authorship, Luther felt that the references in Acts 18:24 to Apollos as "an eloquent man" and "a learned man" were a fitting description of the author of Hebrews. Apollos would likely have communicated in the polished Greek evident in Hebrews. He was known to be "mighty in the Scriptures" and "had been instructed in the way of the Lord."[48] Thus, the Hebrew Scriptures were familiar territory to Apollos, and he could handle them with great skill, as is certainly true of the author of Hebrews.

41. Note Heb 2:3.

42. Gal 1:15–16.

43. Acts 9:15; Eph 3:1.

44. Eusebius, *Ecclesiastical History,* 6.25.11–14.

45. The Latin version of the Bible, 382–405 AD.

46. Tertullian, "For there is extant withal an Epistle to the Hebrews under the name of Barnabas—a man sufficiently accredited by God, as being one whom Paul has stationed next to himself." (Tertullian, *Modesty*, XX).

47. Luther, *Sermons*, 6.167.

48. Acts 18:24–25.

The fact that Apollos was a native of Alexandria[49] might also be relevant. The Septuagint Greek translation of the Hebrew Bible was used exclusively in the many Hebrews quotations, and it originated in Alexandria. Philo, the great Jewish philosopher of the first century, also lived in Alexandria and wrote extensively on biblical interpretation. He may even have had some influence upon the writer of Hebrews, since certain words and phrases, which can be found nowhere else in the Bible except for Hebrews, were used frequently by Philo. One final reference to Apollos in Acts 18 declares that he "powerfully refuted the Jews in public, demonstrating by the Scriptures that Jesus was the Messiah" (Acts 18:28). This is precisely the purpose of the book of Hebrews.

More recently, a suggestion has been made that Priscilla was the author of Hebrews.[50] One significant counter-argument, however, is that the author of Hebrews clearly identifies himself by way of a masculine pronoun in 11:32. In the end, we simply do not know who wrote Hebrews.

The Full Testimony in Summary

- God has spoken in times past.
  - This is our source of direction and confidence.
  - We know who we are because of the prophets.
- God has recently spoken a stronger, better, and clearer message through Jesus.
  - So when we, who live by the prophetic message, hear Jesus, we had better listen.
- Jesus is superior to the angels.
  - The great divine message that formed us came through Moses, but the message itself was delivered to him by angels (Deut 33:2; Acts 7:53).
  - Yet Jesus is superior to angels, and therefore delivers a more important prophetic message than that through the great prophet Moses.

---

49. Acts 18:24.

50. This was Adolph von Harnack's idea in a 1900 article ("Probabilia uber die Addresse"). Ruth Hoppin has recently further endorsed and explained this theory in Hoppin, *Priscilla's Letter*.

- So, stick with Jesus, even though you are tempted to turn away from him.
  - There is no higher authority or source of connection with God.
  - And if our lives are to be connected to God, we turn away from Jesus to our own peril.
- God has made the world subject to Jesus.
  - God never did this with the angels, so, again, Jesus is superior to them.
  - But this only happened because Jesus first fully identified with the world.
- Jesus willingly came into the world to fully experience its pain.
- And this is to our benefit for three reasons:
  - To fully identify with us as sisters and brothers.
  - To make atonement for our sins (which cause the pain of this world).
  - To bring us with him fully into the house of God.
- So Jesus is greater than (over) the angels, but Jesus is also greater than (over) Moses.
- Therefore, be careful that you don't disconnect from Jesus (who is God):
  - Remember how those in our past who disconnected from God came under punishment.
  - The same can happen to you if you do not stay true and committed to Jesus.
- Let God's people in the earlier redemptive sequence be your instructors:
  - Like us, they were saved and led to their "(sabbath) rest" in the promised land.
    - But they failed to stay connected to God by way of the word of the prophet (Moses) and died before reading "rest."
  - Now God has promised us a coming "rest" (i.e., "heaven" when we die).

- But we will receive it only if we remain connected to God by way of the word of the prophet (Jesus) and live faithfully through these trials.

- And, again, the only one who can keep you connected to God is Jesus:

  - He is our true high priest, who will take us boldly to God's merciful throne through his actions on our behalf on the Day of Atonement. He is fully human, so he completely understands the struggles of our lives and sympathizes deeply, to the point of anguished cries.

- In fact, he is as fully committed to fulfilling the mandate and responsibilities of his priestly order as are others.

  - They in their "Aaronic/Levitical priestly order."
  - He in his "Melchizedek priestly order."

- I wish you were getting this. You should be mature enough to teach others, but it seems you have lost your passion for Jesus and are trying only to protect yourselves.

  - Though I write strong words, I am confident that you will continue in our faith in Jesus.
  - After all, God has made absolute promises of care toward us that are our hope.
  - And Jesus is the only anchor we have today to ensure that we will receive what was promise.

- After all, Jesus is a priest after the order of Melchizedek.

  - The Levitical order priests could not fully satisfy needs, since its sacrifices needed repeating.
  - That is why someone from Melchizedek's order was needed.
    - Someone who was a descendant of David (of the tribe of Judah), perfect and never dying.

- This brings us back to the main thing we have been saying: Jesus is the best high priest ever.

  - He is God (seated at the right hand of the majesty in heaven).
  - He is owner of the house of God.
  - He is high priest of the house of God.
    - The true house of God, with dimensions given by God on the mountain.

- The visible house of God, here below (under the care of the Levitical priests), important as it is, is only a shadow of the real thing.
  - He is faultless.
  - He is the mediator of the new covenant (remember Jer 31:31–34?).
- This is very important: God found fault with the old covenant.
  - God is causing the old covenant age to come to an end.
  - Jesus is the only source of hope in the new covenant age.
- These changes are symbolized by the "houses" of the two covenant ages:
  - The tabernacle with God hidden and symbolic actions repeated.
  - The heavenly dwelling with Jesus bringing us directly to the throne.
- Both "houses" required blood sacrifice for God's people to approach God.
  - But in the earthly tabernacle, repeated animal sacrifices by Levitical priests were needed.
  - While in the heavenly dwelling, Jesus offered himself once for all.
- Thus, Jesus is the best mediator and the only source of our eternal security.
  - The tabernacle and Levitical priesthood were only types of this ultimate expression of God's love.
- But keep in mind that there is a symbiotic relationship between first and second expressions of God's covenant:
  - The first is the shadow—the meaningful but repetitious type.
  - While the second is the substance—the perfection of all things through Jesus.
- Jesus has accomplished everything that is necessary and now rules over all, in an age where the new covenant is written on hearts and forgiveness is complete
- So, let's go! Grab each other, keep your focus, and let's let Jesus take us right to God's throne of grace.

- Again, I want to remind you about those in the past who failed to keep faith with God and lost out.

  - You have come through some tough times in the past. Remember how you stayed strong?

  - Some of you seem to be dropping out now, as new threats loom. Remember that Jesus can keep us going.

- Have faith in Jesus.

  - See the example of those who have gone before?

  - Besides, don't you believe that God exists and that he rewards those who seek him?

- Remember how our family's first parents all had faith that God would bring a better future than they experienced at the time.

- Remember how Moses, our greatest hero, chose the difficult path of faith and faithfulness rather than ease and worldly success.

- And don't forget the many among our ancestors who won big for God, or lost greatly in a world that was not worthy of them, seeking by faith what we have recently received in Jesus.

- Most importantly, keep your eyes on Jesus.

  - He ran the race before you did (and a bloody run it was), confident of the joy at the end.

  - Know that the pain of your own race is part of the loving discipline of a Father who is bringing out the best in you.

  - So keep running, and encourage each other on the track.

- The end is near.

  - So keep confidence, and live kindly; beware of bitterness that can tear you apart in these tense times.

  - Remember the two moutains:

    - Sinai, from which God shook the world in terror as he announced judgment.

    - Zion, from which God will shake the world in awe as he announces the consummation of all things.

- Live chaste and ready lives, for God is always with you.

- Blessings. I hope to see you soon.

Message: Blessings as You Suffer and Die

Hebrews is a fascinating book filled with great theology but structured very uniquely, with an incessant movement in its style of presentation toward both ecstatic visions of God's grace and glory, alongside warnings and injunctions to move toward martyrdom with an unfaltering testimony about Jesus. The title reference, "to the Hebrews," was given as early as the second century. Eusebius, the church's first major historian, had information that Clement of Alexandria believed that the document was written by Paul and addressed to Jewish Christians living in Palestine. Clement thought Paul deliberately hid his own identity, because many in the Jewish Christian community resented Paul's main focus of ministry with gentiles and were troubled by Paul's belief that the ceremonial regulations of offerings and purification rites were no longer necessary. Clement was further of the opinion that Paul had written this document in the Hebrew language but that Luke had quickly translated it into polished Greek, in order to serve the many diaspora Jewish communities where the Hellenistic language was primary.[51]

What Kind of Literature Is This?

A linguistic and literary analysis of the book, however, undermines Clement's views, as even Eusebius recognized. First, the theology of Hebrews is certainly compatible with that which Paul expressed in his letters; its phrasing and syntax, however, are so different as to make it impossible to understand how they could emerge from the same person, even if there were amanuenses or letter-writing secretaries involved. Second, the Scripture quotations found in Hebrews are all but one taken directly from the Septuagint (the Greek translation of the Hebrew Bible). In fact, the very selection of Greek texts rather than Hebrew texts provides the nuances for theological points that are made throughout the book. This means that it is highly unlikely that Hebrews was first written in the Hebrew language and then translated into Greek, since the very wording of the arguments and theories in the book depend on the Greek Septuagint. Third, Paul was never shy about identifying himself in his writings, whether to Jews, gentiles, or mixed groups, even when his personality or teachings were being challenged. It is probably for reasons such as these that in the western regions of the early church, where Paul had spent the bulk of his ministry, this document was rarely identified with him, although it was quoted early on as an authoritative teaching for the church.

51. Eusebius, *Ecclesiastical History*, 3.38.

Such is the strange legacy of Hebrews: clear and precise in theology, even while its origins and specific audience are lost from our view. Although Hebrews concludes with a few epistolary notes,[52] the document is not actually a letter. Nor is it a "Gospel" like the Synoptics and John (though it is rigorously focused on Jesus), since it neither outlines aspects of Jesus' movements around Palestine nor summarizes his teachings. Sometimes Hebrews seems to be a sermon, or perhaps a string of sermons stitched together; this may well have been its initial form, before an editorial reworking that created the complex but cohesive document we now have. The final version appears to be an extended written teaching that was designed to be read in public. It is a tightly woven rhetorical interaction between exposition (explaining the meaning of Scripture passages) and exhortation (applying those meanings and values to life situations):

- Exposition (*explaining the meaning of Scripture passages*): 1:1–14; 2:5–8; 3:2–6; 3:14–19; 4:2–10; 5:1–10; 6:13–15; 7:1–22; 8:3–9:10; 9:16–22; 10:1–18; 11

- Exhortation (*applying meanings and values to life situations*): 2:1–4; 3:1; 3:7–13; 4:1; 4:11–16; 5:11–6:12; 6:16–20; 7:23–8:2; 9:11–15; 9:23–28; 10:19–39; 12–13

What Is Its Worldview?

Whatever one might call the literary genre, Hebrews is unquestionably built upon the foundation of Old Testament linear thought. It tells of the progression in God's activities with human history, pointing to specific events like the revelations at Sinai, the construction of the tabernacle, and the ministry of the prophets. This unfolding redemptive work of God has recently reached its apex, according to Hebrews, in the coming of Jesus.[53] Everything—past, present, and future—becomes meaningful only as it intersects with Jesus Christ. Jesus' entrance into human time has changed even our understanding of time, and we are now living in the new messianic era.

Although there are many smaller sections and parenthetical notes, the thrust of Hebrews as a whole is on explaining the unique identity and role of Jesus, and drawing out the implications this has for all who know him:

- Jesus is the Superior Way to God (Heb 1–6):

---

52. Heb 13:22–25.
53. Heb 1:1–4.

- Angels delivered the Torah, but Jesus is himself the living Word (chapters 1–2).

- Moses received the Torah, but Jesus is a new and living symbol (chapters 3–4) of God among us.

- Aaron and the priests sacrificed daily and yearly, but Jesus sacrificed himself once for all (chapters 5–6).

- Therefore Jesus is like Melchizedek, uniquely filling a mediatorial role (Heb 7–10).

- So keep following him in spite of challenges and tribulations (Heb 10–13).

One of the most critical passages expressing this view in summary is found in Hebrews 8:

> But Jesus has now obtained a more excellent ministry, and to that degree he is the mediator of a better covenant, which has been enacted through better promises. For if that first covenant had been faultless, there would have been no need to look for a second one.
>
> God finds fault with them when he says:
>
>> "The days are surely coming, says the Lord, when I will establish a new covenant with the house of Israel and with the house of Judah;not like the covenant that I made with their ancestors, on the day when I took them by the hand to lead them out of the land of Egypt;for they did not continue in my covenant, and so I had no concern for them, says the Lord.This is the covenant that I will make with the house of Israel after those days, says the Lord:I will put my laws in their minds, and write them on their hearts,and I will be their God, and they shall be my people.And they shall not teach one another or say to each other, 'Know the Lord,'for they shall all know me, from the least of them to the greatest.For I will be merciful toward their iniquities, and I will remember their sins no more."
>
> In speaking of "a new covenant," he has made the first one obsolete. And what is obsolete and growing old will soon disappear.[54]

---

54. Heb 8:6–13, quoting from Jer 31:31–34.

In making the comparison between the old and new expressions of the covenant, the author does not criticize the former, but turns common perceptions on their head. He assumes that the recent developments, related to Jesus' coming, were intended all along, with the cultic ceremonies of Israel functioning like a prelude or a preamble:

> Since the law has only a shadow of the good things to come and not the true form of these realities, it can never, by the same sacrifices that are continually offered year after year, make perfect those who approach. Otherwise, would they not have ceased being offered, since the worshipers, cleansed once for all, would no longer have any consciousness of sin? But in these sacrifices there is a reminder of sin year after year. For it is impossible for the blood of bulls and goats to take away sins.[55]

Since Jesus has entered our history as the definitive revelation of God's eternal plans and designs, he has fulfilled the intent of the sacrificial system, and thus made it obsolete. This message, along with the enthusiasm of the divine Spirit, energizes the community of faith that now spreads its witness in this messianic age as the Christian church:

> Therefore, my friends, since we have confidence to enter the sanctuary by the blood of Jesus, by the new and living way that he opened for us through the curtain (that is, through his flesh), and since we have a great priest over the house of God, let us approach with a true heart in full assurance of faith, with our hearts sprinkled clean from an evil conscience and our bodies washed with pure water. Let us hold fast to the confession of our hope without wavering, for he who has promised is faithful. And let us consider how to provoke one another to love and good deeds, not neglecting to meet together, as is the habit of some, but encouraging one another, and all the more as you see the Day approaching.[56]

Steeped as he is in Jewish culture and covenantal outlook, the author reduces all of life to the symbolic representations of the tabernacle. When God took up residence on earth, the furnishings of the tabernacle were designed to provide means by which sinful human beings could approach a holy deity. In the tabernacle courtyard, on the altar of burnt offering, a sacrificial transaction took place, atoning for inner sin and alienation from God. The Bronze Sea standing nearby, although used only by the priests and

55. Heb 10:1–4.
56. Heb 10:19–25.

Levites, symbolized the external cleansing necessary when making contact with Yahweh. In the holy place, the first room of the tabernacle proper, were the visible representations of fellowship—a table always prepared for mealtime hospitality, a lamp giving light for Yahweh and his guests, and the altar of incense which, with its sweet smells, overcame the stench of animal sacrifices outside and created a pleasant atmosphere for relaxed conversation. Finally, intimacy with God could be had by passing through the curtain and stepping into the throne room itself, the most holy place. Here, the ark of the covenant, with its mercy seat throne, was the actual place where Yahweh appeared to his people. Because this spiritual journey was too large a leap for most sinfully compromised humans to make, access was granted and taken only once a year in the person and representative acts of the high priest. Israel, as a people, met Yahweh in the tabernacle (the "house of God") through these symbolic representations.

What Jesus has recently done, according to Hebrews, is short-circuited these feeble and repetitive efforts at renewing human relations with God. He did this by fulfilling all the deep-down meanings of these practices in the grand once-and-for-all activity of his death and resurrection. Now the old meanings, good and proper as they were, are connected to new symbols: the cross becomes the altar of burnt offering; baptism is the cleansing washing that replaces the waters of the Bronze Sea; the Lord's Supper is the on-going experience of the hospitality table; the Holy Spirit is the illuminating presence previously offered by the lamp; prayers (both ours and Jesus') form the new incense that sweetens the atmosphere when we seek God; and the most holy place, with its mercy seat atop the ark of the covenant, is nothing less than God's grand throne room in heaven itself. Indeed, if the microcosm worldview of the tabernacle is expanded and inverted, we can sketch out the meaning of Jesus and the true religion of our lives as a journey from outside the camp into the holy presence of God. As the author notes:

> Since, then, we have a great high priest who has passed through the heavens, Jesus, the Son of God, let us hold fast to our confession. For we do not have a high priest who is unable to sympathize with our weaknesses, but we have one who in every respect has been tested as we are, yet without sin. Let us therefore approach the throne of grace with boldness, so that we may receive mercy and find grace to help in time of need.[57]
>
> Therefore, my friends, since we have confidence to enter the sanctuary by the blood of Jesus, by the new and living way that he opened for us through the curtain (that is, through his

57. Heb 4:14–16.

flesh), and since we have a great priest over the house of God, let us approach with a true heart in full assurance of faith, with our hearts sprinkled clean from an evil conscience and our bodies washed with pure water.[58]

It is obvious from the writer's argument that he and those he is addressing are deeply steeped in the worldview, culture, practices, and religious rites of Judaism. Not only so, but theirs is a conservative, orthodox, and historical understanding of the religion of Israel. The Old Testament is the revelation of God, and Israel holds a special place in transmitting the divine outlook and purposes with the human race. Israel's identity was shaped around its religious ceremonies, which themselves emanated from the tabernacle, its furnishings, and its symbolism.

What Was the Occasion for Writing Hebrews?

Although the author of Hebrews shares these perspectives with his audience, there is one significant difference between them: he fully believes Jesus has ushered in a culminating change that transcends and makes obsolete these previous expressions of religious identity, while they, due to cultural pressures around them, are not so sure of that. This document is written to convince a community which is on the verge of slipping away from Jesus, back into a pre-Jesus Jewish ritualistic context, that such a move would be both unwise and inappropriate.[59]

All of this begs the question: who were the first recipients of this document? Where were they living? What was their background? When were they caught up in these things?

There are a number of clues that come through the author's notes about the experiences they have faced:

- These are second-generation Christians (2:1; 2:3; 13:7).

- Who had come through tough times (10:32):

    - Many were publicly ridiculed (10:33).

    - A number of their leaders apparently were killed (13:7).

    - At least some of them had their property confiscated (10:34).

- Although most had not been martyred, many had spent time in prison (10:34; 13:3).

58. Heb 10:19–22.
59. Heb 10:19–39.

- They knew the Hebrew Scriptures well (obvious from the continual stream of scriptural quotes and allusions).

- They had practiced Hebrew religious ceremonies in the past (13:9–10).

- But they were likely gentile in ethnic background, having come into Judaism in the first place by way of conversion (10:32).

When all of these things are considered together, subtle demographic lines emerge. Because they are well-educated, communicate in Greek, and appear to have come to Judaism from a gentile background, it is likely that these people were proselytes to Judaism who had been seeking moral grounding in an increasingly debauched and debasing Roman society. There were many instances in the first centuries BC and AD where non-Jews became enamored of the rigorous lifestyle found in Jewish communities scattered around the Roman world.[60] After going through years of non-participating observation and instruction, these converts were then officially declared to be Jews through ritual entrance ceremonies.

New adherents of any cause or religion are often the most zealous for their newly adopted perspectives and philosophies. It certainly seems to have been the case with these folks. So it must have been quite exciting and shocking when news about Jesus circulated, announcing the arrival of the Messiah and the coming of God's final act of revelation and transformation. No doubt many of these gentile proselytes to Judaism were quick to take the next step in exploring the messianic fulfillments of the religion they had recently adopted.

Of course, it did not take long before tensions within the Jewish community, and later persecutions from elsewhere, took the glow off these exuberant times. Now, in the face of renewed threats against Christians by the Roman government, a complicating twist had been added. All Christians, whether gentile or Jewish in background, were specifically identified as participants in an illegal religious cult, while Jews who did not believe in Jesus retained official protections as part of an already sanctioned religion.

This heightened the confusion of identity issues for proselyte Jews. If they continued to profess Jesus as Messiah, they would be separated from the rest of the Jewish community and persecuted by the Roman government, perhaps losing their property, their families, and even their lives in the process. If, however, they gave up the Jesus factor in their messianic Judaism, they would be able to return to the safety and camaraderie of the general Jewish community, with all of its religious rigor and righteousness, and, at the same time, escape threats from the Roman officials. The latter

---

60. See, for example, Mishnah Torah: Maimonides, Issurei Biah 13:14.

option was a very tempting choice to make. This seems, in fact, to be the background of one of the last and most specific exhortation of Hebrews:

> Therefore, since we are surrounded by so great a cloud of witnesses, let us also lay aside every weight and the sin that clings so closely, and let us run with perseverance the race that is set before us, looking to Jesus the pioneer and perfecter of our faith, who for the sake of the joy that was set before him endured the cross, disregarding its shame, and has taken his seat at the right hand of the throne of God. Consider him who endured such hostility against himself from sinners, so that you may not grow weary or lose heart. In your struggle against sin you have not yet resisted to the point of shedding your blood . . . Therefore lift your drooping hands and strengthen your weak knees.[61]

The writer of Hebrews points to others, of both Old Testament times and recent difficult circumstances, who chose to keep in step with the messianic progression of God's activities, culminating in the coming of Jesus, the Messiah. If these followers of the right way could keep their faith, even when it cost them everything, you can do it too. And look. They are the ones who are cheering you on. They believe you can remain faithful. In fact, Jesus himself stands at the end of your journey and beckons you on to the finish line. So don't give up now, just when you are achieving a newer depth in your relationship with God. You can continue on. You can make it.

To Whom Was Hebrews Written?

If this is indeed the context that nurtured Hebrews into being written, it is possible to reflect more intelligently on the location of the community in question and the times during which the document was authored. Although the writer of Hebrews talks at length about the sacrifices offered regularly by the priests, there is no indication that either he or his readers were watching these things take place, day in and day out. The ritual systems of the tabernacle are used like intellectual building blocks of a worldview system. They are deeply ingrained in the culture, but not necessarily constantly experienced by those familiar with them, any more than is true for Christians who talk easily about the crucifixion of Jesus.

Because the Scripture passages quoted and exegeted by the author are consistently from the Septuagint, it appears reasonable that the readers were not living in Palestine. The references to Timothy, prison, and people from

---

61. Heb 12:1–4, 12.

Italy in Hebrews 13:23–24 make a Roman connection likely, but do not help in determining whether the author or the audience was located there. What is beneficial, however, is the series of hints about successive waves of persecution. In the remembered past, according to the author, an official government pogrom cost many of them their property and material possessions, landed some in jail, and brought about the death of a few of their leaders. Now they were facing a greater threat, and distinctions were being made between Jews who identified with Jesus as Messiah and those who did not.

The three periods of significant government persecution against the Christian church during the first century were under emperors Claudius (48–49 AD), Nero (64–68 AD) and Domitian (81–96 AD). If this document is written after one attack and shortly before another is reaching its climax, Hebrews was probably penned in either the early sixties or the early eighties. The more limited persecutions under Claudius seem better suited for the past troubles faced by this group, since most of them had come through and were restored to their usual social experiences. Also, it is interesting that the destruction of the temple is nowhere mentioned in this document. Since so much of the theological argument in Hebrews is based upon the idea that the ritual ceremonies of Judaism are no longer needed, the destruction of the tmple would have been a perfect illustration of the author's point. If the temple had been destroyed, it would seem to confirm God's own intent to make null and void the ceremonies at the center of Jewish religious practice. In fact, the very choice made by the writer of Hebrews to talk only about the *tabernacle*, and not the *temple*, may be an indication that the temple was still standing. After all, the author did not want to cast aspersions against the cultic rituals that were taking place daily in Jerusalem, only to go back to their roots and meaning. So he used the tabernacle as his point of reference, knowing that it would serve his theological analogies better than the still-visible rites and customs experienced in the Jerusalem temple by many of them on their pilgrimages. Together, these clues seem to push toward an original date of writing in the early sixties, possibly from Ephesus where Timothy was pastor.[62] Since Apollos had gone there as well,[63] he would be a prime candidate for authorship, but there is simply not enough evidence to make a wise decision about that.

Hebrews compares the two great redemptive interruptions of God into human history and shows how these were paired aspects of God's singular desire to reassert the divine presence and care among an alienated humanity. Setting these two pivotal acts of God against each other makes no sense;

---

62. 1 Tim 1:3.

63. Acts 18:24–26; 1 Cor 16:12.

but neither does remaining handcuffed to the former when its greater replacement has come. True religion is not about how humans can become better people through the ritual acts of even the best of systems; rather, it is about how we can follow Jesus with confidence, especially during times of persecution, since he is the latest and greatest expression of the kindness and majesty of God.

Epilogue

IN OUR MODERN PURSUITS of "God's Word for us," we often read a biblical verse or two and parse out beautiful thoughts or inspiring messages we believe are meant only for us and especially on this day. We might treat several texts in Hebrews in this manner:

- Jesus' wonderful understanding of us when we go through difficult times (Heb 2:17–18).
- Our need for sabbath rest (Heb 4:1).
- How well Jesus knows us and cares about us (Heb 4:15).
- A call for us to be bold when bringing our prayers to God (Heb 4:16).
- God makes promises to us that God keeps (Heb 6:19).
- God's love for us is overwhelming and never-ending (Heb 8:10–12).
- Jesus took away all my sins (Heb 9:28).
- God loves me, even though I have sinned (Heb 10:18).
- Let's keep going to church (Heb 10:25).
- I believe (Heb 11:1).
- We're on our way to heaven (Heb 11:16).
- Pray and God will make it happen (Heb 11:32–34).
- I can run and overcome (Heb 12:1–2).
- These tough times only remind me how much God loves me (Heb 12:5–6).
- You can do it (Heb 12:12–13).
- We can play with angels (Heb 13:2).
- God is always with us (Heb 13:5).
- God will help us with everything we do (Heb 13:6).

- I am blessed (Heb 13:20–21).

Unfortunately, when we read these passages as if they are "Today's Bible Verse for Me," we miss the message of God entirely. None of these "inspiring thoughts" match the actual intent of the writer of this treatise.

A Deeper Message

Hebrews was written to deeply religious Jews who had become profoundly excited by the news that Jesus was the long-promised Messiah, and that the final age of God's good plans had arrived. These people read Scripture daily, in long passages, and not merely to find "my special promise." They were well aware of God's grand designs in creation and ages-wide deliberate acts of redemption. They knew the truth of sin and forgiveness and the call to be faithful servants of God and others. If anything, they were conservative and pious religious folks, a little out of touch with their world because they were consumed by devotion to God.

They even endure ridicule and persecution for their faith. At first, it was part of a shared community experience, since Jews had long been ostracized from gentile neighborhoods. But recently these social attacks heightened and split their old supporting fellowships. Now Jews were not included in the growing public condemnations. The new persecutions were aimed squarely at those who called Jesus "Savior" and "Lord." Jews were allowed to continue living in a gentile world, and do business in the markets and main streets. But "Christians," followers of Jesus, were increasingly sidelined socially and commercially. Moreover, physical attacks and publicly-endorsed bullying was becoming commonplace.

The options were becoming obvious:

- If I stop talking about Jesus and simply devote myself to the deep ethics, profound morality, and meaningful ceremonies and rites of my Jewish identity, I get to be among God's faithful people (as I always desired since I converted to Judaism) and keep my marriage, family, and friendships intact. My business will survive, and I won't be tortured or killed.

- If I keep saying that Jesus is God and the center of my world and faith, I get to be condemned by my family and friends, rejected from my neighborhood, driven out of the marketplace and lose my business, and separated from my spouse and children because they will either disown me or will, with me, be killed by the authorities.

What will be my choice? Be a good religious Jew and survive and thrive in this world? Or continue to say that Jesus is my Savior and lose everything here and die a tortured death?

Martyr's Manual

In our modern pluralistic world of many options, and all of them good, or at least okay, we skim through Hebrews, berry-picking those morsels that make us smile and tell us how much we are loved. But the real message of the book is profoundly dark, even as it is wrapped up in bright hope: "Folks, stick with Jesus, because there is no other source of life or salvation. And, yes, sticking with Jesus means that you are going to be horribly tortured, will lose everything here, and are about to die painfully. But remember, those who really mattered in the past shared the same journey. And Jesus himself walked the way of faith through bloody death."

Those who read the whole of Hebrews and spend time with its implication realize that it has just one theme: "Trust Jesus and die." The promise is that resurrection and a glorious eternity await those who fall faithfully in the coliseum, whispering their martyr's testimony. But that is a promise to be held in faith's abeyance. For now, only a single command: "Keep believing in Jesus and perish under persecution."

Do we have the stomach for this book today? I am deeply challenged every time I reread it. Do I actually believe it is a word for me? Do I actually believe it is a word from God? Do I actually believe it enough to live as if it matters? Do I actually believe in Jesus this much? Will I stake everything, including my life, my possessions, my family, my community, my career, my safety, my lifestyle, my entertainments, on Jesus?

More than any other book in the Bible (except, possibly, for Revelation), Hebrews is a "martyr's manual." It calls out faithful living. And it expects us to die with and for Jesus. Are we ready to read that? Are we ready to live that? Are we ready to die?

Bibliography

Aldrich, Charles Knight. *Introduction to Dynamic Psychiatry*. Columbus, OH: McGraw-Hill, 1966.

Allen, David L. *Hebrews: An Exegetical and Theological Exposition of Holy Scripture*. The New American Commentary. Nashville: B & H Academic, 2010.

_____. *Lukan Authorship of Hebrews*. New American Commentary Studies in Bible and Theology. Nashville: B & H Academic, 2010.

Attridge, Harold W. *Hebrews: A Commentary on the Epistle to the Hebrews*. Hermeneia. Minneapolis: Fortress, 1989.

Baker, David L. *Two Testaments, One Bible: A Study of the Theological Relationship Between the Old & New Testaments*. Downers Grove, IL: InterVarsity, 1976; 1991.

Bancroft, Hubert Howe. *The Native Races*. New York: History Company, 1886.

Basil. *Letters, Volume I: Letters 1-58*. Translated by Roy J. Deferrari. Loeb Classical Library 190. Cambridge, MA: Harvard University Press, 1926.

Bauckham, Richard, Daniel Driver, Trevor Hart, and Nathan MacDonald, eds. *The Epistle to the Hebrews and Christian Theology*. Grand Rapids: Eerdmans, 2009.

Bonhoeffer, Dietrich. *The Cost of Discipleship*. New York: Macmillan, 1966.

Brooke, Rupert. *Collected Poems*. New York: John Lane, 1916.

Brouwer, Wayne. *Covenant Documents: Reading the Bible Again for the First Time*. San Diego: Cognella, 2015.

_____. *Splitting the Day of the Lord: The Cornerstone of Christian Theology*. Eugene, OR: Wipf and Stock, 2018.

Bruce, F. F. *Hebrews*. New International Commentary on the New Testament. Grand Rapids: Eerdmans, 1990.

Buning, Sietze. *Style and Class*. Middleburg, IA: Middleburg Press, 1982.

Cassius Dio. *Roman History, Volume VI: Books 51-55*. Translated by Earnest Cary, Herbert B. Foster. Loeb Classical Library 83. Cambridge: Harvard University Press, 1917.

Crabbe, John. *Hector Berlioz: Rational Romantic*. London: Kahn and Averill, 1980.

Cockerill, Gareth Lee. *The Epistle to the Hebrews*. New International Commentary on the New Testament. Grand Rapids: Eerdmans, 2012.

Dalley, Stephanie. *Myths from Mesopotamia : Creation, the Flood, Gilgamesh, and Others*. Oxford: Oxford University Press 1989.

Darwin, Charles. *The Autobiography of Charles Darwin, 1809-1882*. London: Collins, 1958.

deSilva, David A. *Perseverance in Gratitude: A Socio-Rhetorical Commentary on the Epistle to the Hebrews*. Grand Rapids: Eerdmans, 2000.

Douglas, Lloyd C. *Time to Remember*. New York: Houghton Mifflin, 1951.

Durant, Will, and Ariel Durant. *The Lessons of History*. New York: Simon & Schuster, 2012.

Ellingworth, Paul. *Hebrews*. The New International Greek Testament Commentary. Grand Rapids: Eerdmans, 1993.

Endo, Shusaku. *Silence*. New York: Picador Classics, 2016.

Eusebius. *Ecclesiastical History, Volume I: Books 1–5*. Translated by Kirsopp Lake. Loeb Classical Library 153. Cambridge: Harvard University Press, 1926.

———. *Ecclesiastical History, Volume II: Books 6–10*. Translated by J. E. L. Oulton. Loeb Classical Library 265. Cambridge: Harvard University Press, 1932.

Fosdick, Harry Emerson. *The Power to See it Through*. New York: Harper & Brothers, 1935.

———. *Riverside Sermons*. New York: Harper, 1958.

Frankl, Viktor. *Man's Search for Meaning*. Boston: Beacon, 2006.

Frazer, James. *The Golden Bough: A Study in Magic and Religion*. New York: Wordsworth Reference, 1993.

Frost, Robert. "The Road Not Taken." In *Mountain Interval*, 1. New York: Henry Holt and Company, 1916.

Goppelt, Leonhard *Typos*. Eugene, OR: Wipf & Stock, 2002.

Gossip, Arthur. *The Hero in Thy Soul*. New York: Charles Scribner's Sons, 1930.

Griffiths, Jonathan, editor. *The Perfect Savior: Key Themes in Hebrews*. Downers Grove, IL: InterVarsity, 2012.

Guthrie, Donald. *Hebrews*. Tyndale New Testament Commentaries 15. Downers Grove, IL: InterVarsity, 1983.

Guthrie, George H. *Hebrews*. The NIV Application Commentary. Grand Rapids: Zondervan, 1998.

Hart, George. *Egyptian Myths*. Austin: University of Texas, 2004.

Hermas. "The Pastor of Hermas." In *Ante-Nicene Fathers, vol. 2: Fathers of the Second Century,* edited by Alexander Roberts, James Donaldson, and A. Cleveland Coxe, 1–58. Translated by F. Crombie. New York: Christian Literature Publishing Co., 1885.

Heschel, Abraham Joshua. *The Prophets*. New York: Harper Torchbooks, 1969.

———. *The Sabbath*. New York: Farrar, Strauss and Giroux, 1951.

Hoppin, Ruth. *Priscilla's Letter: Finding the Author of the Epistle to the Hebrews*. Fort Bragg, CA: Lost Coast Press: 2009.

Hughes, Philip E. *A Commentary on the Epistle to the Hebrews*. Grand Rapids: Eerdmans, 1977.

Johnson, Luke Timothy. *Hebrews: A Commentary*. The New Testament Library. Minneapolis: Westminster John Knox, 2006.

Justin Martyr and Irenaeus. *The Ante-Nicene Fathers, vol. 1: The Apostolic Fathers with Justin Martyr and Irenaeus*. Edited by James Donaldson, A. Cleveland Coxe, and Alexander Roberts. Ante-Nicene Christian Library. Edinburgh: T. & T. Clark, 1885.

Kant, Immanuel. *Religion within the Limits of Reason Alone*. Translated by Allen W. Wood. Cambridge: Cambridge University Press, 2001.

———. *Lectures on Philosophical Theology*. Translated by Allen W. Wood and Gertrude M. Clark. Ithica, NY: Cornell University Press, 1986.

Kasser, Rodolphe, Marvin Meyer, Gregor Wurst, and Francois Gaudard, eds. *The Gospel of Judas*. Washington, DC: National Geographic Society, 2006.

Keller, Helen. "My Heart Almost Stood Still." *Letters of Note* (blog), edited by Shaun Usher, March 27, 2014, http://www.lettersofnote.com/2014/03/my-heart-almost-stood-still.html.

Koester, Craig R. *Hebrews: A New Translation with Introduction and Commentary.* Anchor Bible. New York: Doubleday, 2001.

Lane, William. *Hebrews 1–8* (Word Biblical Commentary 47A). Grand Rapids: Zondervan, 2015.

———. *Hebrews 9–13.* Word Biblical Commentary 47B. Grand Rapids: Zondervan, 2015.

Lao Tzu. *Tao Te Ching.* Translated by Stephen A. Mitchell. New York: HarperCollins, 1989.

Leeming, David Adams. *Creation Myths of the World.* Santa Barbara: ABC-CLIO, 2010.

L'Engle, Madeleine. *Dance in the Desert.* New York: Farrar, Straus and Giroux, 1988.

Lewis, C. S. *The Lion, the Witch and the Wardrobe.* New York: HarperCollins, 2000.

———. *Mere Christianity.* San Francisco: Harper, 2009.

———. *Space Trilogy (Out of the Silent Planet, Perlandra, That Hideous Strength).* New York: Scribner, 1996.

Luther, Martin. *The Sermons of Martin Luther.* Grand Rapids: Baker, 1996.

McGinnis, Alan Loy. *Bringing Out the Best in People.* Minneapolis: Augsburg, 1985.

Mueller, George. *The Autobiography of George Mueller.* Glendale, CA: GLH Publication, 2015.

Murphy-O'Connor, Jerome. "Paul and Gallio." *JBL* 112 (1993) 315–17.

Millay, Edna St. Vincent. "Renascence." In *Renascence and Other Poems,* 1. New York: Harper & Brothers, 1917.

Montague, Margaret Prescott. *Closed Doors: Studies of Deaf and Blind Children.* New York: Houghton Mifflin Company, 1915.

———. "Writers of the Day." *The Writer* 25 (February 1913) 23–24.

Nestorius. *The Bazaar of Heraclides.* Translated by G. R. Driver and Leonard Hodgson. Oxford: Oxford University Press, 1925.

Paulus Orosius. *Seven Books of History Against the Pagans.* Translated by A. T. Fear. Liverpool: Liverpool University Press, 2010.

Patterson, James, and Peter Kim. *The Day America Told the Truth.* New York: Prentice Hall, 1991.

Peter of Alexandria. "The Canonical Epistle." In *Ante-Nicene Fathers, vol. 6: Fathers of the Third Century,* edited by Alexander Roberts, James Donaldson, and A. Cleveland Coxe, 269–79. New York: Christian Literature Publishing Co., 1886.

Richardson, Don. *Peace Child.* Glendale, CA: Regal, 1974.

Santayana, George. *Life of Reason.* New York: Charles Scribner's Sons, 1955.

Schenck, Kenneth. *Understanding the Book of Hebrews: The Story Behind the Sermon.* Louisville: Westminster John Knox, 2003.

Schleiermacher, Friedrich. *On Religion: Speeches to Its Cultured Despisers.* Louisville: Westminster John Knox, 1994.

———. *Der christliche Glaube : nach den Grundsätzen der evangelischen Kirche.* Halle: O. Hendel, 1897.

Sexton, Anne. *The Awful Rowing Toward God.* New York: Houghton Mifflin, 1975.

Smallwood, E. Mary. "Domitian's Attitude toward the Jews and Judaism." *Classical Philology* 51 (1956) 1–13.

Smith, Constance Babington. *John Masefield: A Life*. Oxford: Oxford University Press, 1978.

Suetonius. *Lives of Twelve Caesars*. Translated by J. C. Rolfe. Loeb Classical Library. Cambridge, MA: Harvard University Press, 1914.

Swindoll, Charles. *Stress Fractures*. Grand Rapids: Zondervan, 1994.

Taylor, Mary Geraldine Guinness. *Borden of Yale*. Minneapolis: Bethany House, 1988.

Thompson, James W. *Hebrews*. Paideia. Grand Rapids: Baker Academic, 2008.

Tolkien, J. R. R. *The Fellowship of the Ring*. New York: Houghton Mifflin Harcourt, 1954.

von Harnack, Adolph. "Probabilia uber die Addresse und den Verfasser des Habraerbriefes." *Zeitschrift fur die Neutestamentliche Wissenschaft und die Kunde der aelteren Kirche* 1 (1900) 16–41.

Wangerin, Jr., Walter. *Ragman and Other Cries of Faith*. New York: HarperCollins Publishers, 2004.

———. *The Book of the Dun Cow*. New York: HarperCollins, 1978.

———. *The Book of Sorrows*. New York: HarperCollins, 1985.

Weatherhead, Leslie "The Significance of Silence." In *The Significance of Silence and other Sermons*, 21–29. Nashville: Abingdon, 1945.

Weir, Ben, Carol Weir, and Dennis Benson. *Hostage Bound, Hostage Free*. Philadelphia: Westminster, 1987.

Wells, H. G., and Alvin Langdon Coburn. *The Door in the Wall and Other Stories*. London: G. Richards, 1911.

Westcott, B. F. *The Epistle to the Hebrews*. Grand Rapids: Eerdmans, 1973.

Westerholm, Stephen, ed. *The Blackwell Companion to Paul*. Malden, MA: Wiley-Blackwell, 2011.

Wilcken, Andrea, Thomas Keil, and Bruce Dick. "Traditional Male Circumcision in Eastern and Southern Africa: A Systematic Review of Prevalence and Complications." *Bull World Health Organ.* 88 (December 2010) 907–914.

Wilde, Oscar. *The Picture of Dorian Gray*. London: Ward, Lock and Company, 1891.

Witherington, Ben. *Letters and Homilies for Jewish Christians: A Socio-Rhetorical Commentary on Hebrews, James and Jude*. Downers Grove, IL: InterVarsity, 2006.

Printed in the USA
CPSIA information can be obtained
at www.ICGtesting.com
LVHW022038040124
768061LV00003B/130